Stories, Pictures and Reality

Stories, Pictures and Reality is a naturalistic study by a mother who documented her children's encounters with literature from their earliest months to adolescence and beyond. It is ground-breaking in its triumphant challenge to the commonly held belief among cognitive psychologists, that children have no understanding of reality and pretence before they are at least seven. Through a mother's fascinating observations of the development of the love of books in her children, the book becomes a compelling exploration of children's relationships with literature.

Stories, Pictures and Reality records how the children develop an understanding of the way pictures relate to the 'real' world, the role of the author and illustrator, and how (via literary characters) they develop an awareness and sensitivity to other people's thoughts and emotions. Through a convincing demonstration that young children can enjoy complex words and plots, the book places an emphasis on the benefits of actually reading words to young children, rather than just labelling or talking about pictures.

Students, researchers and academics involved in early literacy will value this book, yet anyone with an interest in children's cognitive abilities and children's literature will read the text with fascination and delight. It will develop in the reader an understanding of how brilliantly such young minds can think and reason about subjects that puzzle even the most sophisticated thinkers.

Virginia Lowe is an independent expert on literature for children, and Honorary Associate at Monash University, Australia. She operates a manuscript assessment agency – http://createakidsbook.alphalink.com.au.

Stories, Pictures and Reality

Two children tell

Virginia Lowe

Routledge
Taylor & Francis Group

LONDON AND NEW YORK

First published 2007
by Routledge
2 Park Square, Milton Park, Abingdon, Oxon OX14 4RN

Simultaneously published in the USA and Canada
by Routledge
270 Madison Avenue, New York, NY 10016

Routledge is an imprint of the Taylor & Francis Group, an informa business

© 2007 Virginia Lowe

Cover by Jacqui Young

Typeset in Garamond Three by
RefineCatch Limited, Bungay, Suffolk
Printed and bound in Great Britain by
MPG Books Ltd, Bodmin

British Library Cataloguing in Publication Data
A catalogue record for this book is available from the British Library

Library of Congress Cataloging in Publication Data
A catalog record has been requested for this book

ISBN10: 0–415–39723–5 (hbk)
ISBN10: 0–415–39724–3 (pbk)

ISBN13: 978–0–415–39723–0 (hbk)
ISBN13: 978–0–415–39724–7 (pbk)

To Rebecca and Ralph, who have become delightful, responsible, courageous book-loving adults.

And to their loving, caring, considerate and knowledgeable father, John.

Contents

Figures

Foreword

The more we have come to know about children's first approaches to literacy, the more we are confronted by evidence of the historical, social and linguistic complexities of the topic. In an ever-increasing range of cultural settings, current research reveals the variety and importance of the preschool experience and knowledge that children gain from early acquaintance with stories and books. The contents, characters, and ways of telling, reading and listening to stories emerge in children's play as features of their linguistic growth. As the result of this, parents are now encouraged, officially, to read with their children in the years before school assumes responsibility for their progress. Thus, pre-school reading activity has now become a research area of its own.

However, one particular strand of evidence has a longer history. Where parents have had a professional rather than a passing interest in their children's early encounters with books, stories and nursery tales and rhymes, and have kept detailed journals of these, we see how individual differences contribute to more general understandings. There is a kind of collaborative curiosity about 'what happens next'. For the novice reader, this concern is about events in the story; for the adult, it confirms a belief that the young reader's attention has been captured in a way that bodes well for a continuing interest in reading. As these inquiries have different ways of collecting evidence of what happens to individual children, they 'count' as naturalistic evidence in research of a particular, insightful kind. My first awareness of this reportage of young children's views of the task of understanding what happens in books came with Dorothy Butler's *Cushla and Her Books* in 1979, an exploration of the part picture books played in the early life of a severely handicapped child. Also revealed in the details of these naturalistic studies are reflections on current social, cultural and moral aspects of contemporary life in a multicultural society.

Each single example of this kind of reading research displays the author's particular interest in carrying out these long, detailed observations over time. Each has a range of relevance to current matters of literacy and literature. Dr Lowe's studies of siblings offer distinctive evidence of her children's responses to books as 'real' or 'imaginary'. As the children engage in conversations about particular aspects of particular texts, we see the cognitive and imaginative capacities of young children as they explore the world of fiction. Among other things, they show that they can discuss the reality-status of stories, characters and situations before the age of 5. This study is a significant addition to the distinctive collection of its kind.

Margaret Meek
Reader Emeritus
London University Institute of Education

Preface

Stories, Pictures and Reality argues that young children are underestimated by many of those who speak and act on their behalf. It challenges us to recognise the capacities of children, specifically in the areas of their understanding of reality and their book appreciation.

The book is unique. No other studies the book contacts of children from birth to adulthood. Although I have chosen to stop at 8 years old, I can make comparisons and comments about Rebecca and Ralph as adolescents and adults. No study in monograph form has dealt with a boy, nor with a second child in the same detail as the first. Neither has there been a study which covers infant book behaviour in such detail (most of the previous studies have begun records at age 2). And there has not been a monograph-length study of an individual child's understanding of reality.

In exploring these capacities through the longitudinal study of Rebecca and Ralph, there are three fields to which significant contributions are offered. The first is that of the cognitive psychologists and other researchers and theorists in the understanding of reality, particularly those who study the reality of the words and the pictures that make up the secondary worlds of literature. As well as data on young children's understanding of the reality-status of books, there is information about their concept of reality in general and also other aspects of development, such as the understanding of emotions and of the existence of other minds, about causality and humour. The study challenges the expectation that one can discover a smooth developmental sequence in the children's growth in understanding.

Second, the book makes a contribution to critical theory in children's literature, adding to the body of knowledge available to the under-resourced area of childist criticism.

> Although most people agree that the paradox of children's literature is its domination by adults in all spheres of its production, few are yet persuaded that what children say about the books they are offered has any critical significance.
>
> (Meek 1995: 6)

Finally, and more generally, there is the desire to influence those involved in the selection of books, and the reading of them to young children. It aims to prevent the stultifying effects of underestimation, to urge the reading of the actual words, and to encourage the sharing of challenging illustrative styles and stories. The many results that can arise from this practice include the lifelong enjoyment of books, exposure to the enriched language of literature, and training in narrative, the 'primary act of mind' (Hardy 1977: 12). Among teachers, publishers, librarians and parents there is a tendency to diminish or dismiss in advance the potential capacity of the child for a sophisticated and engaged response to an appropriate text. *Stories, Pictures and Reality* demonstrates to this diverse audience that very young children can respond to books and stories and enjoy them for themselves, for the worlds they create, and for the language and pictures in which this is done.

The reality question is of vital interest to developmental psychologists, to philosophers and to literary critics as well. In fact, this study is cross-disciplinary. It is to be hoped that those who study humour, theory of mind, narratology, imaginary play and also the ontological status of everything will find relevant chapters and gain something from them. Together the chapters make up a case for not underestimating the young child.

Rebecca and Ralph's book contacts, 'the books we've had for ever', have been recorded more thoroughly, for a longer period and in greater detail than those of other children in previous studies. Both children, with their different tastes, different responses, different environments, as well as their interactions with each other, are drawn upon, and the study also builds on those that have preceded it. Certainly Rebecca and Ralph were articulate, privileged children in a Western environment, so one cannot generalise from them. On the other hand, the aim of the study is to see what is possible for children at the peak of their ability – both what they are capable of taking from books, and how they understand the reality-status of them as well – and this aim could only have been fulfilled by articulate children in a book-rich environment.

Sections of this book have appeared in different forms and in greater detail in a number of other publications. These are listed in the bibliography.

I owe gratitude to my children for allowing me to make use of their words and ideas, and reveal them to the world. And none of it would have been possible without the loving care and meticulous research of their father, John.

Acknowledgements

Rebecca and Ralph for allowing me to use their words and ideas.

Margaret Gill for her invaluable supervision of the PhD thesis on which this book is based.

Margaret Meek for her unfailing support and encouragement.

Monash University for the facilities and assistance it has made available.

I should like to thank the authors and publishers who have kindly given permission to reproduce illustrations as follows:

Illustration of Lion from *B is for Bear* by Dick Bruna, © Mercis bv, 1967 (Figure 3.1).

Illustration of Eskimo from *B is for Bear* by Dick Bruna, © Mercis bv, 1964 (Figure 3.2).

'Illustration', copyright 1928 by Wanda Gag, renewed © 1956 by Robert Janssen, from MILLIONS OF CATS by Wanda Gag. Used by permission of Coward-McCann, A Division of Penguin Young Readers Group, A Member of Penguin Group (USA) Inc., 345 Hudson Street, New York, NY 10014. All rights reserved (Figure 3.4).

Illustration from *The Cow Who Fell In The Canal*. Illustration Copyright 1957 by Peter Spier. First Published by Doubleday and Company, New York, NY, USA. (Figure 3.5)

Illustration from *Where the Wild Things Are* copyright © 1963 Maurice Sendak. Used with permission of HarperCollins Publishers Ltd. (Figure 4.1)

Illustrations from *Moominland Midwinter* by Tove Jansson, Penguin/Puffin edition (1971), reproduced by permission of Oy Moomin Characters Ltd (Figures 4.2 and 5.9).

Illustration from *The Quinkins* by Percy Trezise and Dick Roughsey, reproduced by permission of HarperCollins Australia (Figure 4.3).

Illustrations from *Barbapapa's Ark* and *Barbapapa*, reproduced by permission of Talus Taylor (Figures 4.4, 4.5 and 5.12).

Illustration from *Muffel and Plums*, reproduced by permission of Lilo Fromm (Figure 5.1).

Illustration from *Mother Goose: A Collection of Nursery Rhymes* by Brian Wildsmith, (OUP, 1987), copyright © Brian Wildsmith 1964, reprinted by permission of Oxford University Press (Figure 5.2).

Illustrations from WHISTLE FOR WILLIE by Ezra Jack Keats, copyright © 1964 by Ezra Jack Keats, renewed © 1992 by Martin Pope, Executor. Used by permission of Viking Penguin, A Division of Penguin Young Readers Group (USA) Inc., 345 Hudson Street, New York, NY 10014. All rights reserved (Figures 5.3 and 5.4).

Illustration from *The Elephant and the Bad Baby* by Elfrida Vipont, illustrated by Raymond Briggs, (Hamish Hamilton 1969, London). Text copyright © Elfrida Vipont Foulds, 1969 reproduced by permission of Penguin Books Ltd (Figure 5.5).

Illustrations from *The Tale of Tom Kitten* and *The Tale of Samuel Whiskers* by Beatrix Potter, copyright © Frederick Warne & Co., 1907, 2002. Reproduced with permission of Frederick Warne & Co. (Figures 5.6 and A.1).

Illustration from *The Hare and the Tortoise* by Brian Wildsmith (OUP, 1999), copyright © Brian Wildsmith 1966, reprinted by permission of Oxford University Press (Figure 5.7).

Illustration from *Angus and the Cat* by Marjorie Flack © 1933. Used with permission of Harold Ober Associates Incorporated and Farrar Straus & Giroux. (Figure 5.8)

Illustration from MADELINE by Ludwig Bemelmans, copyright 1939 by Ludwig Bemelmans, renewed © 1967 by Madeline Bemelmans and Barbara Bemelmans Marciano. Used by permission of Viking Penguin, A Division of Penguin Young Readers Group (USA) Inc., 345 Hudson Street, New York, NY 10014. All rights reserved (Figure 5.10).

Illustration from *John Brown, Rose and the Midnight Cat*, reproduced by permission of Ron Brooks (Figure 5.11).

Illustration from *Crazy Cowboy* by Guillermo Mordillo, reproduced by permission of Dotin BV (Figure 6.1).

Illustration from *Patatrac* by Jean Jacques Loup, published by Jonathan Cape. Reprinted by permission of The Random House Group Ltd (Figure 6.2).

Illustration from *The Mouse with the Daisy Hat* © Ruth Hürlimann. Licensed by VISCOPY, Australia, 2006 (Figure 6.3).

Illustration from SUMMER by Alice Low illustrated by Roy McKie, copyright © 1963 by Alice Low. Copyright renewed 1991 by Alice Low and Random House, Inc. Used by permission of Random House Children's Books, a division of Random House, Inc. (Figure 6.4).

Every effort has been made to contact copyright holders for their permission to reprint material in this book. The publishers would be grateful to hear from any copyright holder who is not here acknowledged and will undertake to rectify any errors or omissions in future editions of this book.

1 'Is this a real story?'

The study and its methodology

'Is this a real story?' 'But animals can't talk!' 'These are my favourite not-real persons.' When does a child reach awareness of the reality-status of the literary world? This is a study of two children as they work towards this understanding, by way of a diet rich in books, a careful parent-observer – and a Reading Journal kept from their first weeks of life, up to independent reading and beyond.

While I was studying librarianship I encountered Dorothy Neil White's *Books before Five* (1954), in which she discussed her daughter Carol's encounters with books. I was enchanted, and determined that when I had children, I would carry out a similar study. In the interim, as a children's librarian, I was soon surrounded by children's books as I selected the collection needed for a large new municipal library.

Some years later I was married to John, a librarian, who could not have been more supportive of my plan. He was just as eager as I was to read to our first child, Rebecca, and to keep the record of the process too. We began almost at once to introduce her to books and to record her responses. Three years later our son Ralph was born, and we continued with the Reading Journal for him as well.

It is perhaps fortunate that I had not reread *Books before Five* when I embarked on this, because White did not begin her study until Carol was about 2, by which time the first books (and her reactions) had 'vanished along with lost dolls and feeding bottles' (White 1954: 1). This might have influenced me, but as it was, I started making notes at first book contact – which was 13 weeks for Rebecca (1 week for Ralph).

I continued to keep regular field notes until the children were reading at their interest level, at about 8, and sporadically until they each left home at 18. The Journal consists of 6,318 handwritten pages, with 1,842 books mentioned. From the start, I kept a bibliography of all the books read, indexed by date, so I could relocate each entry. When I began my PhD thesis the Journal was annotated with marginalia, and indexed under 317 topics.

As well as the delight their father and I both took in sharing books with the children, I enjoyed the observation and recording. In fact, when they were old enough to ask what I was doing, I often told them I was writing a book about children's books (though not that it was about their own reactions to them). As writing was part of what happened in the home (this was before computers – though we owned a typewriter, I didn't use it for the entries), this method seemed a more natural way to keep the record than using a tape recorder. I kept notes at least weekly until Rebecca was 3, and daily for the next five years, covering both children, until Ralph started school and I returned to paid employment. From then it was back to keeping the record several times a week, daily during holidays. When they were respectively 13 and 10, we all went to Europe for three months (our second trip), and the record was kept daily during this period also. The observations frequently ran to ten or more pages – on occasions over twenty, though the average for a year was never greater than three and a half a day. (The observation and recording process is explained in greater detail in Lowe 1994a.)

Why didn't I tape the reading sessions? Most other parent-observers who have studied children and books have used a tape recorder (or even, more recently, a video recorder), and certainly that would make it all verifiable. If the tape is there, you have proof that it actually happened. On the other hand, transcription of an hour of child-talk on a tape can take three or four hours, or perhaps up to ten. I preferred to spend this transcription time reading more books to the children. Others have insisted that if they did not have the words exactly correct, they preferred not to record the incident (the Cragos say 'When in doubt, leave out' (1983: xx). But my emphasis was on recording as many incidents as possible, and if the language was not exact, at least there would be the sense of what the children said. Also, I find a tape recorder intrusive, and the taped children (Anna Crago and Lesley Wolf) were certainly aware of it, often even performing for it.

The reader has to take it on trust that I have captured the gist of what the children were trying to convey. There were several cases where I jotted notes immediately, then subsequently misplaced the piece of paper when I came to write up the Journal in the evening. I recorded the incident as I remembered it, but when the jotted notes reappeared some time later, I could compare them. In each case, what I had recorded in the evening was the sense of the exchange, but was in simpler language than the children had actually used. It appears that when in doubt about their words, I would take their language development back several steps rather than exaggerate it.

There are several levels of interpretation of the child's language. First there is the understanding of the actual words – easier for a parent than any other researcher – then of the actual meaning. These two levels can be illustrated with an incident when Rebecca was 17 months old. She was on my hip as I talked with a children's librarian about Ezra Jack Keats's books, including *Whistle for Willie*. Rebecca joined in the adult conversation with 'ff, ff' urgently. I interpreted this to mean 'woof woof', as I knew this was her word for 'dog'. The further level of interpretation is that she meant by this: '*Whistle for Willie* is about a dog.' A mother interprets the intention of a baby via the complex accumulation of expertise developed through interaction and observation. On this basis, the reader must accept (1) that 'ff, ff' was her 'word' for 'dog'; (2) that there was no sound of a dog barking, or picture of a dog within sight; and (3) that when I responded 'Yes, *Whistle for Willie* is about a dog', she smiled and relaxed, and showed with her body language that this was the message she had been trying to convey. Similar assumptions must be made by the reader with all the incidents retold about the children.

There is an observer's paradox in recording language and behaviour. The material that you want to collect is ideally gathered when the subjects are unaware of being studied. This is never completely possible, but a parent-observer comes closest, because what a parent does, year in year out, will be considered unquestioningly as what the parent does. There is no disruption in the child's actual behaviour. There is also the question of 'speaking for the other'. All children are 'other' to adults, and even a silenced other, in that there would be no way of their opinions being heard at all, if devoted adults did not collect and record them. Peter Hunt coined the term 'childist criticism', on the model of 'feminist', for criticism that attempts to 'see what is really happening on the child's terms rather than dealing in ingrained assumptions about children's perceptions and competences' (1991: 192).

This is not a linguistic study, and could not be used as such. It is the children's understanding of concepts that has always fascinated me. I was, naturally, also interested in their level of speech and vocabulary, but what I was recording mainly was their responses to the books they encountered. It is not possible to generalise from this study. From a book-exposure point of view, Rebecca and Ralph were exceptionally advantaged children. They were healthy, intelligent, privileged children, living in an affluent Western society. They lived in a comfortable house with a back garden on a quiet street; they never knew hunger; they had parents devoted both to them and to each other. The study shows what children are capable of, not necessarily what is possible for the average child, though my hope is that all readers will look at all young children with a new expectation of their abilities and understandings.

Eventually, when I used this mass of data as the basis for my PhD thesis (begun when the younger child was about 18), the aspect I chose to study was that of their understanding of the reality of the text and pictures. Although a number of other studies of young children and books have been published, there is no other that looks specifically at this aspect, although the Cragos do have a chapter on it (Crago and Crago 1983: ch. 13, pp. 200–214).

A few remarks on the previous studies which have been published by parent-observers are essential, as I occasionally cite them, and compare the studied children with mine. White is the foremother of them all with *Books before Five*, and in fact when that was first published in 1954, the idea of even reading to young children was not universally accepted, let alone recording these book encounters. Others have been the Cragos' *Prelude to Literacy* (1983), Butler's *Cushla and Her Books* (1979) and Wolf and Heath's *The Braid of Literature* (1992), hereafter referred to respectively as *BbF*, *Prelude*, *Cushla* and *Braid*.

There have also been studies in articles, and even series of articles, on book development, several theses by parent-observers, an ongoing column in *Books for Keeps*, and developmental case studies that touch on books in passing – for instance on learning to read and write (Bissex 1980; Baghban 1984; Schickendanz 1990), and on the development of scientific concepts in a child (Navarra 1973).

The Child That Books Built (2002) is Spufford's impressive attempt to record his own childhood reading, by rereading the books he remembered. It is a fascinating record, but does not touch on his earliest book contacts, beginning only when he could read for himself, with a few earlier musings on *Winnie-the-Pooh* and fairy tales. (He is only a few years older than my children, and would certainly have had some of the same picture books, for instance, but none are mentioned.)

Recently there has been renewed interest in observing children with books in group situations in kindergartens or schools. Of particular note are Arizpe and Styles's *Children Reading Pictures* (2003) and Kiefer's *The Potential of Picturebooks* (1995). Others are Jalongo (1988), Hungerford (1993), Bromley (1996), Watson and Styles (1996) and Sipe (2002). It is heartening that children's responses – through reader response theory or Hunt's childist criticism – have been taken up in this way. These are fascinating and show what children are capable of taking from stories, and how they can discuss them. Nevertheless, none of them begins in infancy, nor has the chronological depth to demonstrate an individual child's responses over years.

It is noteworthy that of the individual children whose book encounters have been studied and published in book form, none has been male (although there are a couple in articles, including a book section by Michael Rosen on his son teaching himself to read at 5, 1996), making my record of Ralph unique. Furthermore, although there were second children (all girls) while the first was being studied, none of the other parents actually records the responses of both children in the same amount of detail. As the environment, and hence the behaviour and responses, of a subsequent child are always quite different from those of a first, this aspect is also unique to my study. Similarly, the quantity of data collected, and the length of time over which records were kept, seem to be unique. Of course the handwritten records are less accurate than audio or video ones, but the quantity and chronological range make up for this. Others who kept electronic records have done so only once or twice a day, or even once a week, whereas I recorded as many as possible of the book encounters or references, whether we adults were involved or not, day in, day out.

I have always been intensely interested in the question of reality – what is real – possibly because I was short-sighted from birth, so presumably always aware, at one level, that what other people saw was different from what I did – that reality depends on perception. (Jerome Bruner was not able to see until he was 2; Bruner 1983: 7. This may similarly have influenced his interest in reality and how the mind works.) Much later there was epistemology in philosophy at university (I did not begin undergraduate studies until I was 38, even though I had already for some years been lecturing in tertiary institutions on English and children's literature). There were the philosophical questions, such as Berkeley's. And the whole idea of solipsism – I cannot prove that anything external to me exists, because I only have the images that my senses build in my brain. Or, as Descartes puts it, 'I think, therefore I am' – yes, that's me – but what of the rest of the world?

A compulsive reader, I have always enjoyed the playful self-referential texts – 'postmodern' ones, or the older ones like Sterne's *Tristram Shandy* – where the reality of the text itself is deliberately brought into question. I have pondered for years Coleridge's 'willing suspension of disbelief' – to what extent does one believe in a story, 'live' within it?

The question of what is real not only is one that engages philosophers, but is one of the earliest concepts that must be mastered for infants to thrive in the world. They must be able to recognise that people and objects exist in the external world, even when out of sight; that a reflection or photograph or picture is not the object or person; that their own thoughts and memories and dreams are internal, not externalised. This is not the place for a philosophical discussion of reality as such. Suffice it to state that we will speak as though there is an external world shared with other people, although this is, in many ways, a great assumption. And that there are secondary worlds created by artists – writers and illustrators in this case – that have a form of reality as well. As Bruner puts it, 'At our most unguarded, we are all Naïve Realists' (1986: 64). Look at the way everyone is able to hold two (or more) completely differing or contrasting ideas in their mind at the same time (we know that the earth circles the sun, but we still talk about the sun 'coming up').

There is a long history of case studies of child development, but Piaget was one of the first people to study the young child's knowledge of reality, most thoroughly in *The Construction of Reality in the Child* (1954). His view that infants do not understand reality thoroughly – or even think about it – until about 7, the 'concrete operational' stage, has been shown to be flawed. My own view is that he, along with most of the developmental psychologists who have followed him, put too much weight on what young children actually say. Young children find no compelling reason to tell what we would see as 'the truth'. Their guiding principle is to not appear stupid – to learn what is being offered as quickly as possible, and to show that they have learned it. So when they are asked a tricky question in an experimental situation, they do as they do in real life. They ask themselves what this question really means, rather than what it actually says, and answer accordingly. (Donaldson 1984 demonstrates this convincingly.) Another drawback of experimental work, especially on the understanding of reality and of the theory of (other) minds, is that psychologists frequently use stories and pictures in their tests without evaluating, or often even considering, the reality-status these hold for the children, a point I shall return to.

As it is cognitive psychologists who most often discuss the child's understanding of reality, and as they almost always conclude that the child can only understand various forms of reality at a much older age than any observant parent could demonstrate, a digression must now be made to look at the sort of experiments that lead to these conclusions. In a false belief experiment, the child is shown a cookie box with pencils in it, and cookies hidden in a basket. Then a puppet is introduced. A child of 3 will say the puppet will look for cookies in the basket where they are. A 5-year-old will say that the puppet will look in the box where they should be. (Flavell 2000 summarises these experiments.) But the young child (though she couldn't express it) knows that the only mind a puppet has is the mind of the person who is working it, so the puppet does 'know' that the cookies are not in the cookie box even though it didn't 'see' the removal of them. It is only after 4 that children understand that the experimenter is expecting them to *pretend* that the puppet has a mind – that because the puppet wasn't there to see the transposition, it couldn't have known. When they have grasped what the experimenter wants of them, then they can solve the problem easily. It does not test whether they understand about the false belief but whether they can answer tricky questions. There is also the matter of whether they choose to tell the truth or not, when they feel the truth will make them look silly in front of an adult. A researcher may say 'this is really and truly a white lamb' when it is actually a toy, even though it is white, which was the point the researcher was making. The non-verbal tests of false belief now being devised (for instance by Clements and Perner 1994) have apparently shown in experimental situations that children of 3 or below can pass them.

The change at age 4, is in the way the children handle speech, and how willing they are to risk looking foolish in front of strange adults. The experiments are about whether literally they can *tell* the difference. Most of the things that puzzle developmental psychologists depend on this sort of fact. The result is that they find that children do not understand about other minds or reality generally until much later than any parent can demonstrate in the home. Donaldson (1984) and Wellman (1990: 262) clarify these ideas.

Gardner has pointed out how often developmental psychologists use pictures and stories (usually created for the experiment, not for aesthetic reasons) to examine theory of mind and reality without considering the child's understanding of the fictional world at all. They expect the child to talk about, and treat, the fictional world as if it is the real world, but it is not until about 4 that children are able to articulate what they already know. Generally they know much more about the reality-status of the items presented to them than the examiners imagine they do. 'The stories are denuded of aesthetic components, there is little style, figurative language, dialogue. The very aroma of literature has largely evaporated' (Gardner *et al.* 1980: 107).

While Donaldson and many others have overturned Piaget's findings, Piaget must be acknowledged as the first person to find young children worthy of academic study. Vygotsky (1978) argued that children are capable of more when they have a scaffold, when the behaviour is supported. This is what book reading was doing for Rebecca and Ralph.

The next chapter is a general description of the two children, their environment, and the selection of their books. Chapter 3 is devoted to book behaviour in infancy, because this is the least studied period. There are few actual comments by the children in this period; instead, their behaviour and my musings on their understanding of the reality concept are given up to the age of 2. It includes a section on their recognition of objects in pictures. Chapter 4 looks at the children's understanding of reality generally, and how this applied to books. It includes the influence of language, dreams and logic. This is followed by the book's reality through interpretation of pictures, specifically the conventions of direction of regard and perspective (Chapter 5), the role of the illustrator (Chapter 6) and of the author (Chapter 7), the understanding of other minds (the theory of mind applied to characters, Chapter 8), identification with characters and pretend play (Chapter 9), and the children's understanding of humour and irony (Chapter 10). Differences in the children are obvious throughout, but the final chapter foregrounds these. Are the differences based on gender, on position in family, on personality generally? It also looks at the relevance of the results in today's vastly different world. Throughout there is the joy of sharing literature with the children, and comments on their pleasure as well. One of my most firmly held beliefs is that we must never underestimate children. They deserve complex characters, complex language, delicious big unusual words to taste and grow on, and many different styles of visual art.

Throughout this work the children's ages are given in years and months (4–2 = 4 years 2 months). In passages of dialogue their words are given in inverted commas, as I am reasonably sure I captured these accurately. The adult side of the conversation, though, is given in square brackets – this is to indicate that I am not sure of the wording. Often in the Journal I would just put '?' to indicate that I asked a question – their answer would indicate the topic. As it was hard work to remember the children's words, I rarely managed to record the adult ones at all (and I acknowledge this as another shortcoming of the study – the actual words that the adult says are obviously significant in many cases). Nevertheless, I am sure that if I was aware of influencing responses in particular cases, I recorded this. The actual children's books will be mentioned by title (sometimes a shortened one – for instance, *The Tale of Benjamin Bunny* becomes *Benjamin Bunny*). Their authors and illustrators can be found in the list of children's books arranged by title.

All these unverifiable variables leave one with the question 'Is this a real story?' Did it happen in the way I described it in the Reading Journal? Or in the thesis? Or here? All I have is my own perception, my own recorded memories and my musings in the intervening years, but I offer them here as something unique and possibly useful to many people as well. Rebecca in her Afterword shows that parental interpretation can disagree with children's actual memory. She reveals a little of the effect that the process had on her.

I must here acknowledge the people whose work has been most influential for this study: Margaret Meek, who has always called for more studies of children's actual responses to books; Jerome Bruner in his studies of narrative and also reality; and Hugh and Maureen Crago, whose first observational study I read when Ralph was born, and who alerted me to the fact that my reading record could be much more detailed. The Cragos have remained friends, and when their children and mine were small we compared their reactions.

2 'The books we've had for ever'

The environment, the books,
the children

The two children, their reading environment and their books are discussed in this chapter in broad sweeps, to provide the background for the rest of the study. I will start with a look at us parents and our attitudes.

I had a great interest in books as a child. I was read to, but as my mother was a musician, mainly I was sung to while she played the piano. Her baby diary of me records that at 1–9 I sang the ends of the lines of about thirty nursery rhymes, and by 2–4 I could sing while she played 'some 89 nursery songs'. My mother continues:

> A quaint little habit of hers is to think of a song and sing it to almost any word one likes to say such as today – I went to help her out of her cot and said 'oh you are stuck' and straight away she sings 'Yankee doodle' commencing with 'stuck a feather in his hat'.

This resembles Rebecca's year-long period of intense quotation at around 2 (see p. 11). Both my mother and grandmother read to me, and at 2–3 I knew when to turn the pages of *Milly-Molly-Mandy* (Brisley). I learned to read easily, and was a compulsive reader from then on, moving from Enid Blyton to Charles Dickens almost seamlessly at 11.

My parents didn't care for fantasy, though, so I heard no fairy stories and no fantasy until I could read them for myself at 5 or 6. Also – and this may be significant – they did not tell us the Father Christmas myth – let alone about fairies and other imaginary beings that are often presented to children, such as the Tooth Fairy. So this perhaps made easier our own choice to tell our children only the truth, as far as we knew it and they could understand. We always made a clear distinction between stories in books, imagination, and what happens in 'real life'.

So perhaps we unconsciously coached them in their early understanding of the reality-status of stories and pictures. Certainly they were both able to understand reality, and articulate it, much earlier than is generally expected. Again, it may be that they were in fact no younger at this stage than most children, but just had the language for the concepts, and a mother who was a parent-observer to keep the record.

Rosenblatt distinguishes between efferent (cognitive) and aesthetic (emotional) reading (1978: 23), but, as Kiefer (1988: 266) points out, both cognition and emotion are involved in responding to picture books, or any sort of fiction. In general, with a similar upbringing (in so far as a second child's is similar to the first's) but completely different personalities, Rebecca overall reacted cognitively to the stories, Ralph with emotion.

There are people, children's literature people even, who feel children should never question fiction, that they will lose the pleasure in narrative if they see it as story rather than reality. My feeling is that all children do, unless specifically told otherwise, and certainly this did not destroy Rebecca and Ralph's enjoyment of literature. They constantly demanded books as infants, and have both grown into readers, if not quite as compulsive as their mother.

When they were young, on most days there would be several reading sessions. Before bed was an established one, and there was almost always another first thing in the morning, as they were got up from the cot, or got out of bed, clutching the books I had selected to put in with them that night. I usually chose ones that were relevant from yesterday's activities, or alternatively ones that they hadn't looked at for quite some time. In the period before they started school, and also later in the school holidays, when we were at home, there would be several reading sessions during the day, often taking about an hour and a half in total.

The other major influence on their environment was their father. John had learned to read before school, and reads a lot of fiction, as I do. But he also enjoys non-fiction, is quick to consult reference books – the household's eight dictionaries are his domain. As befits two librarians, we have a large reference collection, and John consults it often. He also reads the newspaper fairly thoroughly, which I rarely do.

Having been a children's librarian, I was of course interested in what our children read, and already had a collection of children's books. I cared a great deal about which stories they had access to. We used the public library extensively but I felt that we should own the books that became firm favourites, so their personal libraries grew apace also. Of course, other books, not of our literary or aesthetic standard, came into the house – often as presents, but also, regrettably, from the library.

Wolf and Heath comment extensively on the use of literature as a manipulative device by both parents and children (*Braid*: 21, 110). The Lowe adults very rarely used this ploy to jolly along chores or get things done, although a book reading could always be used to comfort or cheer and lighten a dark mood. My occasional attempts to draw a moral lesson from a story were likely to misfire. Trying to persuade Rebecca not to fight with her friend Justin, I reminded her that Frances's best friend was a boy (*Best Friends for Frances* – Frances is an anthropomorphised badger): 'Well, it's different for animals!' she said firmly (4–9).

Rebecca was born on 6 December 1971 and Ralph on 27 February

1975 – 3 years 2 months apart. Box 2.2 (p. 21) is a chart of their development, both language and physical, and also some book-handling skills.

One wonders how their intense diet of books affected them. (See Rebecca's Afterword, p. 165) Certainly neither of them learned to read easily. (The literature at the time said that they would if they had been read to extensively, but it was not so. Both were close to 8 before they could read at their interest level.) However, the book exposure affected their vocabularies as one would expect, and acted as a framework for complex language structures.

Neither of the children spoke particularly early, either – another thing I expected would come naturally with so much book contact. Perhaps this was a direct result of our eschewing the labelling game. There was little of the 'What's this?' 'Show me the cat' in the diet of Rebecca, though she supplied it herself in the case of her baby brother. (See examples in Boxes 3.1 and 3.2, pp. 27 and 31.)

When we moved to Melbourne from the rural city of Bathurst and Rebecca was just 2, people began commenting on her 'English accent', and eventually I realised that she was using the best language in her environment – the language we read to her from books – as her model. We read with expression, though with few dramatic moments. John sometimes assumed different voices but I very rarely did. However, Rebecca had adopted the slightly exaggerated intonation, and complete sentences and an elevated vocabulary, that she was used to from the readings. At 2½ she took this one stage further, moving into a stage of extensive quotation, either direct quotations from the texts of books, or adapted ones.

Her earliest quotation from a book was at 2–0. One meal, she complained that her food was hot. I said no, it was warm. 'Warm and cosy,' she countered. This was not a phrase we used, certainly not with reference to food. John and I both recognised it as a quotation, but didn't know where from. 'Say-a' she told us, but we couldn't understand, so she got down from her high chair, went into her room, and pushed all the books off her low table until she found Bruna's *The Sailor* and brought it to us triumphantly. Sure enough, 'the igloo was warm and cosy'.

From this age on she quoted occasionally. 'Where are you going this nice fine day?' was a favourite, from Milne's 'Puppy and I'. In the car at 2–2: 'I saw a horse. He was black and [mumble]'. I offered, '[He] was black and very beautiful' (from *Millions of Cats*). This was it and throughout the trip she used the construction, including 'I saw a caravan. It was purple and very beautiful'.

However, at about 2–3 she began quoting extensively, larding all her conversation with literary phrases. It seemed to be particularly unusual experiences that inspired quotation. A trip at 2–4 encompassing the bush, the beach, boats, a pier, and froth left on the beach by the wild surf led to many quotations, including 'I'll take a boat and I'll sail away' (from *The Sailor*), 'Baby Doll wants to go on a boat to market' (*The Cow Who Fell in the Canal*) and 'I went down to the fluffy sea' (adapted from 'Sand between the toes' in *When We Were Very Young*). Occasionally it was single words from her books. At the strange phenomenon of baby spiders flying on silk in the wind, we told her they were called 'lerps'. After a moment she said 'I think I'll call them nightingales' – a word encountered only in *Inch by Inch*.

Ralph didn't quote, probably because his book experiences were less intense though more varied. He had an early awareness of the written words in a book, pointing at the words on a pictureless page I was reading to Rebecca at 1–1 (p. 34), but there was less quoting and reciting.

He often referred to 'the words' of a book, which seemed to mean the printed words as opposed to what the reader was articulating. In Oxenbury's *Cakes and Custard* nursery rhyme book, he looked for 'the cat and the fiddle', which are just not in her illustration, and complained 'But the words say it' (2–7). Similarly, to Dr Seuss's 'A fish in a tree, how can that be?' he answered seriously 'It's just a word' – in other words, a book can say anything, it doesn't have to be plausible (*One Fish, Two Fish, Red Fish, Blue Fish*, 2–6).

It was eventually quite clear that he had the concept of the printed words carrying the spoken ones in reading aloud, and also that someone had written them, when he addressed the author as 'read-maker' at 4–0 (p. 108).

Margaret Meek says that most adults sharing books with children 'keep the reading whole' (1992b: 177), which does not agree with a perceived emphasis on labelling found in the work of other commentators. However, the two bookish parents in this study believed that the sooner the child could get inside the story, in the book's own language, the better. The picture book was viewed as a work of art, with the words and the pictures belonging together, so that to some extent the words were inviolate. We preferred to read the text, even to a young baby, and keep the interest by pointing out details in the picture as the words mentioned them. We disliked quizzing the child, to ask for a demonstration of knowledge that they knew we knew they knew. The labelling game is a form of coaching. In our family books were for pleasure, aesthetic pleasure. Any learning that happened thereby was incidental. This, at least, was the idealised point of view, the theory.

In practice there was some labelling (different animals, say, or parts of the body), but this was separate from the process of reading the story. The labelling game did happen (see the references to pointing on pp. 36–41 and Box 3.4 on p. 31), but it occurred outside the frame of the story itself, and it was not our only mode of sharing books with infants. Instead, the words of the text would be read either as written, or abridged, depending on the concentration of the child, but rarely altered or retold in our own words. Our expectation was that the children would enjoy the literary language, just as their parents did.

Despite the Lowe parents' penchant for the actual words of the story, meanings were still negotiated. The example of Ralph at 2–0 maintaining that there is raw egg inside an egg, rather than a duckling (p. 106), is one example of many where he initially denied the veracity of the printed word.

Some aspects of the reading process were inevitably affected by the fact of my recording them. I often chose books that I thought would be in print for years, for instance, and I chose reading as my favourite activity with them. However, these aspects were only intensifying behaviour that would have been a normal part of our lifestyle, anyway.

That our relatively undramatised style of reading affected the children's verbal responses is obvious when they are compared with Anna Crago's. Many of Anna's first quotations were exclamations (*Prelude*: 257), something which our children rarely quoted. Also, Anna asked many questions throughout the stories, Rebecca very few up to about 3–2, probably because we endeavoured not to have the story interrupted (*Prelude*: xxiv–xxv; Lowe 1977a: 142). However, Ralph, with a younger sibling's different environment, did ask questions.

Some of the previous case studies have been mainly interested in the actual process of learning to read, especially where the parent-observers were educationalists. We were interested in the books as literature and in the illustrations as works of art, and it was aesthetic appreciation we were concerned with, rather than the ability to decode words, believing that this would eventually happen with exposure. Neither child being an early reader, they were happy for us to continue the supply of complex fiction by reading aloud well into the middle primary years.

I shall now give a brief sketch of both children: their personalities, book interests, book-related games and also their learning to read. This will put the study into context. The children's infancy is treated at length in Chapter 3, which traces their book development up to the age of 2.

The environment of the two children was different, as is inevitable. The younger shared most of his reading sessions with his sibling, which brought exposure to a much wider range of titles, and more complex ones, than were offered to the older child at the same age. His reading experience was also different, in that it was more social and more lively, being shared with another child. However, both Rebecca's and Ralph's earliest book experiences were, apparently, unlike those of most other children, as we usually read the words of the book, rather than merely playing the labelling game with pictures: naming and requesting names.

Born into a bookish, middle-class, educated home, with devoted parents who were committed book people, they were of course very advantaged in this area. The house was full of books, both adults' and children's, and, as we are chronically untidy, books tended to be found on the floor, on chairs and tables and beds as well as on the bookshelves.

Our style of parenting was fairly non-authoritarian. We did not have many rules, and those that we did have involved the children's safety. However, books were another matter. It seemed easier to teach the children to respect them, rather than cure ourselves of untidiness, so they were forbidden to tear or draw on books, or to stand on the pages. We were, however, quite happy for books to be used as building material, or as substitute groceries in shopping games, for instance. In fact, books were one of the most familiar items in the house.

An interesting comment on this is Ralph at 3–11 (Box 2.1) when he refused to believe that there had been a time when the house had no books in – this was apparently outside his ability to imagine.

Box 2.1 'The books we had forever'

Reading Journal, volume 21: Ralph 3–11 to 4–1

Ralph bouncing boisterously from room to room on a large orange rubber ball with a handle.

Ralph: This is a small house. A small house but a good one.
Virginia: You like it, do you?
Ralph: Yeah. It's got lots of books and stuff.

One week later:
Ralph: How do your own books get into your house?
Virginia: Someone buys them and gives them to you. What did you think?
Ralph: I thought when the builder builded the house he made them, too.

This was not a flight of fancy, but quite serious. It is clearly a combination of his experience with the new room being added, and his inability to imagine a house without books.

One month later, Ralph 4–1:
Ralph: How did books come, which are our books?
Virginia: We bought them or brought them from Bathurst.
Ralph: No, the ones we had for ever. I mean the ones in the house when we came here.

It seems that nothing convinces him that the house was once bookless.

So, the children had ready access to books. We put library books, and precious signed copies, safely on a high shelf for protection, to be shared only with parents, and kept pencils and pens separated from books as much as possible. However, even when the children were infants there was very little damage. There were only one or two incidents of deliberate tearing throughout the childhood of both, despite the fact that Rebecca had had books in her cot to look at when she awoke, and often spent half an hour or longer alone with them, from 12 months.

Rebecca coped well with the advent of Ralph when she was aged 3 years 2 months. She enjoyed talking to him and showing him the pictures as Lucy does Tom in *Lucy and Tom's Day* (Hughes). She treated him almost as an adult would. She knew I was pregnant as soon as we did. She felt Baby Sibling kick, and talked to him *in utero*, following the development of the foetus in *Where Do Babies Come From?* We tried to prepare her carefully by explaining that living with a baby, though looked forward to eagerly, was not all fun. Not long before his birth I felt I had perhaps overdone this, when she told me a story about her pretend mouse Brownie's mother (Whitey), who has 'fifty-three twins'. She has so many babies that she has to put their cots in the hall and the bathroom and the toilet, and they all cry together and lose their dummies at once and she and Brownie's Daddy 'come and kiss them all over, but they still cry a little bit' (3–1).

Their respective methods of learning to walk are indicative of their personalities. Rebecca taught herself to walk, holding on to the bars of the playpen (where she had to be confined in the kitchen while I cooked, in the Bathurst house). She did it by what appeared to be measured stages, as if she knew exactly what she was teaching herself. She could walk at 10 months, run at 11. Ralph impulsively took his first steps – six of them – at Rebecca's fourth birthday party when he was 9 months old. Then he returned to cruising around furniture and crawling for several more months. He was almost walking when we left Australia's summer (and bare feet) for Europe's booted winter, and he was 13 months before he was walking independently (though he was able to run – after or away from Rebecca – very shortly afterwards).

Neither child spoke early. Rebecca's understood vocabulary was very large but she refused to use any word until she was sure it would be understood, and was 1–7 before she was using many words (Box 2.2 and p. 33).

Later she was acutely aware of her pronunciation. At 2–2 she came to me in the kitchen asking for a banana, and for the first time pronounced it correctly instead of 'bana'. She was very excited: 'Mummy, Mummy, I can say it with my tongue! Banana!' pronouncing it with delight, slowly and carefully. A week later she also remarked on the fact that she had at last learned to pronounce /l/ – anyway at the beginning of words ('libry' instead of 'yibry'). Talking to the cat (with a partial quotation about cats from *Benjamin Bunny*): '/l/. I can say /l/. When I was a little girl I had no opinion whatever of /l/s. I took an enormous jump . . .' and paused, realising the rest of the quotation was not relevant. We had never criticised her mispronunciation, or drawn attention to it, other than making sure our reply used the word correctly, but she was just very self-conscious and aware.

Ralph's language development could not have been more different. The level of talk in the house was so much greater with another articulate child present. Rebecca enjoyed chatting to the baby, and especially showing him books. She supplied much of the labelling game which had been almost absent in her own earliest book contacts. So, there was a different level of language for fun, and of laughter, in his environment. He was not particularly concerned if he was misunderstood. In fact, much of his language was jargon for many months. Rebecca used jargon only to 'read' handwritten letters at 12 months. Other than that, she didn't say something until she was sure it would be understood. If she couldn't be understood, what was the point of speaking?

Ralph of course knew what the point of speaking was – it was to socialise. Actual communication of meaning took a back seat for many months. Nevertheless, both of their vocabularies were quite extensive by 21 months (see Box 2.2).

Naturally, their book experiences were different too. We spent less time reading to Ralph as an infant. He was less rewarding to share books with than Rebecca had been, because he was so active: he wanted to be playing with the cover, chewing the pages, or simply bouncing on the adult's knee. Also, he 'talked' throughout – jargoned – so our reading of the words continued under this constant chatter. Nevertheless, I did persist. I believed everyone had to have contact with books and stories – and he never had to be persuaded to hear a book.

Once he started talking conventionally, he also began to ask questions related to the books – something Rebecca had rarely done. Generally we discouraged questions. We would turn them back onto the child – 'What do you think?' – or, if we could see the answer coming in the text: 'Wait, it will tell you.' Rebecca rarely asked vocabulary questions, preferring to taste interesting words, and try them out. Some time later – even weeks – when she had been chanting the word as she played, she would suddenly ask 'what does mackintosh [or fortnight, or camomile tea] mean?' She seemed to want to work out the meanings herself first, before she asked us.

This was probably because we adults treated the book as an aesthetic whole, with the words read as far as possible straight through. Most people who have published studies of young children with books are more interested in the child understanding the meaning of the word (possibly because most have been teachers). Of the studied children, only Cushla's parents seemed to treat books the way we did – to be enjoyed, and to grow into the understanding of them (*Cushla*: 28ff.).

Rebecca was 3 before she started to question books, and when she did it was the concepts she was interested in, not the facts of the story (which presumably were clear to her anyway). *Barbapapa's Ark* was by far her favourite book from 3 up to 7. Thinking of logical questions to ask about it was definitely part of the pleasure of this book (p. 59).

As an aside, it is worth considering how much influence childhood reading has on the adult. We cannot know whether the child's favourite book is a favourite because it relates to something in their personality, or whether the book itself influences the adult. Did Rebecca's passion for the environment arise from or lead to her love of *Barbapapa's Ark*? Her year after school (18) was spent in the forest trying to save the old growth from being logged, including ten days in prison for her pains. Today she farms without chemicals and with no cruelty to the animals she is surrounded by. Hugh Crago (1993) published an article on her identification with Snufkin (from Jansson's Moomintrolls series) and Jansson's identification with Tarzan at a similar age. In the same way, Ralph's determination to 'save' book characters can be seen as a precursor to his career today as an ambulance paramedic.

In all things Rebecca was a perfectionist. She loved to draw and to create things with play dough or paper, sticky tape, staples and glue – clothes for herself and baby Ralph, little books for her doll's house. Her output was prodigious. However, at 3–2 she stopped drawing for almost a year. When she started again I commented 'You used to draw all the time.' She pointed dismissively to the two sketches that had been attached to the front of the refrigerator for almost a year, explaining that 'they don't look anything like a cow and a cat' (4–1). As long as they were there to remind her of her shortcomings, she chose not to do any more. Fortunately, she started kindergarten at 4–2 and took up art again with a vengeance, seldom returning with fewer than two paintings. Always if I praised something that she was not happy with, be it a block building, a paper construction or some pencil work, she would knock it down or tear it up. I had to learn to hold in my instinctive and quite genuine enthusiasm and ask 'Are you happy with it?' or 'Tell me about it.' On the other hand, Ralph did little in the way of drawing and constructing, though his drawing level was equivalent to Rebecca's when he did do it. When he did, I had to respond with enormous enthusiasm if he was to return to the task. I had to unlearn my hard-won reticence.

Rebecca had an impressive colour sense. Even before she could say the names of the colours she would pick out the exact shade in two disparate places and say 'match' (one of her first words). One day it was one of the colours in her floral dress and a car just that exact shade of aqua passing us (1–3 – 'match'). Ralph was slower in this regard. He knew colours were important, and when we were out he'd always comment on Minis we saw as 'Mamma car' (because the nearby grandparents owned one). Then in anticipation of my next question, he would chant 'Blue Mamma car, yellow Mamma car, red Mamma car' – quite at random. He was 2–3 before he had the colours accurate.

Rather than draw or create, Ralph was a dramatist. His games were all acted out, either by himself or with model figures. He loved imaginative adventures, and in late primary years he started a continuing fascination with role-playing games.

Their attitude to books was in similar contrast. Rebecca seemed to consider the words inviolate. Away from the book she would quote, even deliberately adapt the quotations and misquote, but she always accepted what the book said. Ralph, on the other hand, queried everything. To him there was nothing sacred about the book's words. He was quite happy to argue with the author or the interpreting adult, and as our policy was to give all opinions equal weight, he tended to feel he was right. He would disagree that there was a duckling in Bruna's eponymous egg (p. 106), or would offer to marry the little lame boy left behind by the Pied Piper, or to take a ladder and climb the steeple and rescue the little half-chick in the story in *Fairy Tale Treasury*.

A moment of insight occurred at 4–2. Listening with Rebecca, Ralph had heard many isolated chapters, especially of the Narnia Chronicles, over the previous three months. *Moominland Midwinter* was the first non-episodic 'chapter book' read specifically for him. At bedtime the first night he wanted to know 'How will we remember what we were up to?' [That was the first chapter.] 'Is it pretending to join on to the next chapter?' [It is one story right through the book.] 'Does it go on and on and on?' He was clearly delighted with this new concept. From then on he listened to novels, and he and Rebecca frequently shared them, with readings usually delayed until both were present to listen.

They had differing books as their favourites also, although both heard plenty of their sibling's choices. Speaking generally, Rebecca preferred stories of the everyday, or of normal people having fantastic adventures. Ralph loved fantasy, and thrived on myths and legends when we began reading them to him at around 4. The next section lists their favourite titles with a few comments on the reading patterns, to give some flavour of the intensity of some reading periods. As can be seen, both children heard many stories over and over. As Dombey points out (1992: 33), familiarity with the outcome does not prevent the child, and even the reading adult, from joining in, becoming again (or still) the implied reader, who feels the tension, looks ahead and creates hypotheses.

Despite recognising all the letters of the alphabet and knowing many words that started with each letter, and despite being able to read the little books I made for them, they both found learning to read quite difficult, and were about 8 before they could read at their interest level. Part of the problem with Rebecca was that her first school used the ITA method, with different symbols for the sounds, so she was cut off from the familiar print and the thirty words she recognised by sight. Also, she was very aware of the level of reading ability of the others in the grade (two or three being able to read when they started school), and saw herself as a poor reader (again typical of her perfectionist personality).

When Ralph started school it was at Montessori, and he was never pushed to read, so there was not the drama with the school readers that made reading practice so unpleasant with Rebecca (of course she hated getting things wrong, and hated being taught as well). When they both changed back to a conventional school, it seemed Ralph couldn't read at all, so they put him into the grade below his age level. However, by the end of the year he was reading at the level of the others, so he skipped a year to go in with his peers.

This was all rather a surprise, as I had expected them to read easily. I suspect that the level of the readers they had to begin on seemed boring and banal after the sort of narratives they were used to hearing. Perhaps the effort to read themselves seemed unrewarding compared with the stories they listened to every night. As they were already into C.S. Lewis and the *Moomintrolls* (Ralph) and *Five Dolls* and Rumer Godden (Rebecca), the readers must have held nothing but hard and unpleasant work.

Underpinning all this book activity was the period when they were infants, which is described in the chapter which follows.

Favourite books

Here are brief summaries of a few of Rebecca's and Ralph's favourite books, and also some of the reading patterns, so that the intensity of the book contact can be gauged. They are organised under the child's name, followed by a section on the ones important to both the children. Remember that as soon as Ralph was capable of listening to full picture books, Rebecca usually listened in to his readings too, and that later – when he was about 3½ – he would listen in to the longer chapter books being read to her. The net result is that Rebecca heard the picture books over a longer period of time, while Ralph began to hear the longer stories at an earlier age. Between them they encountered 1,842 titles up to the age of 8 – 1,178 for Rebecca and 1,175 for Ralph.

Rebecca

Bruna's *B is for Bear* (see Box 3.1), and also the Brian Wildsmith titles *The Hare and the Tortoise* and *Mother Goose* were important to Rebecca as a baby. *The Hare and the Tortoise* was requested almost routinely for the night-time read – two or three times a week – during the year she was 2 (Figures 5.2, 5.7).

Millions of Cats by Wanda Gag was borrowed from the library at 1–4, and given, wrapped as a present, at 1–6. She opened it with the back up, but recognised the yellow cover with black writing and no picture, and began to say 'miaow, miaow' at once (Figure 3.4).

Make Way for Ducklings and especially *Blueberries for Sal* by Robert McCloskey were important.

The Tale of Samuel Whiskers was her favourite Beatrix Potter, after she received it at 3–2. Prior to that it was *The Tale of Tom Kitten*.

Barbapapa's Ark by Annette Tison and Talus Taylor was her favourite book from 3–5 up until it was usurped by the Moomintroll books at 6–4. At 7 it was still a security object, and one of the two books she chose to take away to Brownie camp (Figures 4.4 and 4.5).

Five Dolls and Their Friends (Helen Clare) was loved for its wordplay and outrageous characters at 4–10.

Alice in Wonderland and *Through the Looking Glass* by Lewis Carroll were influential from 5–5. When she set up home for herself at 19, the books she felt every home should have, besides a good dictionary, were *Winnie-the-Pooh* and *Alice*, and she searched for second-hand copies.

Other favourites within the time frame of this book were *Ramona the Pest* (Beverley Cleary) and the rest of this series from 5–7 (she identified closely with Ramona's school adventures); Green Knowe series (Lucy Boston) from 6–2; Little House series (Laura Ingalls Wilder) from 7–6; *The Secret Garden* (Frances Hodgson Burnett) from 7–10. (Rebecca was known as 'Dick' from 'Dickon', and spoken of as 'he', for over a year at the Montessori school.)

Ralph

The Elephant and the Bad Baby by Elfrida Vipont and Raymond Briggs was one of Ralph's first loves (Figure 5.5).

Richard Scarry's Best Word Book Ever he received at 1–10, and spent hours poring over it from then on. He was fascinated by all titles by Scarry.

Crazy Cowboy (Guillermo Mordillo) from 3–8 and *Patatrac* by Jean Jacques Loup from 4–0 were favorites. He learned to distinguish styles of drawing from these (Figures 6.1 and 6.2).

Myths and Legends (Anne Terry White and Alice and Martin Provensen) was important from 3–9.

Others were: *The Hobbit* by Tolkien (he heard this at 4–11. Rebecca at 8–2 usually declined to listen – too much fighting, she said; but see her comments on p. 166); *Charlie and the Chocolate Factory* (Roald Dahl) at 3–6 and again at 7–1; *A Wizard of Earthsea* (Ursula Le Guin) Ralph at 7–5 (with Rebecca 10–8).

Both

As infants, there were *Mother Goose* (Brian Wildsmith – Figure 5.2), Dick Bruna's *B is for Bear* (Figure 3.1 and 3.2), *The Sailor, The Egg, Miffy at the Zoo, Miffy's Birthday*.

Later they shared *Winnie-the-Pooh* and *The House at Pooh Corner* (Milne). From the age of about 2, both of them would always listen to another of these episodic chapters. They also had several of the stories on tape.

Both spent a lot of time with Asterix titles (Goscinny and Uderzo) also (often the two of them without an adult) from when Ralph was 5–6, especially as Rebecca (8–8) could now read them for both.

The Mouse and His Child (Russell Hoban) was enjoyed with Ralph 7–4, Rebecca 10–7.

Tove Jansson's Moomintroll books were important to both. Rebecca first heard the picture book *Who Will Comfort Toffle?* several times at 4, then again with Ralph (3–1) at 6–4. This was also the age at which we read her the first of the series, *Finn Family Moomintroll*. It was completed in eight days. Ralph, at 3–1 to 3–4, overhead some of it, and was aware of Rebecca's fascination. Once it was finished, Rebecca asked for individual chapters to be read until we got the next book (a pattern repeated throughout the reading of the whole series). She bought each of the other books with her meagre pocket money and kept them with her in a little blue case, and the current one under her pillow. The second one she acquired was *Comet in Moominland*. This was read over five days, followed by the other five in the series over the next two months. She was 6–7 when we completed the last one. *Moominland Midwinter* took only two days to read (days without school, obviously). This was the first title Ralph heard right through specifically for himself at 4–2. It took eight days to read. He heard the rest over the next three months, and *Comet* again ten months later (5–1) (see pp. 134–137).

Box 2.2 The children's development

Behaviour	Rebecca	Ralph
First book contact	0–3	0–0
Crawls	0–7	0–7
Walks	0–10	1–1
Weaned from breast	0–10	2–5
Identifies five body parts	0–11	
'Bup bup' for any animal		0–11
14 words in use	1–2	1–1
Pictures right way up	1–0	1–8
Identifies 15 body parts	1–2	
29 words in use		1–4
35 words in use	1–7	
Two-word sentences	1–7	1–5
68 words		1–9
350 words	1–9	
Three-word sentences	1–9	
Possessive, plural 's'	1–9	1–11
Names colours (4)	1–10	2–3
203 words		2–0
First-person pronoun 'I'	2–0	2–2
'I can say it with my tongue'	2–3	
Recognises figures 1 to 9	2–2	2–3
Counts to 5	2–2	2–8
1,147 words (excluding names and inflected verbs)	2–3	
Recognises 26 letters (upper-case)	2–3	
Recognises 3 objects without counting	2–6	2–6
Reads at interest level	7–6	8–0

C.S. Lewis's Narnia chronicles were also significant to both. Rebecca heard *The Lion, the Witch and the Wardrobe* at 7–2, and Ralph, then 4–1, often sat through the chapters read as well. The whole series was finished in three months. When Ralph was 5–11 we started the series again, and continued to read them aloud regularly until he was 8–6 (see pp. 116–119).

3 'More book'

Infant book behaviour

The period of book development from birth to 2 is the one that has received the least recorded consideration. In the first of the reading diaries, Dorothy White began her recording only when Carol was 2 (*BbF*), and even the Cragos, the most meticulous and thorough observers to date (*Prelude*), have very few records before this age, and did not keep records of Anna or her sister Morwenna as infants. Shelby Wolf began her records when Lindsey was 3–2 (Wolf 1988: 2), and despite the fact that she had a second child while she was working on the Lindsey material, there are no infant records of Ashley either. Cushla is the only child for whom there is a record of book behaviour as an infant (*Cushla*: 15–58).

Prior to the age of 2, naturally there are few comments from the children themselves on reality – in books or in life. However, there is behaviour that indicates how the infant is thinking. There is also a lot of book behaviour: recognition of pictures, book handling skills and the influence of books on language development. It seems apposite to devote a chapter to this period. Not only is it almost completely uncharted territory, but it also underpins the remainder of the observations.

There have been quite a few individual children whose language acquisition has been recorded, most notably the crib monologues of Wier (1962) and Nelson (1989). I cannot compete with these records, of course, if only because I did not actually use an electronic recording device. However, my record covers a much greater length of time and many more situations.

Dorothy Butler's record of her granddaughter (*Cushla*) is the only one that deals with babyhood, and Cushla, although definitely advanced in book handling skills and understanding stories, was indeed a special child (she had a genetic abnormality), so the record is unusual in many ways. This babyhood record may exist because Cushla heard the actual words read, as our children did, rather than mainly playing the labelling game, so in both cases there was much more to record.

By the time Rebecca and Ralph were a year old, the pictures were not collections of things to name, but already part of a cohesive story, which, if not understood fully, was at least predictable – the characters reappearing and the words always following the same pattern. The story was already marked as a different type of discourse from conversation, because, unlike the labelling game of others, it was not in dialogue form, not colloquial. When only labelling is involved, 'no gross modification of the adult's customary use of language is required in carrying out book-reading. The mother is acting in a linguistically conventional manner' (Ninio and Bruner 1976: 8). This did not apply to our behaviour. The Cragos observe that 'the written narrative spoken aloud must have sounded quite different to Anna from the book talk of the "outside" model' (*Prelude*: 8). In Ninio and Bruner's terminology, we were clearly behaving in a linguistically 'unconventional' way by actually reading.

DeLoache remarks 'Since picture book reading sessions are most often terminated by the child's losing interest, a major part of the mother's role is trying to keep the interaction going' (1984: 18). Perhaps this is another result of the labelling process, because in our house it was almost always the officiating adult who terminated the sessions; the children, from about 10 months, would have shared books for as long as the adult would cooperate. There were occasions when something else drew their attention, or they were tired and their concentration was poor, but generally the demands, both to start the reading sessions and to continue them, came from the children themselves.

The children did practise labelling alone. As a parent-researcher I was confident that when they sat and pointed to things in the pictures, they were labelling for themselves, even before they could say the words. Rebecca used labelling routines in her interactions with baby Ralph, so this aspect of his

Figure 3.1 B is for Bear Dick Bruna.

book experience resembled that of the other studied children more closely than her own did. Box 3.4 contains the transcription of a session where Rebecca at 4–6 is sharing a book with Ralph 1–4, with some direct quotations from the text but plenty of the labelling game as well. Words and pictures belong together from an aesthetic point of view, which is why we adults read the words (occasionally abridged) rather than talked about the pictures. Also, we disliked the sort of test questions inherent in the 'labelling game'.

They were full-term healthy babies, lengthily breastfed. As has already been mentioned, both walked quite early, but neither was a particularly early speaker, with Ralph producing his first words younger than Rebecca, but she gaining vocabulary more quickly thereafter. Language development up to 2 is recorded in this chapter.

When Rebecca was born, John was the librarian of a large rural tertiary college. She was 13 weeks old when, waiting for him in the library, I began idly turning the pages of a big atlas on a stand as I held her. I noticed her head moving as she followed the pages turning. I took this as readiness for books, and started to read to her as soon as I returned home. Her first book was *B is for Bear*, which I thought would interest her because of the bright primary colours, heavy outlines and lots of white space around each object. She was interested, and reading became a regular activity from then on. I soon added several other Bruna books and Wildsmith's *Mother Goose*. The experience of sitting on a lap, and listening and feeling the vibrations of the voice, accompanied by bright visual input, proved irresistible, and before long we used books not only to amuse, but to cheer, comfort and distract her, just as we used them ourselves.

Her first clear love was the yellow lion in *B is for Bear* (Figure 3.1). At 6 months she would stare and pat it, then scratch at it, perhaps thinking it

---

Box 3.1 Infant encounters with *B is for Bear*

Reading Journal, volume 1: Rebecca 0–3 (13 weeks).

Several times has sat right through *B is for Bear* with every sign of interest. 26 openings seem a long span of concentration.

Tries to reach out to touch favourite pictures – seems to like the yellow lion best (or is that just wishful thinking on our part?). Seems enthusiastic and interested in yellow and some red pictures, but just passing glance at grey ones, or even ignores them. Certainly looks longest at the red and yellow ones (yellow bear and lion, red pig). Follows the picture with her eyes when turn over the page, and seems to wonder where the picture has gone to. Then she moves her eyes over to the right-hand page again and discovers the new picture. She has touched and held the pages, and the cover. One day I let her push the front cover shut over and over (did it by accident the first time, but seemed deliberate later).

was three-dimensional and could be grasped. (This behaviour can be seen more clearly with Ralph – see Box 3.2.) She also showed enthusiasm for the yellow bear and red pig, and least interest in the grey mouse. Unlike Cushla, she had no interest in the single letter on the left-hand page, but waited eagerly for the page to be turned to reveal the next picture.

Bruna's pictures are brightly coloured and very stylised – not likely to be recognised by a baby as representing anything in the external world. They have heavy black outlines, and stand out against the white pages. The second edition has coloured backgrounds instead of white, and in my opinion the pictures are not as arresting. Also, the Eskimo, which featured largely in Ralph's infant responses – see Box 3.2 – has been replaced by an elephant.

Presumably it was the colours and designs that fascinated the children, but it is interesting that quite different pictures attracted them as babies, and coincidently also aligned with their interests and personality types as they were revealed in later years. Ralph's intense interest in people seemed to fit in with his fascination with the first of the Bruna pictures which illustrated a person ('Eskimo', Figure 3.2), just as Rebecca at 14 weeks (her third

Figure 3.2 B is for Bear Dick Bruna.

'reading') had shown a strong preference for the 'lion' (Figure 3.1). At the time, we put Rebecca's preference down to the yellow colour and interesting spiky pattern, but the lion remained her favourite page for the next six months, and animals fascinated her throughout her infancy and childhood (and indeed as an adult also). She preferred the single-colour pictures (the bear, the lion and the pig). There is no mention of the Eskimo in her early encounters. The Eskimo, in contrast to the lion, has many colours and quite complex patterns. Ralph's fixation with it was not repeated, but two months later, with only one reading in between, it was the queen who held his attention – another of the three people pictured in the twenty-six openings.

Box 3.2 Infant encounters with *B is for Bear*

Reading Journal, volume 3: Ralph 0–3 (16 weeks).

[Ralph's first 'reading' of Bruna's B is for Bear *had been at 14 weeks, when he watched the pages turning and looked at a couple of the pictures, though not very fixedly. He did not sit through it all. Two weeks later I tried again.]*

In bed this morning, after his feed, I showed it to him. He was lying beside me, so I could see him easily in profile and watch his eye movements. We went through the apple, bear, castle and duck with minimal interest. He was lying still, with a glance at the picture and then away to another section of the page or right off the book altogether. I was just telling myself that he and Rebecca are two different children, and comparisons are odious, when we reached the Eskimo. This time the reaction was completely different. He stared and stared at it, with his eyes going from the feet up to the face over and over again. I didn't count how many times this happened, but certainly more than ten. After about six of these, he started vocalising to it, making three or four cheerful 'ah's, and began to move his arms excitedly, too. At first it was generalised arm waving and kicking, but gradually his left arm waved closer and closer to the book, until it was right on the picture, hitting it quite hard with his fist. He also smiled at it several times. He seemed completely fascinated. I've never seen him smile at any object before, only people. After a long time – at least several minutes – his concentration was not broken, but I wanted to see if the same interest was apparent on other pages. His waving continued during the fish and the grapes, and he grasped the bottom of the book with his left hand several times, but not the same concentrated looking. He used the bottom-to-top eye sweep again on the fish once or twice, so it may be an automatic picture scanning reaction, but then looked right off the book. At the hammer he made an unhappy sound, so I turned back to the Eskimo and he was excited again and repeated his happy noise. This time he looked steadily but only for several seconds, then away, so I continued. We got to the owl, when he grizzled again. I returned to the Eskimo, but there was minimal interest, and I assumed he had had enough 'reading' for one day.

Box 3.3 Shared encounters with *B is for Bear*

Reading Journal, volume 4: Ralph 0–6, Rebecca 3–9

[*With three 'readings' to Ralph in between, I here share the book with both children.*]

Showed him *B is for Bear* again. Very interested in the pictures themselves, this time, and much less manipulation. Main response to all was to scratch with fingers of both hands over picture. No response at all to the letters on the left-hand side. Also picking motions with his thumb and forefinger on the pictures, as if trying to pick up bits – e.g. mouse's tail. At 'lion', and a couple of the others, scratched first and then a long pause to stare before back to scratching – seemed to do that to those of most interest. After some time, on most, he would sit back, still looking at the picture, then look away. He would lose concentration at last, if I left him on one page for too long. I lifted each page to get him to help turn. It was more like crumpling, not really grasped, just part of the scratching, usually. Less trying to get mouth to them than last time, though (and he is inhibiting that reflex himself now – not *all* his toys go straight to his mouth – uses his eyes first quite often).

He first put his mouth on the book ('kissed', as Rebecca had it) at the red 'pig'. Did the same to the red 'toadstool', and to the black 'umbrella' immediately afterwards. Concentration was decreasing by this time (largely due to Rebecca's comments). She asked me to turn over the pages while he was still in his first interest, several times. Rebecca's comments, telling him about the pictures, I rather enjoyed. I find in *B is for Bear* I tend to just say the word and sometimes the letter, e.g. 'C is for castle'. However, Rebecca's commentary went like this:

Rebecca: That's called a castle, Little Man. You go in there. You look out of those.
            Those are windows to see.

At the grey 'duck' Ralph picked at the eye (black spot) and the yellow beak. I seem to remember Rebecca more or less ignored the grey ones at his age. No special response to the 'Eskimo' this time, not even response directed mainly to the face, which I somehow expected to see. More interest in colours and patterns on clothes, especially the pants. 'Fish' and 'grapes' little response, but at once tried to grasp (or anyway looked like it) the handle of 'hammer' – reached directly out to it with his hand open.

Rebecca: That's to hammer nails into wood, Baby!
            That's a key. It's to open doors with.

At 'lion', he showed the most interest in the face – staring, then picking at eyes and other spots. Then pause to stare, and back to scratching again.
    Picked at the mouse's tail with thumb and finger of one hand.
    Yellow and black eyes on 'owl' reached for specifically, then:

Rebecca: Yes, that's his nose [beak], Little Baby!

She laughed at him kissing the 'pig'. At 'queen', he showed most interest in her red skirts at the bottom, though touched face also. At 'violin' Rebecca's breakfast was brought and his interest waned. Got him to look briefly at the remaining pictures by turning the page myself, saying 'look' and tapping the picture. He'd feel each briefly, then back to watching Rebecca's scrambled egg. Even under these circumstances, I could tell he liked the 'zebra', though, and he also singled out the white eye and blue water of the 'whale'.

No attempt to grab book, suck corners etc., but content and interested to feel and examine pictures. Not even very much interest in helping turn pages – much more interest in the picture on the turning page than the feel and manipulation of holding and turning the paper, which is a real advance over the last time.

Boxes 3.1, 3.2 and 3.3 contain both children's early encounters with the same book at similar ages, for comparison. Detailed descriptions of young infants and books are rare. I reproduce here three entries from the Journal for *B is for Bear*, first with Rebecca at 0–3, then Ralph at 0–3 and again at 0–6, being shown it by Rebecca. This latter demonstrates how the same book can be used in quite different ways by different mediating 'adults'. By the time of Ralph's infant book experiences I was recording Rebecca's book responses in the Journal every night, so his record is fuller.

Whereas Rebecca's first encounters with books had been the atlas in the library at 13 weeks, and then *B is for Bear*, Ralph had books from as soon as we came home from hospital. Rebecca put books in the bassinette beside him, open at a picture, so he was surrounded by pictures from 10 days. However, it was not until 14 weeks that he first showed a real interest in a picture. He stared, fascinated, at a poster of Humpty Dumpty in a change room in the city, and on returning home he looked with interest at the Galt rag book I then showed him. Two weeks later came his first encounter with *B is for Bear*. His second experience with it at 16 weeks is recorded in Box 3.1. DeLoache (1998) spells out the 9-month-old infant's grasping response to pictures as if they were real objects, as common in both American and African environments.

Ralph's overall book experience was completely different from Rebecca's too. For one thing, we read to him less frequently than we had to her. At 16 weeks she was already hearing books for pleasure and comfort several times a week, but he was so active that we read less, and his book experiences with us were often several weeks apart. He was much more difficult to share books with. Certainly Rebecca at 0–6 had gone through a period of wanting to chew the corners, so for a few weeks there was a lull in book activity. But I noted that Ralph at 0–6 tended to bounce all the time. He also vocalised throughout, whereas Rebecca had just listened to our voices. All of this made sharing books with him less rewarding for us, so we did so less frequently at first.

Another difference was Rebecca's interaction with him. From well before his birth, following *Lucy and Tom's Day*, she had decided that the role of an older sister was to 'show him the pictures', as Lucy does Tom. Consequently, he had much more of the typical 'labelling game' than she had had herself. She talked to Ralph about the pictures, even in those cases where she could have recited the words. One example is her telling him about *B is for Bear* (Box 3.3). Another is her sharing Bruna's *The Sailor* with him (Box 3.4). This demonstrates the 'labelling game', which had been largely missing from her own baby book experience.

Box 3.4 The labelling game

Reading Journal, volume 9: Ralph 1–4, Rebecca 4–6

This was transcribed as Rebecca spoke, in volume 9 of the Journal. She is showing him The Sailor *by Dick Bruna.*

Rebecca:	I think I'll read Ralph a book. 'Once there was a sailor with a smart new ship. I'll sail away and see the world, he said.' [quoting the opening lines of the book].
	Look at the flag, Ralph.
	See all the smoke it's making?
	One, two, three [counting the portholes].
	There's the sailor, Ralph.
	There's the lighthouse. See the tiny lighthouse door?
	Great big sun.
	Drip drip drip – there's as many drips as that on the other side [to the whale's spout].
	Pup pup – look, Ralph, there's a pup pup [his word for dog].
Ralph:	Bup bup bup.
Rebecca:	Where's the sun, Ralph? Where's the sun?
	That's called an igloo.
	Want something to eat? [to pot on the fire].
	Look, Ralph, look. Look what else he's going to get. [Ralph looks, then goes away. She continues anyway.]
Rebecca:	'The end'. That's the end, Ralph.

Baby Rebecca's interest in pictures was intense. At 0–4 I took her to the official opening of John's new college library. She sat through the hour of formal speeches and presentations, occupied throughout with the plastic book *Things I See*. She sat on my lap, helping turn the pages and gazing at each picture. Similarly, at 0–5 she accompanied us to a Library Association of Australia cocktail party, and sat in her carry basket looking at a book throughout (to the delight of all the librarians, needless to say). Ralph, a much more active child, would not have had the same intense, quiet concentration.

She had books among her toys from 0–4 and often chose to study them. One which I commonly left with her was Esmé Eve's *Mother Goose* (Figure 3.3). This was a library reject and damaged in places, so I did not mind her using it as a toy. However, there is no record of her mistreating it.

When she was 0–11, I felt she was choosing to look at this the right way up. Sometimes I watched her crawl around the open book on the floor until it was right way up for her. I could not be sure of this, however, until at 1–0 she was looking at the simple raised sketch on the base of her set of beakers. She was holding the blue one, and I told her 'That's a bear.' She turned it slowly round in her hands then stopped, and when I looked over her shoulder, she had it right way up. This seemed a remarkable feat to me, as there was no colour. It was just a raised line of the same blue plastic. It was an outline, with no horizon indicated, nor anything else but the teddy bear seated, to give the clue to which way up it should be. I had never shown it to her before, either, though she had doubtless noticed it herself. Anyway, there was now no doubt in my mind that what appeared to be orientating books correctly for herself, was just that.

Again Ralph's experience was completely different. The first child hears stories from the adult's lap, or possibly sitting or lying beside them. As a second child, Ralph often was involved with the book being read to Rebecca, but as it was not specifically for him, he often joined in by coming to the adult's knee and looking at the book upside down. So, a fair proportion of his book experience would have been upside down, whereas none of the first child's was. It is not surprising, then, that he was 1–8 before he could orientate books correctly. He also had books among his toys, but whereas Rebecca had spent a time every day in her playpen, Ralph had the run of the house, and Rebecca's fascinating activities to watch, so very seldom chose to look at books alone. In fact, when he was truly mobile we put Rebecca (4) back in the playpen – setting it up with a small table, her pencils, paper and scissors, so she could come and go by climbing over, and Ralph could watch her through the bars but not spoil her creative activities.

Neither child was an early speaker, but Rebecca's noises for animals gave me some insight into her interpretation of pictures, with '[woo]ff, [woo]ff and 'miaow' noises appropriately, also 'baa' and 'moo' and a hopping motion with her hand for kangaroos and rabbits. She began to use these noises to her picture books with pointing. It is noteworthy that in the very familiar Eve *Mother Goose* she could identify the cats, even standing on their hind legs and wearing hats (Figure 3.3), as she showed by her pointing and enthusiastic 'miaow' sounds (1–1). And of course this was one of our book games – pointing to each of the animals and giving its sound. She became imperious at 1–1, pointing to animals and demanding their sound (and yes, I admit this is a form of labelling, though the sounds were for amusement, not instruction).

Figure 3.3 Mother Goose Nursery Rhymes Esmé Eve.

Ralph's first spoken word, apart from 'Mummum' and 'Dada', was 'bup bup', made to any sort of animal. (Rebecca, typically of her, either got the sound correct for the animal, or said nothing.) Ralph was enthusiastic and indiscriminate. I noted that in one day at 0–11 he made his 'bup bup' sound to a pig and a leopard on *Sesame Street*, a neighbour's hen, and to the book *Whistle for Willie* seen on the floor.

Rebecca has always had her father's prodigious memory. I vividly remember a day trip by car from Bathurst to Melbourne (about 500 kilometres) in which I amused her for an hour or more by singing nursery rhymes (0–11). I could repeat each ditty twice in succession, but then if I ran out of inspiration later and returned to, say, 'Baa Baa Black Sheep', she complained vehemently – no repeats! It was a long car trip!

Rebecca would sit for a long time just looking through books. She had a small table on which her most familiar ones were piled. At 1–0 I started the habit of putting three books in her cot when I went to bed. In the morning she would spend twenty minutes or more looking at them (once, at 1–1, it was forty-five minutes) before she called and was brought into the big bed to hear them read. Only once or twice did I leave her too long, and a page was torn. The next morning, her distress at having no books (I told her she wasn't old enough if she couldn't look at them without tearing) was sufficient to ensure that damage was minimal.

Books were read at bedtime, but usually on several other occasions during every day as well. Among their earliest words were pleas or demands for books to be read, with the child following the adult – clutching a book, or with it held out enticingly, and saying 'Wead! Wead!' (Rebecca 1–6) or 'Book! Book!' (Ralph 1–7). Of course such requests were rarely denied. They enjoyed their stories, but also knew well how to get their parents' attention!

A few words on their language development. All parents can tell similar stories about their children; the only difference is that I have kept a record of it. Again, their developmental patterns were very different, but I think not because of gender but because of their position in the family, and their personalities. All children, all people, are at the same time alike and different.

In her speech development Rebecca seems atypical, but no doubt there are many others like her.

Rebecca's understood vocabulary was extensive, even though she did not use the words herself. The Reading Journal reports that at 10 months she could obey thirty directions without physical clues – she could 'put the bear behind the television' or 'shut the drawer', etc. However, she never did like to do something unless she was sure she could do it properly. At 1–4 she was using only fifteen words. Hungry one morning, she came grizzling to me working in the laundry. I told her to go and ask Daddy for her bib, and she went off to find him, saying 'bibibi', a sound we had never heard her make before. Because John hadn't heard my original instruction, he didn't understand and had to come and ask me anyway, which may be why, although she could certainly pronounce the word, it didn't enter her lexicon until months later. She had to get it right *and* be understood. For her, language was to communicate, and if she couldn't say something and be understood at once, she just didn't attempt it.

Similarly, although she had been able to show us 'eyes, nose, mouth, hair' since 10 months, and had added many other parts of the body subsequently, the one she chose to say first was 'e-bow' at 1–7, not presumably because of its importance to her, but because she could say it to her own satisfaction.

This was the age when she began to use words consistently. She had thirty-five in regular use, with occasional two-word sentences ('Mummy more'), and also began filling in words in the texts she knew: 'grew' and 'no' in *Where the Wild Things Are* and the rhyming words in some nursery rhymes. In the next three weeks her lexicon had jumped to 102 words, and by 1–9 I counted 350 over two days, with new ones being produced constantly. By then her usual statements were of two words, some three, and some even longer. She regularly used both the possessive and plural 's'. She could 'read' ten letters and numbers correctly. At 2–0 she first used the first-person pronoun – 'I catched it'.

We seldom used babytalk ('Motherese', as Bruner calls it. He points out its importance to the infant in learning language, and perhaps its absence was what kept Rebecca from trying out her understood language aloud – who can tell?). Generally we spoke to her as one would speak to an adult, just as we read the words of her books rather than talking about the pictures. By 2–0 her language was clear, and she was largely using the literary language she heard us reading. Rebecca was intensely aware of her own pronunciation, though, needless to say, we didn't overtly correct her (see p. 15).

As a second child, Ralph heard much more unintelligible and incomplete dialogue, and had fewer books shared with adults too (though he heard more overall, as Rebecca frequently spent time with him and books, and he often listened in when we read to her as well). By 1–1 he had fourteen words and at 1–4 twenty-nine (twice the number of Rebecca at the same age). These were all used consistently, but many were difficult to distinguish. His first two-word sentence was 'more bears' to *Blueberries for Sal* at 1–5, and he confined this usage to books for some weeks. By 1–7 he was demanding 'more book' at the end of each one we read. At 1–9 his vocabulary was sixty-eight words, but he still used jargon also. At his second birthday he was using 205, by now much more clearly, often in three- to five-word sentences.

This language development was more conventional than Rebecca's. He used jargon in the usual way, and mixed it quite happily with real words. He was always noisy and garrulous, and physically active too. He did not seem conscious of pronunciation in the same way Rebecca had been. We speculated that, apart from his outgoing nature, he also actually heard more language that he didn't understand. Adults are careful to address a baby in clear words, but of course his young sibling did not always do so. Anyway, there was a greater amount of speech in his environment not addressed to him than there was with the first child, so we were not at all surprised by his jargoning.

However, he was particularly interesting in his development of an aware-ness of the printed word. There seems to be universal agreement that young children do not understand that the printing in books 'carries' the words that are read aloud. They apparently think that you 'read' the pictures. This may be another consequence of most parents not actually reading the words, but instead labelling to teach vocabulary until their children are 2.

Neither of these children showed Cushla's interest in the letters in *B is for Bear*, but there were other examples in Ralph's case as early as 1–1. I was reading a book with some openings without pictures (a Rumer Godden) to Rebecca. One of Ralph's few words at the time was 'bir' for 'bird'. I read a sentence that included 'bird' and Ralph came across to look. He was obviously expecting a picture to match the word, but when all he encountered was text, he pointed to the page and said 'bir', not as a question but as a statement. It seemed to me that he clearly understood that the spoken word originated with the text, rather than with the pictures or with me the reader.

As we have seen in Box 3.2, Rebecca supplied much of the labelling to Ralph which we had not given her. Unlike for her parents, though, it was not a serious undertaking, but a game. Another example of this is the 'eyes open, eyes shut' game (p.130).

An incident that demonstrates just how different the environment of subsequent children is, and how this influences their view of themselves, occurred when Ralph was 1–1. Rebecca (4–4) was sharing *Lucy and Tom's Day* with him. He had a vocabulary of no more than ten words. On the opening where Lucy and Tom play in the park, there are a number of wheeled toys pictured. Ralph pointed to the block truck and announced 'buh!' [bus], his generic term for all wheeled vehicles. Rebecca did the good big sister reinforcing behaviour of 'Yes, it's a bus!' but she then continued pointing out the other toys one by one, then moved on to other objects such as the tree, asking 'what's that?' and 'reinforcing' each in exactly the same way: 'A bus, is it? Yes!', being highly entertained by his consistent wildly inappropriate reply. She said aside to me 'He says everything I ask him is a bus!' Just as I was contemplating intervention, and wondering how on earth a second child actually manages to learn anything, Ralph sorted it out for himself. With careful deliberation he pointed back to the block truck and declared 'buh' firmly – yes, he did know all the time.

There is no way to tell whether this began as a genuine mistake, but whether or no, it quickly developed into a game to amuse Rebecca. Paradoxically, Ralph's misuse of the word shows that he does understand that there is a right name for everything, even if in practice he can't produce it himself. And Rebecca's hilarity would have brought this home very vividly to him.

At a reading of *Millions of Cats* (Figure 3.4) at 1–6, I almost completed the text, but noted:

> He is a lot more talkative than Rebecca during readings. I find my text goes on underneath his constant exclaiming. In this case it was 'beow beow' to all the cats, and 'Daddy' to each appearance of the very old man. On the first picture of the hill 'covered with cats' he discovered all the cats for the first time. Previously he has just miaowed to the clear ones in the foreground, but today he realised that all the head/ear shapes over the hill are more cats. He was very excited and pointed and pointed with 'beow', even to the most distant wriggly-line representations.

Figure 3.4 Millions of Cats Wanda Gag.

Despite not appearing to listen to the actual words, he was very enthusiastic about the book-reading process. He would drop whatever he was occupied with, at the offer of a book, and if anyone began reading to another child, he was on their lap instantly. I noted at 1–10 that, given the opportunity, he would listen to as many books as Rebecca had. When she started school, just before his second birthday, there was more time to spend with him and books, and as he was growing out of the constant chatter (or perhaps just learning the advantages of listening), it was more satisfying for the reader, too.

His 'talking' through books may have been the result of his hearing a higher proportion of talk than Rebecca, because she chatted to him so much of the time, and especially when sharing books. But it may equally have been that he was naturally a more garrulous person. He also heard proportionately less literary language, because reading time had to be divided between the two of them, and though Rebecca would usually still listen in to his stories, he rarely stayed the distance for her much longer ones.

Pictures and reality: recognition

Despite a minimum of the labelling game, the children did learn to recognise, and also name, objects in pictures.

Learning to name actual physical items runs parallel to recognising and labelling pictured ones. This is one of the first book activities for a child in most Western, middle-class families (Heath 1986: 99). The first few 'words' are likely to be the names of people or animals in the baby's immediate environment, but the ducks and cows that are often among the earliest recognised pictures may not be met by the child for years (Nodelman 1988: 35).

The pictured world is one aspect of the secondary world created by the author and illustrator of a picture book, but on another level it is also a reproduction of the external physical world and its myriad objects, and it is this aspect that we will examine here.

Initially, a baby has to learn to 'read', or make meaning of, pictures as representing three-dimensional objects, and shortly afterwards relate them to the verbal signs with which they are surrounded by attending adults – to the words, whether simple naming or the author's text. This recognition of the pictures precedes the relevant language being produced, but can be demonstrated by the child pointing on demand.

Rebecca's consistent preference for the yellow lion in *B is for Bear* (Figure 3.1, Box 3.1) from 0–3 to 0–9, over many readings, indicates an ability to recognise and remember a pattern, even if it was not yet related to an object in the external world. As we saw, Ralph's response was quite different and he selected a person rather than an animal for his close attention (Figure 3.2, Box 3.1). Similarly, Rebecca's intense staring at pages in Eve's *Mother Goose* and the Mulder board books of animals, while on the floor by herself from 0–8, also seemed to demonstrate a nascent ability to identify specific things in them, especially once she began pointing to characters in the pictures for herself.

Rebecca's fascination with animals emerged with her first words being the animal sounds that she used to ask us to perform to pictures in books. The 'moo', 'miaow' and '[woo]f, [woo]f' sounds were applied first to animals in pictures and a week or so later to animals met in the street or seen from the car. It also for the first time showed me what Rebecca could recognise, as she could now say 'miaow', or whichever sound was relevant, while she was pointing to pictures.

A number of experiments have shown conclusively that infants can recognise and respond to pictured faces. As early as 0–3 they notice that photos of two strangers are different (Barrera and Maurer 1981a), and look longer at a photo of their mother than that of a stranger (Barrera and Maurer 1981b). At 0–4 they look longer at a photo of a person as opposed to other patterns, and at 0–5 even recognise the same person in colour and black-and-white photos, and in a line drawing (Cohen *et al.* 1979: 417–418). However, this knowledge seems not to have been passed down (or up?) to those in the picture-book world back then, some of whom were still dogmatising on the topic of what children are capable of, often implying that children cannot recognise anything in pictures even until about 1–6 perhaps (e.g. Alderson 1973: 9). For this reason, Rebecca's first recognition of pictured faces at 0–8 surprised me. Bruna's stylised, strong-coloured pictures had furnished both children with their first excited responses to pictures at 0–3; however, faces soon became important, and demonstrated their first actual recognition of pictured items as relating to their counterparts in the real world.

It does in fact seem that recognition of pictures is inherent, as Bloom explains (2004: 72). To test this, two psychologists tried to keep all pictures from their baby, but had to stop at 19 months because of his desperate attempts to look at the picture on his high chair (incidentally, I don't know how they could maintain that he saw no pictures when there was one on his chair! But they were careful that he never saw television, and his curtains and other furnishings in the house had no pictures on. How deprived a child!). Eventually, with absolutely no instruction and very limited exposure, he was able at once to identify the simple line drawings they showed him (Hochberg and Brooks 1962).

Ralph at 0–6, held up to a poster-sized black-and-white photograph of myself with Rebecca as a baby, looked and looked, smiled, vocalised, waved his hands, and in general exhibited great excitement. He appeared to recognise me. As Barrera and Maurer (1981b: 715) confirmed with infants of 0–3, recognising a photograph of his mother was well within his chronological ability.

Three days later he suddenly stopped moving and stared fixedly at a packet of baby cereal ('Farax'), the side of which bore a large coloured picture of a baby's face. When we gave the box to him he looked at the picture searchingly, then scratched at the mouth with his forefinger, as if he were trying to insert it, as was his wont with actual mouths. His interest was clearly in the picture itself. There was very little manipulation, and the other interesting aspects of the box – the torn top, the inside and its contents – were ignored. Although he tried to push his finger into the mouth, there was no loud protest when it would not go in, as there was when a person denied this insertion. He seemed already aware that this was a representation of a baby, not the baby itself. After all, it did not move or smell or make a sound or feel like a 'real' baby (still 0–6).

Rebecca's first unambiguous recognition of a picture was her excitement over pictured babies at 0–8, with exactly the same response to them as to actual babies met in the street, but not to other pictures. Both children could locate 'nose' and 'eye' correctly on pictured faces at 0–10. Rebecca had had extensive tutoring in this, in the form of a ritual devised by her grandmother to all large pictured faces: 'Eyes, nose, mouth, HAIR!' This game was not played with Ralph, but his ability to identify the features was the same. By 1–2 she could also point to 'hand', 'ear', 'eyebrow', 'teeth', 'tongue', 'toe', 'knee', 'leg', 'foot', 'finger' and 'navel' on pictures, people or dolls (although she didn't produce a word for any body part for another five months).

Mimicking an expression shows that the face is recognised as more than a collection of specific features. At 1–0 Rebecca was studying the cover of a crochet pattern book, and, while I watched her, she began putting her tongue right out and in again, over and over. One of the little models in the photograph has her tongue right out, about to lick a lollipop. Two weeks later (1–1), looking by herself at *The Story about Ping*, she opened her mouth wide in imitation of the boat boy shouting in the water. She was able to mimic the sketchy water-colour painting as easily as she had the bright photograph.

A similar example of mimicry by Ralph was at 1–7. He was listening to *The Elephant and the Bad Baby* when Rebecca noticed he was frowning, an expression none of us had seen on his face before. He was staring intently at the page of the angry people pointing at the Bad Baby, many with frowns on their faces. As his expression was unique, we assumed he was mimicking a specific face, or registering their emotion in an empathetic way, rather than feeling anxious for the Bad Baby. Once he found the Baby on the right-hand side of the opening, his face lit up – 'Bubby!' – and he relaxed.

The children could also locate specific people, with Rebecca at 1–3 being able to find the 'boy running' from more than eight very small figures on one opening of *The Cow Who Fell in the Canal* (Figure 3.5).

Recognition of animals followed soon after that of faces and people. There was confusion at 0–8 when I pointed out the 'pussy' in Wildsmith's *Mother Goose*, with Rebecca transferring her excited looking from the book to the floor, in search of our cat. Both children at 0–11 could locate the dog in *Whistle for Willie* when asked (or even without being prompted). The fact that both grandmothers owned dachshunds like Willie may have contributed. Ralph was able to articulate 'bup bup bup' (his 'word' for dog) as well. Rebecca at 1–1 became most insistent in her requests for animal noises. 'Ah!'

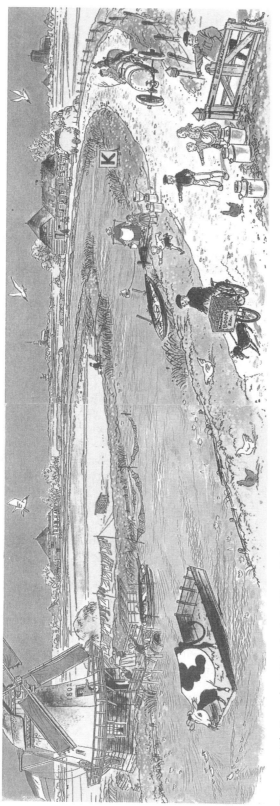

Figure 3.5 The Cow who Fell in the Canal Peter Spier.

she would shout imperiously, pointing to an animal in Eve's *Mother Goose*. There is at least one cat on every double-page opening, but most are sketches with one colour wash, not at all naturalistic. Often the cats stand on their hind legs and wear hats or carry umbrellas, but this made no difference to her ability to recognise them (Figure 3.3). Ralph learned to point out animals and ask for their noises in *Fast–Slow, High–Low* at the same age (1–1), and he could also volunteer 'moo' or 'baa' for himself, though indiscriminately.

Rebecca first encountered *Orlando Buys a Farm* at 1–1. The first time through I paraphrased the lengthy story and pointed out the animals for her, making their noises. Three days later I went through it again, then she spent a lot of time looking at it by herself, turning the pages. At the double-page spread of the farmyard, she pointed out each animal for me to make the noise, carefully identifying just the animals, ignoring all the other details on this crowded page. On another crowded opening, the market, she looked for a long time and eventually located Orlando in the middle, quite small, upright, with only his head and front paws showing. The lithographs have flat, subtle colours, though clear outlines.

Being able to locate an animal on a crowded page, even without being able to name it, demonstrates that the pictures are recognised – if not relating to the real world, at least as something that will inspire an adult into an exciting and noisy performance. Two weeks later Rebecca attempted to label them herself, in the process unequivocally demonstrating her ability to recognise in pictures cats, dogs and ducks (1–2). Very soon she made the same noise to actual animals encountered, showing that she saw the correspondence. She could even produce the 'word' when the book was mentioned without its being present, as seen in the library conversation about Ezra Jack Keats recorded in Chapter 1 (p. 2). Ralph could recognise wheeled vehicles ('bus') at 1–1, whereas Rebecca at the same age could not orientate the car, pram or house correctly on her beakers, although she had no trouble with the teddy bear or any of the other animals. I presumed that her inability to turn the inanimate objects the right way up was caused by her inability to recognise them.

It appears that initial recognition of pictures may come, as with faces, because they resemble familiar things in the environment. There is unlikely to be any conscious comparing of these two versions of reality (the pictured and the actual), nor even a realisation that there is supposed to be any relationship between them. Baby Ralph was not demanding and frustrated when his finger was not given mouth-room by the pictured Farax baby, as he was if an actual mouth denied his finger. Already the pictured world was a different, a parallel world. Similarly, the clothed cats did not confuse Rebecca. She knew our cat did not wear clothes. Nevertheless, she could still recognise the cat shape immediately, however it was disguised in books, just as Ralph later recognised the wriggly lines in *Millions of Cats*, Figure 3.4.

A number of other aspects of early picture recognition – perspective, obscured objects and direction of regard – are explored in Chapter 5. These responses are each part of a continuum, and their development is traced.

In the words of the title of Butler's study, babies need books, and they need them not just for practising vocabulary skills, but to hear the stories, to begin to understand what makes a narrative – that people (characters) have desires and beliefs which drive these stories, that books are created by authors and illustrators. They also need to learn about the reality-status of the stories. The beginning of all these understandings is here, before they are 2.

4 'This one's exotic and not real too!'

What is real, what is pretend?

'Ghosts aren't real but witches are.' 'He wants to be a *real* tortoise.' 'I can't touch that spider because it's not real.' 'That's not a real one – it's just a page of it!' These were all produced by Ralph before he was 4.

Coleridge spoke of the 'willing suspension of disbelief', and it is this belief and disbelief in the worlds created in fiction, and how the children reached these states, that is studied here. Tolkien takes issue with this suspension. He says that children are 'capable of *literary belief*' and that the 'story-maker' creates a secondary world

> which your mind can enter. Inside it, what he relates is 'true': it accords with the laws of that world. You therefore believe it, while you are, as it were, inside. The moment disbelief arises, the spell is broken; the magic, or rather art, has failed.
>
> (1964: 36).

Rosenblatt, the distinguished literary theorist, explained that the worlds of fiction are created by others and recreated in our minds when we read or evoke the literary work of art from the text (1978: 31). She suggests that an aesthetic stance is required for reading fiction, and an efferent one – gleaning information – for reading non-fiction. The example she gives is of an 8-year-old querying the White Rabbit's pocket watch ('he was listening with an efferent attitude') and deplores his 'literal-mindedness' (1978: 39). It appears that she would have disapproved when my two children queried the reality of stories. She does admit that it is a continuum, and that each reading is a combination of both stances. And certainly my children did not insist on the unreality of characters during the actual story. They usually listened aesthetically during the reading, but carried on their efferent investigations afterwards.

All children query reality unless they are deliberately discouraged from doing so. Most people are happy to tell children untruths; Father Christmas is the traditional one. We would have felt uncomfortable telling our children that there really was a Father Christmas when there patently wasn't, so they missed out on this common element of childhood. Adults who uphold this myth discourage its questioning, and perhaps this also discourages the querying of other fictions.

It is probable that both parents also encouraged, even rewarded, the querying of the reality of stories. I have never seen this as spoiling the story, and the two children, now adult readers, agree. Stories and books were inherently interesting, and the reality status of them just added to the interest. Recognising a story as fantasy or nonsense (or, as I would phrase it when they were little, 'pretend' as opposed to factual, or even as opposed to a realistic story) was part of the fascination.

It was our belief that it is an important life skill that children learn, to differentiate what is possible from what is imaginary. They need to understand that not everything they hear is true. They need, as far as books are concerned, to understand the difference between fiction and non-fiction, and between a realistic story and a fantasy one.

In the beginning, books are accepted by infants as merely another form of reality, with no testing of the parameters of how the secondary world compares with the external one, except in recognising that pictured objects can be labelled with the same terms as their counterparts in the physical world. Eventually, however, children begin to realise that comparisons between the two types of worlds can be made. Then fantasy and nonsense begin to be questioned.

It was Ralph who was the more astute about and aware of the real/pretend dichotomy, possibly because of his position as the second child. Rebecca's pattern had usually been to accept a story without queries or comments, and when learning to talk she didn't pass through the usual interminable 'why' stage. She generally asked a question only after she had worked out the answer for herself.

However, by the time Ralph was beginning to talk, she, at 4, was very involved with discussing reality. She assigned roles to Ralph. As soon as he could follow in the most rudimentary way, games would start with 'Hey Ralphie, let's pretend that . . .' She talked and sang to him about reality. So Ralph had the concepts presented to him continuously, obviously seen as important by the most interesting person in his environment, Rebecca. He had her terminology on which to build his understanding.

At the same time as they were working out the parameters of the real in the external physical world, they worked on the reality status of the fictional, secondary one.

Reality terms

The terms 'real', 'pretend', 'imaginary' and 'true' are particularly problematical and ambiguous, because they can be, and indeed were, used in quite different ways even within the family.

'Real', for instance, could be contrasted with 'pretend': Rebecca's Brownie was a pretend mouse, in contrast to those that occasionally invaded our kitchen. But 'real' could also be used as 'genuine' in contrast with 'artificial', as in real cream, or a real fire in winter. Closely related to this is our speaking of the 'real version' of a story, as opposed to, say, a parody on *Sesame Street*, or the Disney version of *Winnie-the-Pooh*. This was usually applied to fairy tales, myths and legends, and, with hindsight, must have been a confusing use of the word. Occasionally it would even be applied to imaginary creatures. We were capable, for instance, of discussion about how 'real' griffins look (based on the ones carved on European cathedrals).

Rebecca worked on these differences, producing dichotomies such as 'I'm pretending to dry myself with a real towel' and 'I drove a *real* pretend car' (at 3–8 and 4–1), both similar to Carol White's 'Will you real come to my pretendy house?' (4–9, *BbF*: 184). When Rebecca, in grade Prep, told Ralph (2–8) that she had been to a farm and milked a cow, he asked her, wide-eyed, 'Was it a real cow, Becca?' . . . 'Was it real milk?' Talking about a forthcoming visit to the zoo, we mentioned the fairy penguins. Rebecca joked 'Well, if they're called fairies, they can't be real!' (4–10). At 7–0 she explained to Ralph (3–9) that fairies were 'really pretend'. He agreed: 'Yes! They're not in this part of Australia!' She corrected him: 'They're not anywhere 'cause they're pretend.' Rebecca made a fine distinction about her imaginary companions at 5–1: 'They're not pretend, they're invisible!' This could show confusion about the concept of 'pretend' but was more likely to have been conscious pretence in itself.

When we adults talked about something being 'real' in the story, to us this meant 'alive in the story' (as Ralph later phrased it) – part of the story world. However, the children sometimes interpreted it as something like 'tangible' instead. For Rebecca at 5–3, Olga the guinea pig met a 'real' dragon, because it was not imaginary, whereas I would have called it a 'pretend' one because it was a dragon *kite* (*Olga Meets Her Match*). As is the way with so much language, this ambiguity remained, and was not even noticed at the time.

Stories could be 'only pretend' for Rebecca at 4–0 and Ralph at 3–4, but they would still ask 'Is this a real story?' Again this term was slightly ambiguous. What did they mean by 'a real story'? We generally answered as if they had meant 'Could it really happen' – that is, is it a *realistic* story? After all, the other possibility, '*Had* it really happened?', was very rare in their experience. Probably only the stories we told of our own childhoods could be considered 'real stories' by this definition.

The family's use of the terms is obviously what the children will use. When Carol asked 'Is that Farmer Jones' house?', White agreed (*BbF*: 138). Just as we avoided Father Christmas and the Tooth Fairy, we tried to be accurate about the real and the pretend. There were lots of pretend games, of course, but they were known and acknowledged as 'pretend'.

Rebecca and reality

I will begin with Rebecca. Not only is she the first sibling, but also her case is the more straightforward. We rarely discussed reality with her, unless and until she asked, so, unlike Ralph, she had to work it out almost by herself.

Her first recorded use of a reality word in a game was at 2–10: 'I'm Tigger pretending to be Eeyore.' There were earlier remarks referring to other people: 'You're making it up!' (2–2); 'Sometimes he pretends to take your toy' (of our jovial butcher, 2–7). No doubt she had pretended to be someone, long before she was pretending to be someone who was pretending to be someone else, but this was her first use of the word to apply to the activity. Her identifications with characters were particularly intense and long-lived. Several years later she was Snufkin from Jansson's Moomintroll books for some months (from 6–4 – pp. 146–147).

Bloom discusses children's imaginary companions, which he says 'can offer companionship, alleviate loneliness, allow for the development of rich and enjoyable fantasies'. Children, however, are the first to point out that they are imaginary if it seems anyone is getting too serious about them (2004: 219). Rebecca often blamed events and accidents on her imaginary friend Brownie the mouse, who was her companion from about 2–10. However, when I once tried to use the concept: 'I wonder how *x* happened? Perhaps Brownie did it?', she told me firmly 'Brownie is pretend.' She was 3–0 at the time. Next day when she spilt a glass of milk, she accused Brownie as she often had previously. I objected 'But Brownie is pretend!' However, he was her mouse, and she was in control: 'He's getting realler and realler!' A month later, when I expressed surprise at some unlikely biological feats ascribed to Brownie and his family, she assured me 'That's how it is with pretend mouses' (3–1). At the same age she spoke about characters in books 'pretending' to be something else when they were dressed up, and at 3–4 described (correctly) a character 'imagining' something. The concept of pretending as an activity was firmly established.

However, it was not until 3–5 that she began to question the pretend as the basis of fantasy in books, and it was 3–7 before she queried a whole story rather than a character. Halfway through *The Man Who Took the Indoors Out*, an exceptionally fantastic tale, she interrupted to ask 'Is this a true story?', to which my reply was 'No, it couldn't really have happened.'

One of the most common of the fantasies that inhabit children's books is the anthropomorphised animal. It is possible that humanised animals are accepted by children who live with actual animals, as Rebecca and Ralph did. Anthropomorphism was widely practised, with the adults addressing the pets quite naturally, and articulating their imagined replies as well, so stories about speaking animals could be seen as a natural extension. This may explain why they had less difficulty with the concept, and were consequently slower to articulate it as a problem, than children in petless households. (Anna Crago declared 'Animals don't usually wear clothes' at 2–11 – *Prelude*: 201.)

Rebecca's first delighted comment on anthropomorphised animals was on the mouse protagonists in *So Small* at 2–6: 'I've never seen mice do that!' She didn't pursue this concept in other books until a year later, when concerning her well-loved *The Hare and the Tortoise* she remarked 'Owls can't talk.' This (3–6) was the beginning of an intense interest lasting a year.

Two weeks after this (3–7) she had a sudden illumination, during *Miffy at the Zoo*, that 'Animals can't talk.' It was probably the contrast of Miffy's thoroughly anthropomorphised rabbit family being able to converse with the zoo animals that brought her to this realisation. She found the whole process highly amusing once it had occurred to her, and remarked on it with hilarity at every reading for almost a year, though she didn't bother to state the obvious to any other book.

Other expressions of this reality interest were using Max's dreaming to explain *Where the Wild Things Are* (see p. 57) and explaining of a song of her own 'It's just a nonsense poem' (both some weeks later at 3–8).

By 3–9 'Is it really?' or 'Is this a real book?' had become 'almost a routine question', though only applied to a book with a strong fantasy element such as *Lord Rex*, or where the contrast between realistic and anthropomorphised behaviour is emphasised, as in Potter's *Two Bad Mice*. Concerning the familiar *Tom Kitten* she asked 'Were they really in bed with the measles?' (3–10), although she well knew Potter's own answer: 'Quite the contrary; they were not in bed: *not* in the least' (see Figure 5.6).

By 4–0 she was able to demonstrate her understanding of the reality status quite clearly. *Barbapapa's Ark* was 'only a pretend book, anyway . . . because barbapapas aren't real'. In a conversation about zoo animals, I mentioned bears saying something: 'Bears can't talk,' she said, and I parried 'What about Teddy Robinson?' (*Dear Teddy Robinson* was very popular at the time). 'He's just pretend!' (4–1).

Eventually Rebecca realised that there could be 'real' items from the external world in a fantasy story, and she began, at 4–2, asking 'Is there such a thing as a space ark? A rocket?' (*Barbapapa's Ark*). By 4–7 she was using the knowledge acquired from this book. In a general discussion with no book present:

Rebecca: Is the sky part of the earth?
Virginia: Well the air is – it's attached to the earth.
Rebecca: Is it stuck down with glue?
Virginia: No, it's held down with gravity.
Rebecca: Do other planets have air?
Virginia: Yes, but it's not usually air you can breathe. [*Mars, Venus and Jupiter were mentioned.*]
Rebecca: But could a planet – a green and white planet like a playground – could some planet have air you could breathe?

Virginia: Yes, there's sure to be planets with breathable air. They just haven't been discovered yet.
Rebecca: Well, the planet Barbapapa went to, that surely had air you could breathe.
Virginia: Yes, it surely did. But that's only a story.
Rebecca: They're *all* only stories.

It was not clear what she meant by this. Perhaps that all the stories in books were made up? Or could she have thought that the whole concept of 'other planets' was pretend? Later conversations showed this to be unlikely, but it's now far too late to find out.

Rebecca did not begin to ask generalised questions about the reality of whole classes of creatures, rather than specifics, until she was 4–9.

Rebecca: Are ghosts real?
Virginia: No, they're just imaginary things.
Rebecca: Are there other imaginary things?
Virginia: There's fairies and dragons and giants.

Two days later she asked 'Are unicorns real?' [No, they're pretend, like dragons.] 'Well, why do they put their picture in?' (this in an alphabet workbook with realistic pictures, under U). And at 4–11 'Monsters are only pretend.'

One of the ways of testing ideas about the reality of the fictional world is to question the reality of objects rather than characters, as above with *Barbapapa's Ark*. She also queried the reality of the fictional world in her first Moomin book, *Finn Family Moomintroll*, when she asked if the Mameluke was a 'real fish' (6–4).

Another way of examining reality was to consider where stories are set. She asked 'When can we go to Finland?' (6–5), and at 6–6 she spelled this out further, in a dictated essay on 'My favourite author':

> I wish I could go to Finland for a holiday, because I want to see it because it is in the books, to see if the forest really looks like it. Tove Jansson lives in Finland where Moomintroll lives.

There is no suggestion here that she thinks she can actually visit Moominland itself. She knows it is possible to visit Finland, but not Moominland.

Perhaps her most sophisticated version of the question came at 4–11 with her stating the concept of belief. 'I don't believe in mermaids' was a phrase she acquired from the story 'Teddy Robinson and the Mermaid' in *Teddy Robinson Himself*. At 6–2 she encountered it again in *Alice* (p. 56).

Ralph and reality

The fact that Ralph's contacts with the concept of reality began much earlier is epitomised by Rebecca explaining earnestly to him that 'Little Jack Horner' was 'just nonsense, Little Man', when he was only 0–9. She (3–11) had just asked of Jack Horner's 'what a good boy am I', 'Why was he good?' and been told it was nonsense.

She often sang her own songs to Ralph. A lullaby at 4–5 (he 1–3):

> When you wake in the morning you'll find a lamb in your cot.
> You'll find a mouse.
> A sheep, a mouse and a horse in your cot.
> The horse is a toy one,
> But the lamb and the mouse are real.
> Baa baa, squeak squeak, neigh.
> Little boy go back to sleep now – I've sung to you.
> (adapted from the lullaby 'All the pretty little horses')

This early tutoring by his sibling probably explains his younger understanding. He queried the possessions and behaviour of anthropomorphised animals before he did their speech or clothing. As early as 2–5 he often mentioned this in his beloved *Scarry*, including 'Pussy cats don't have kites!', 'Dogs can't drive!' and 'But animals don't do that' (2–8). It was an audio tape rather than a book which brought his first statement that animals don't talk. While listening to 'A Frog he would a-wooing go' at 3–3, he remarked 'It must be pretend 'acause it's really people. They can't talk, can they? Animals can't talk.' The same month he applied the concept to books. To his grandmother, who was reading *John Brown, Rose and the Midnight Cat* (Figure 5.11), he explained 'Dogs can't really talk – or open doors.'

The unreality of texts was in fact one of his basic interests. At 2–7 he exclaimed of a pictured spider 'I can't touch [presumably meaning "feel"] that spider, 'acause it's not real.' He also had to come to terms with the teasing of the older sibling. To a picture of a skeleton, Rebecca (5–10) threatened Ralph (2–8): 'It will get you!', but he replied with equanimity 'No. It's in a book. It's stuck down!' On another occasion Rebecca had almost frightened herself with 'Help, it's a blue-ringed octopus! I don't want to touch it!' (6–1) in a factual animal book. Ralph (2–11) said with some puzzlement 'But it's only 'tend!' A similar event happened when he was 4–0, but now it was he doing the teasing – to a sponge on the sea floor in *How Life Began*:

Ralph: That's poisonous. If you saw a real one of those and you touched it, you'd die!

Rebecca: I am touching a real one.

Ralph: That's not a real one. It's just a page of it.

Ralph asked many more questions about stories and poems than Rebecca, even 'why?' to nursery rhymes (2–7). If there was an answer that was logical within the frame of the rhyme or story, we would give that, but were often forced back on to 'It's just a nonsense rhyme' or 'It's just a pretend story.' Consequently, he heard these explanations much more often than Rebecca, and internalised them earlier.

Like Rebecca at 3–1 ('That one's pretending to be a sheep'), he was able to recognise when characters were acting in books: 'He's pretending to be a lion' (2–11) to the boy in a mask in *May I Bring a Friend?*

We had an alphabet jigsaw with T as a tortoise at 3–1:

Ralph: That tortoise is looking sad.
Virginia: Is he? Why?
Ralph: Because he wants to be a *real* tortoise. Don't cry, tortoise, I'll make you real with my magic thing.

(perhaps as had happened with a magic pebble in *Alexander and the Wind-Up Mouse*).

He also queried the reality-status of characters, with several insights being inspired by feet. Some anthropomorphised characters are like soft toys, with 'clothes' that to adult eyes are clearly part of their construction. The 3-year-olds at Playgroup often maintained that the Wild Thing with feet (the familiar blue bull-headed one, Figure 4.1) was 'a person dressed up' because they could see the feet sticking out. Ralph at 3–3 pointed out 'He's got real toes' but didn't therefore assume he was a person (*Where the Wild Things Are*).

Feet were an issue in the 'reality' of another character at 4–5. Ralph was being read *Moominland Midwinter* and was interested in the status of Too-ticky, who is human-looking and clothed, as opposed to the rest of the cast of gloriously varied creatures (mostly naked). He tried to explain 'He's [*sic*] a real kind of person. No he's not, 'cause he hasn't got the right sort of feet' (Figure 4.2). The reverse of the Wild Thing, she has paw-like feet on a human body. Ralph paused for a minute then decided 'But he [*sic*, i.e. the artist] could have just drawn them that way.' In other words, Ralph, struggling to make meaning of the two different worlds, saw a fictional world with a 'rightness' of its own, 'free-standing, independent of the text's language' (McHale 1987: 156), to which the author/illustrator as transcriber or describer had privileged but not omniscient access (the 'actual' Too-ticky could have had human feet, after all; Lowe 1991a).

Gradually he worked out his own terminology, seeming determined to be able to denote something that couldn't exist in our world, but did in the secondary world of the book. He used it first in *The Quinkins* (one of Roughsey and Trezise's Aboriginal Dreaming stories), which fascinated him. Before it was even read he wanted to know 'Are they alive, Mummy?' The Quinkins, spirit creatures, are illustrated in what is clearly rock art being painted at the beginning (Figure 4.3). This artistic activity was probably what foregrounded

WHERE THE WILD THINGS ARE

STORY AND PICTURES BY MAURICE SENDAK

Figure 4.1 Where the Wild Things Are Maurice Sendak.

the reality issue for him in the book. Then he continued 'They're drawing pictures of what's Quinkins actually' (4–5). The next day, at a school performance of *The Wizard of Oz*, he asked:

Ralph: Is the Wiz-a-Woz alive?
Virginia: No, pretend.
Ralph: Are the other things alive?
Virginia: It's only a pretend story.
Ralph: Are they alive in the *story?*

Two months later he was still using the same phraseology, asking of the ogre in 'Puss in Boots' (*Velvet Paws and Whiskers*) 'Is it real? Is it alive in the story?' (4–7).

   He spelled out his view on the reality of creatures at 4–2, using Jansson's threatening Groke. In his first of the series, *Moominland Midwinter*, he announced reassuringly 'She's not real', but a few days later he asked out of the blue if the Groke was 'always awake'. My reply was 'perhaps she's asleep

Figure 4.2 Moominland Midwinter Tove Jansson.

sometimes and awake sometimes', but he disagreed. He went off chanting to himself 'We don't know and we don't know, 'cause we've never seen one and there's nothing real about them.'

At 4–9, at the height of his interest in myths, he asked 'What if the Gorgon was real? Jason and Bradley [friends] have got a friend with hair like that.' He seemed fairly confident, however, that the Gorgon was not real, nor, as he said a few days later, was Father Christmas. Tarzan he had encountered at a friend's place, and predictably taken to his heart: 'Tarzan is my favourite not-real person' (4–10).

He played with the concept of the stories' reality in a way quite different from that of Rebecca. Part of his reading pattern was to propose alternative outcomes, inserting himself into the stories to make brave rescues, for instance. He usually did this in stories that had touched him deeply, but it was to the nonsense of *Wacky Wednesday* that he spelt it out explicitly. Of the babies who appear to be in danger: 'Perhaps we could be in the story and get all the babies out' (3–1).

Ralph's first reference to the reality status of a whole story came at 3–2, to one of Lobel's *Mouse Tales*. 'This is only a pretend story, isn't it?' At the same reading at which he queried the Quinkins as imaginary characters (4–5), he described the book itself (Figure 4.3) as 'It's Chinese, isn't it? This one's exotic and not real too!' (having confused Chinese and Aboriginal cultures). Certainly we would not have applied the word 'exotic' to any story, so this was his own description.

Figure 4.3 The Quinkins Dick Roughsey.

He would also ask whether stories were myths or legends, because he was so familiar with these genres. The trailer for the film *The Black Stallion* maintains that 'most of all, you'll believe in – The Black Stallion'. Ralph replied scathingly 'I wouldn't believe in the Black Stallion. It's only a legend' (5.2). The 'belief' concept occurred to him again at 5–10 'Why do some people believe in heaven?' After the long description of Elves and Wood-Elves in *The Hobbit* he asked 'Is that a myth?' (5–7).

In reply to the lion's 'Some stories are true, and some aren't' in the first edition of *The Lion in the Meadow*, Ralph (3–7) answered: 'No stories are true. None of our stories are true.' Presumably he meant no stories in books actually happened. He continued that if he had a dragon of his own like the boy in the story, he would prefer not to let it out of its matchbox. It is not a true story, but nevertheless he wouldn't take the risk, if he were that little boy.

Ralph was an anxious child, and often refused to hear the scary parts of a story that was being read to both children, leaving the room or seeking refuge on the other parent's knee. Often the parts that worried him were the protagonist being naughty and punished, or being in danger – especially from an overpowering adult. He would not allow the page of Tabitha Twitchit bearing down on her recalcitrant son even to be opened in *Tom Kitten* at 3–4, and was disturbed by the little dog in *Madeline's Rescue* who was thrown out of the school by an adult.

He identified strongly with the protagonists of stories. He was 2–5 when he first reacted in a frightened way to a book. At 2–11 he said 'I'm scared of the wolf' in *Peter and the Wolf*, and beat a hasty retreat from the room during the relevant part of the reading. He often found it expedient to articulate his fears and his understanding that scary characters in books did not really exist. Television could be even more threatening than books. He assured me that in *Doctor Who*, 'they're people inside clothes' (meanwhile switching the television firmly off, 4–4).

In some cases his fear was caused by the way the story was read. At 3–3, he said – 'Not *The Three Bears*, 'cause when he gruffs I'm scared, you see', referring to John's dramatic rendition of Big Bear's 'great rough gruff voice' (demonstrating that we did dramatise readings sometimes).

Ralph's ability to handle the 'pretend' concept did not seem to allay his anxieties. The fictionally created fearful episode seems to have been frightening in itself, even when he knew it would not impinge on his actual world. At 3–5 he told me about monsters who lived in our house and came out in the dark. He assured me that they were 'pretend', but when I asked if they were scary nevertheless, he answered 'yes' fervently. Only when he discovered the violent wonders of the Greek and Norse myths (3–9) did his anxieties gradually disappear. Monsters like Grendel and his mother, the Minotaur and the Gorgon were popular – listened to, talked about and acted out with enthusiasm (p. 149). Of a Christmas present he exclaimed (4–10) 'The one with all the scary monsters is my favourite book!' (D'Aulaires' *Book of Greek Myths*).

The reality status of the fictional world depends to a large extent on the reality or realism of its characters, so Ralph's comment 'She's not real' on the frightening Groke, when he encountered her in his first Moomintroll book (*Moominland Midwinter* 4–2), was significant as a way of mitigating her threat. In a somewhat similar way, attempting to alleviate threat, Ralph worked out possible plots at anxious moments in the stories, for instance: 'Moominmamma will come and open the cage, or else how could Moomintroll get out?' (*Moominsummer Madness*, also 4–2). The question of the reality status of Jansson's inimitable characters will be discussed in Chapter 9, with a section devoted to the moomintrolls.

His suggested rescues of characters in trouble were sometimes from within the book, as in the Moominmamma example, and sometimes external, such as his offer to bring the little half-chick down from his spire, using a ladder, three months previously (p. 18) He quite often devised ways of alleviating the situation for a character. Of course, this is the normal creation of texts – speculation and anticipation – which we all do when we read, but most adults do it silently.

The idea of a comet's effect on our world produced anxiety in *Comet in Moominland*, partly because of the relative size of Moominland objects and ours. The first time he heard the book – listening to a chapter or so each night – Ralph several times reminded his father 'Ah ha, Daddy! I just remembered – I said I don't want the comet bits.' On one occasion Rebecca (also listening – for the second or third time) reassured him 'It isn't really scary' (though she had tensed up when first hearing it, some months before) but he answered 'It is for me!' (4–3). Fortunately, after a few days' break, and with me reading instead of his father, he was happy to hear the story to the end. On his rehearing it at 5–1, long before we got to the final chapter, he anticipated it, now calling it the 'best' chapter. But he went on to apply his ideas and his fears to our world:

> 'Mum, seeing they [the moomin creatures] are so small, the rock would be that high, and their house about that high [holding his hand about 10 centimetres above the floor], so the comet would have come down that close and gone back up to another country. So if it had been our house it would have come to there [pointing out the height on the wall], and we would have exploded!'

What light do Ralph's fears throw on the question of the reality of books? It did not always help him to know they were 'only pretend'. Clearly, the imaginary world was often just as disturbing. His empathy for the protagonist, even if it was only Harry the dirty dog in the story of that name being unrecognisable to his family when dirty (he refused to have this opening read, calling it 'the bad part' at 3–3), demonstrated that the characters did have a very distinct reality in his mind (see also Lowe 1992).

As we have seen, Rebecca was 4–9 before she began to ask about the reality of classes of beings. Ralph at 3–1 was already working on the classification of fairytale people: 'There used to be people who were kings and queens. There aren't kings or – um – mermaids, any more.' In other words, at this stage he saw them as having had some form of reality in the past, which, according to Applebee (1978: 38), is one of the common ways children explain fantasy. And at 3–5 Ralph produced another list: 'I'll tell you what's pretend: unicorns, Batman, Robin, Superman, pirates, cowboys, Indians.' At 3–11 he announced that 'ghosts aren't real, but witches are', and at 4–1 asked, with reference to the brownie in *When We Were Very Young* (though the book was not present), 'Are there any sorts of fairies in the world?' Monsters were ambiguous at 4–5. His friend David said 'Monsters are only pretend' but Ralph countered 'No they aren't. Some are really alive, and I'll tell you how the pretend ones are. Pretend ones are really people dressed up, but some are really alive.' It is not clear what he meant by some being 'really alive', but the realisation about dressing up may have been helped by his understanding of the grotesque in *Doctor Who* six weeks before.

Language and reality

One way of exploring the children's understanding of the relationship between language and reality is through their referring to words as such. This self-conscious understanding appeared much earlier than has previously been recorded.

Ralph at 2–6 was able to use the concept of a 'word' to define what is real, what not. In a joking authorial-intrusive question, Dr Seuss asks 'Fish in a tree? How can that be?' Ralph was hearing *Hop on Pop* for the first time in about a year. He gave the question serious consideration and replied 'It's just a word!' His terminology shows that this was not a learned phrase. If asked, his parents' (and sibling's) response would have been something like 'it's just nonsense'. He knew that the way the nonsense world is created is with 'words', and he chose this to explain the authorial query.

By 4–9 Rebecca had reached a more complex stage of thinking about language and reality. As often, when playing in the back yard, she was picking clover as 'blueberries' and 'bottling them for next winter' (*Blueberries for Sal*). She left her bottling jars with me, 'Sal's mother', and when she returned to 'bottle' her harvest, she complained that baby Ralph, sitting on my lap, was in her way. I joked:

Virginia: I'm bottling *Ralphs* for next winter.
Rebecca: You can't. Ralph's a little boy. You can't eat boys! (pauses, thinking) Ralph's a boy's *name*. You can't bottle *names*!

On the subject of names, she also spoke about when the word 'pea' was invented at 4–4 (p. 112).

From 2–7 on, Rebecca would invent words and often add their definitions. A non-figurative drawing might be pronounced to be 'an abstract' but more often 'a gong gong' or some other neologism. 'I "swapped" me. That means when you bump your head' (2–7) or 'I'm "chambering" – that means turning over the pages sideways' (2–10). These were offered quite earnestly, as words to fill gaps she perceived in the English language. On another occasion I told her to stop scratching at her rash. She answered hopefully 'I'm not scratching, I'm *honing*. Is that all right?' (2–7), this time with a grin, knowing that a renaming would hardly be accepted by her mother as legitimising the action. Like the children Chukovsky quotes (1963: 4), Rebecca sometimes 'invented' a word that actually did exist in the language.

These selective examples of the children's language awareness demonstrate their nascent understanding that the relationship between words and the things they stand for is tenuous, and that in the case of books there need be no connection between the words and the external world.

On the other hand, recognition of the external world does happen through words, just as it does through pictures. As Paul has it, mimesis 'is about how the language of poetry makes animals recognizable' (1992: 73). The child sees the 'real' through the lens of the literary words he or she knows. As just one instance, Rebecca, when discussing the forthcoming Agricultural Show and the grand parade in the ring, remarked 'That's what Wilbur did!' (7–9, *Charlotte's Web*).

Dreaming

Dreams create a secondary world, though a world only shared when it is retold as a story. Rebecca often swapped dreams with us in the morning, but hers were so long and involved that they were clearly inventions, even if based on a dream image initially. They often included give-away story elements, such as 'and the next morning, they . . .' (2–9). Probably even then she understood that dreams are not 'real', but the first recorded statement on the topic was at 3–6. To my 'Do you remember . . .?' she replied 'No. Not at all. You dreamt it!' Two weeks later she first used this explanation about a book's fantasy.

Ralph described his dreams in a similar way from 3–4 on, although not in the long, complicated, obviously extended versions until 3–8. He never made the connection between dreaming and stories, preferring to think of fantasy incidents 'really' happening to the character in the story.

Through the Looking Glass led Rebecca at 6–1 to another insight. She was fascinated with the idea of the characters being part of the Red King's dream, and the day after hearing this chapter she commented 'Wouldn't it be funny if we were all just in a dream?' [Like Alice being the Red King's dream?] 'Yes!' Two days later she tried this concept and another from *Alice* on a friend, with a laugh to show she was joking: 'Sarah, I don't believe in you!' [Sarah laughs too, rather puzzled.] 'Sarah, wouldn't it be funny if we were all in a dream? Just in somebody's dream?' Three weeks later (6–2), she reached a further point in this journey through a concept. In the course of a long discussion that she began with 'What is God?', a topic inspired by the religious instruction at school, she came up with the idea that 'Perhaps we're just in God's dream?' I told her that some people do, in fact, believe something very like that. She then wanted to know 'What would happen if we were part of God's dream?' and my reply was that there was really no way you would be able to tell (Lowe 1994b).

Dreams are themselves a form of secondary world, although one not shared with other people. Rebecca in particular was very aware of the dreaming process and compared dreaming with fantasy sequences in her books. I will examine this process mainly using one title, *Where the Wild Things Are*.

Aidan Chambers has said of this book that 'the profound meaning' cannot be discovered unless one realises that 'Max has dreamt his journey to the Wild Things, that in fact the Wild Things are Max's own creation' (1985: 48). Other critics also find the dream explanation compelling. I prefer to read the story as fantasy rather than as a dream. One knows that the Wild Things are part of Max, an extension of his aggressive impulses which he has to learn to bring under conscious control, but this is a different level of interpretation from that of accepting the story as a dream (Lowe 1979b). If one reads it as a dream – that Max fell asleep and all this was only a dream rather than an alternative world – the book loses its impact. We never suggested the 'dream' explanation.

Rebecca had known the book since 1–6, but had not heard it for some four months at 2–11 when I chose to read it at playgroup. At the end she asked 'How did the forest get away from his bedroom?' This was her first querying of the basis of fantasy, in any book. Up to then she had accepted the fantasy elements without query, as part of the story. My answer was 'Perhaps it was just pretend' – meaning the whole story was a fantasy story, and logical explanations were unnecessary. She was 3–8 before the topic came up again, again at playgroup, where this time it was one of the boys who asked how the trees got into his bedroom. I suggested as before that it was just pretend, but Rebecca volunteered that it was a dream, which neither John nor I had suggested to her. (Anna Crago at 3–9 asked of Max 'Did he have a dream?' When her parents asked if she thought so, she replied 'Yes'; *Prelude*: 209.) By this stage Rebecca had been querying fantasy elements, such as animals talking, for some months. For several weeks thereafter she used the 'dream' explanation for fantasy or inexplicable incidents. For instance, in *Lord Rex*, at Rex's most ridiculous wish, to get a giraffe's neck, she was slightly puzzled and asked 'Was it a dream?' [I don't know. Perhaps we'll see at the end] and at the finish she decided 'I think it was a dream really.' [It could have been. Or perhaps it's just a pretend story.]

When Ralph was 2–1, in a period of enormous enthusiasm for the *The Wild Things*, hearing it several times a day for about a week, Rebecca explained to him on the first page of the forest growing: 'He had a dream!' (5–4).

At another reading (Ralph 2–5, Rebecca 5–8), she remarked 'I wonder what he ate?' [I don't know.] 'Anyway, it was just a dream.' [Who said so?] 'Ruth.' [Well, she shouldn't have. We don't know that!] I was sorry this suggestion had been put into Ralph's mind, because for me it would spoil the story, and anyway did not allow him to come to the conclusion for himself. She added 'Well, it must have been [a dream], because it couldn't really have happened!' I had forgotten that Rebecca had offered the dream explanation four months previously, and also two years before, so that she in fact was not just quoting her kindergarten teacher of the previous year.

Ralph looked for logical explanations within the story-frame, rather than using the dream explanation. Beginning at 2–7, he began to query the events: 'Where's the bed gone?' and by 3–3: 'Why did a forest come there?' At 3–10 he asked of the forest's appearance 'How did that happen?' [I don't know], and volunteered a different sort of explanation. 'Perhaps somebody planted some seeds and then somebody built a house there' (i.e. on top of the seeds). At the same reading he wanted to know 'What happened to the trees?' and when I turned it back on him [What do you think?] he said crossly 'You tell me! You think of something!' 'The place where the Wild Things are' was the setting for one of his own dreams, although it was a different version from Max's (people could 'walk on the top of houses', 3–8).

Ralph never gave the dream explanation himself, or referred to it again, even with Rebecca present. He never found it satisfying and logical, as she had, and apparently her influence was less significant than his own natural way of reading a story. Almost at the end of the period under discussion, Rebecca expressed her understanding clearly: 'All books are real, even fantasy books, because you could say fantasy books are dreams' (a propos of nothing) and, eleven days later, '*The Wizard of Oz* is a true story, you know, because it was all a dream' (7–10).

I am not sure how Bruner's 'vicissitudes of human intention' would apply to a dream. Perhaps that's why I always find stories that end with the waking child, unsatisfying – and it was all a dream. If there is no intentionality, there is no real pleasure in the plot.

Causation and reality

The concept of causality, the emerging cognitive pattern of 'Why . . . Because . . .', is learned with difficulty in the external world. Once they had grasped it, however, Rebecca and Ralph expected it to apply equally in the fictional world. The general rules of causation are necessary to understand a plot. Something has happened, or will happen, because of something else (Rabinowitz 1987: 104–109). Children tend to assume that, within the fictional world, there is a reason for each incident. This aspect of book behaviour is represented best by *Barbapapa's Ark*, the popularity and influence of which need to be considered first.

The barbapapas' world was perhaps a surprising one for logical and scientific understanding to flourish. Barbapapa (appropriately French for 'fairy floss' – I capitalise it as a name, but not when talking about the whole 'species') has an amoebic pale pink body and his spouse and daughters have twee, sexist distinguishing characteristics of a permanent wreath of flowers, preternaturally long eyelashes and curves (Figure 4.5). Barbapapas can change their shapes to become anything they want. Each of the stories had a message that agreed with our family ideology, expressed in a witty way, and the pictures were full of detail to be pored over. They offered concepts new to Rebecca such as space travel, which she did not query at the first encounter with *Barbapapa's Voyage* (2–9), but were briefly explained. She and Ralph encountered a total of seven books about the barbapapa family, and they were extremely popular and influential.

Rebecca was 3–5 when she borrowed *Barbapapa's Ark*. The book went through four distinct phases of popularity, each of about a month's duration. When we first had it from the library, it was popular from 3–5 to 3–6 (thirteen readings). Later she was given it for her birthday, and the next month of intensive enthusiasm covered sixteen readings, 4–0. It was lost for a month, and on being found again at 4–2, went through another intensive phase (seven readings). At 4–5 it was again lost, this time for only a week, but this led to her final phase of intensive reading covering 4–6 to 4–7 (eight readings). By then she knew it so thoroughly that, as she said at 4–11, 'I don't need it read', but she still pored over it daily, even at 5–3, and referred to it as 'my favourite book'. A total of fifty-two readings are recorded up to 5–0, and certainly some would have been missed, especially on the days when it was read three or four times. Most of these readings have comments and questions recorded at some length. There were no readings, though quite a few quotations from it, references to it, games based on it, and looking at it alone, in the intervening periods. It had become a security object, and when we left it behind on a Christmas trip to Sydney when she was 4–0, every day, she begged, with tears, to go home for it. Even at 7–11 it was one of two books she took away to Brownie camp with her. When Ralph had it read to him she would join in if she was at home. It remained a popular book to share with visitors, seeming to fascinate them as well. In all, some contact with either child was recorded on 170 days.

Ralph encountered the books and their creatures at a much younger age than Rebecca, and his responses would have been influenced by his knowledge that they were special to her. He heard them almost as often as Rebecca did up to age 5 (forty-three recorded readings). He asked questions and explored the text in somewhat the same way that she had, but it never reached the status of books-one-must-have-by-one-always.

Barbapapa's Ark concerns the effect of pollution and hunting on the animals of the world. After saving the animals and taking them to their Refuge, the barbapapas find 'the dark city' still pressing in on them, so they build a rocket and escape with the animals to a 'quiet green planet'. The absence of animal life brings humanity to its senses and they clean up the world, whereupon the barbapapas and all the animals return, amid general rejoicing.

Rebecca had asked the usual 'why?' and 'how?' questions of the external world, but she did not begin to query her books until about 3–1, and then never on their first few readings. The questioning that occurred almost at once with *Barbapapa's Ark* was atypical. It appeared that the thinking up of more and more 'logical' questions was a type of game with her – a fact that she revealed once at 4–0, in the middle of one of the interminable discussions on the book, by saying, with some satisfaction, 'And another question . . .' This section will cover just a few of the causation problems that the book presented to both her and Ralph, and the steps they took to solve them.

The second opening, the polluted lake, defines the problem (Figure 4.4). The text asks 'Why were so many of them sick?' We answered this question for Rebecca at first, giving her the word 'pollution'. By 4–0 she could answer it herself: 'That's why!' pointing to the pollution in the water. At 4–2 her answer was 'Because of the pollution. That's the pollution pipe', and at 4–3 she included both the air and the water in her pointing as she said 'Because of the pollution'. Ralph at 2–11 gave 'because of that poison, that's why' and by 4–0 had a more complex answer: 'Because of the pollution and the horrible people' (there are no people in the picture, but we had previously discussed its being people who were causing the problem). The mother duck is calling her ducklings from the water, and they do not appear to be ill. Rebecca was interested in this phenomenon, and tried various solutions: 'It's lucky the ducks didn't get sick! They're getting out just in time, aren't they?' (4–0);

Figure 4.4 Barbapapa's Ark Talus Taylor.

'The ducks didn't get sick because they escaped just in time' (4–2) and the same day, at another reading, 'They're not sick because they came down here' (tracing a clean route down the stream), this time creating an antecedent for her explanation. The hedgehog's illness, on the next opening, puzzled her. As she explained, 'The hedgehog is the only on-path animal to get sick – because he dipped his nose into the water with pollution in.' To my query she elaborated: 'The zebras and the other animals didn't go in the water. All the other sick ones were water animals' – so it appeared that 'on-path animals' was a neologism for 'land animals' at 4–6. This is also the picture that puzzled Ralph into spelling out the direction of regard (p. 75).

The knowledge gained from the book was applied to the external world at 4–0. At a friend's house Rebecca came and told me in some distress: 'All the fish will get sick!' then explained 'They use blue toilet paper!' Polluting the seas was the reason we gave for using only white paper ourselves. Three weeks later, in their shared bath, Ralph (0–10) vomited some of his tomato from tea: 'Red pollution!' Rebecca shouted (4–1), and even in the clean water we gave her, she continued to wash her owl 'to get the red pollution off'.

The concept of hunting and killing was unknown to Rebecca (except perhaps with predatory animals). When the barbapapas frighten the hunters away, she remarked 'But hunters aren't afraid, never!' then added 'Perhaps

they [the hunters, or more likely the authors] forgot that hunters aren't afraid' (4–0). At 4–2 she objected 'But deers are gentle animals' [Yes, they are] 'So why are they hunting them?' She had apparently decided that only fierce or harmful animals could be hunted. For the first time I explained the sad facts of blood sports, so when the hunters drop their guns and run away from the giant barbapapa animals, she was puzzled: 'But hunters kill animals.' She could see no reason why they didn't shoot before they ran. At 4–6 she was still puzzled: 'Why didn't the hunters try to kill the barbapapas?' This is a case where the adult accepts the incident as quite logical within the framework of the story, but the child's query points to a logical flaw.

The 'quiet green planet' where the Ark eventually takes the animals seems a paradise. Perhaps it would have been better to stay there and let the world and the humans look after themselves, a cynical adult thinks. This idea eventually occurred to Rebecca at 4–0.

Text: *Barbabright had built a telescope on the planet, so he was the first to notice that Earth was growing green once more. Everyone was overjoyed.*

Rebecca: She wasn't! [overjoyed – the female one milking]
Virginia: Why not?
Rebecca: Because it [i.e. the new planet] was all shiny and there wasn't any pollution.

At 4–6 she discovered another problem. The text says that the people cleaned up the world and 'promised not to hunt animals any more'.

Rebecca: How would they know they had promised?
Virginia: [misinterpreting her 'they' as 'people on earth']. I suppose they talked about it together.
Rebecca: But how would they [the barbapapas] know when they were so far away? (She reasoned that their telescope could show Earth's greenness, but not that the people had made their promise.)

Looking at it alone, but describing it to me, at 4–6 she suddenly spotted a new illogicality.

Rebecca: Look, she's hammering in a sign. The signs say 'Barbapapa Refuge' (correctly). All the animals are following the signs. They are following the signs, but they don't know what a barbapapa is! The animals are following the signs, but the hunters aren't.

There are two problems here. One is how the animals know that the barbapapas will save them when they have never seen one, and the second is why the hunters do not follow the signs as well. The overtones of safety in 'refuge', clear to an adult, probably escaped her.

The whale, which was 'chased right out of the ocean', taken to the Refuge and subsequently installed in the Space Ark, engaged her in much thinking about the logistics of the process. In the Refuge the whale is shown in a lake, isolated from the polluted river. At 3–6 she first queried how the whale could have got there, commenting that its other inhabitants, the ducks and the hippopotamus, could have walked across from the stream, but how could the whale and the swordfish have managed, needing to stay in the water? I made a few suggestions involving big tanks, and later John suggested that the barbapapas might have turned themselves into helicopters (as they do on another page) and lifted them across. At 4–0 she was asking again, and I suggested that they might have dug a channel from the stream to the lake, which explanation she gave back to me three days later. She also wanted to know how the whale got into the Ark, and how it, and indeed all the animals, got out again (at 3–6). At 4–0 when she asked I said that there must be a door for them to get out of, and she agreed 'It's around the back of the Ark' (hence it cannot be seen).

Classification of the animals inspired much discussion at all ages, especially on the page showing the Ark itself, cut away to reveal the various compartments, some with deep water, some with shallow, some with none, and different animals being loaded into each. She talked about which animal would go with which, and how much water the various ones needed, and also asked, at 3–5, why the hunters' dogs did not go to the Refuge with the other animals. It is possible that Ralph's 'Are fleas animals?' at 3–1, when the barbapapas have cunningly used fleas to chase away another group of hunters, was playing with the same idea. If they were animals, why weren't they protected too?

This book also provided a broader perspective on the subject of anthropomorphism. Here the animals are usually not anthropomorphised, needing to be clearly distinguishable from the barbapapas, who often assume animal shapes. Consequently, the final opening, where the animals dance with the barbapapas and the people in their 'barba-celebration', suddenly behaving in a much more human way, caused some discussion. Ralph: 'But animals don't do that!' (2–8. The book had been missing for six months). This was among the earliest examples of his objecting to a fantasy element. At 3–1 he was able to put it more clearly: 'Animals can't dance.' At 3–4 he objected that 'He couldn't really walk' (the seal, dancing on its back flippers). Rebecca came upon me making notes on the same opening when she was 4–0, and asked me 'Do you have to write down how that one can dance?' [How do they dance?] 'It's only a pretend book, anyway.' [How do you know it's only pretend?] 'Because barbapapas are not real'. Where Ralph had queried what the animals could do, Rebecca's comment (at a rather older age) concerned the reality status of the whole story.

Barbapapas are peculiar creatures and their anatomy and physiology puzzled Rebecca, too. At one of the earliest readings at 3–5, it was the cover that caused confusion, as it illustrates both animals and barbapapas disguised as animals. The difference is clear to an adult by the barbapapas' unlikely colours and blobby, unformed appearance.

Rebecca: There is a daddy elephant (the adult one), a mummy elephant (the yellow barbababy) and a baby elephant (the little elephant held by Barbapapa).

Figure 4.5 Barbapapa's Ark Talus Taylor.

Virginia: That one hasn't got any feet. I think it might be a barbapapa really.
Rebecca: No. Perhaps they [the illustrators] were in a hurry and didn't have
          time to draw his feet. (Then, after more discussion, a logical and
          face-saving solution for the lack of visible legs.) Actually, he's
          kneeling!

At 3–11 she noted that 'Barbapapa has no legs – he must move like a
snake', but, as Ralph pointed out at the same age, 'Barbapapas can change
their shape so they can change into feet. So they *can* have feet!' (having
noticed as early as 3–4 'He hasn't got any legs. How can he walk?').

At 4–0 Rebecca remarked on one cleaning the animals:

Rebecca: He's being a shower, isn't he? He drank the water first. (Then,
          presumably by association with things coming out of the body)
          Where do they do bowels? (i.e. excrete).
Virginia: I don't know. Perhaps underneath somewhere?
Rebecca: But where do they do bowels where no one will see? (i.e. where is
          the lavatory?).
Virginia: Perhaps there's a toilet in the house (which is in the picture).

Whether the initial question was about anatomy or plumbing was impossible
to tell.

Another physiological problem linked to causation concerned their repro-
ductive biology. The books themselves set this up. In *Barbapapa*, the first
in the series, Barbapapa is born in a garden, fully grown. In the second,
Barbapapa's Voyage, he is looking everywhere for a Barbamama, but eventually
finds her, also underground but fully grown, in his own back yard. But then
the book explains that 'Barbapapas lay eggs like turtles' and shows the eggs
being placed in the ground, the barbababies growing there, and eventually
being 'born' – as infants, not adults. She objected to this at 7–1 and again at
7–3: 'There's something wrong here! Barbapapa came out of the ground
grown up, but the children are little.'

In many other stories there were examples of the children's application of
strict logic. Owl is riding on the witch's broomstick in *Meg's Eggs*. 'Why
didn't Owl fly?' (Ralph, 2–9). In *Orlando Buys a Farm* the kittens are dressed
as Indians. One has a doll on her back: 'Why is that a baby?' [You mean it
should be a *kitten*?] 'Yes!' (Ralph, 2–10). On *Stone Soup*: 'But how could they
put in milk when they had filled it up with water?' (Rebecca 3–8). When the
animals in *Leo the Late Bloomer* make snow statues of themselves: 'But how do
they know what they look like?' (I suggested perhaps they had a mirror to see
themselves; Rebecca, 4–1). Barbapapa is searching the planets and encounters
aliens in *Barbapapa's Voyage*: 'One of those planets has got water' [How do you
know?] 'See his feet?' (Rebecca pointing to the web-footed creature at 4–6).
When wild animals called to Petunia to entice her away from the farm: 'How
did the Wilds know what her name was?' (*Petunia Beware*; Rebecca, 4–8).

Rebecca argued at 7–1 that there could be giants that were too big for us to see, just as we are too big for ants to perceive, or alternatively they might stand still and camouflage themselves as trees, like the one in *The River at Green Knowe*.

The nonsense of nursery rhymes is particularly hard to rationalise, but if the children were in a 'why' mood, they did attempt to. Rebecca: 'Why did the dish and the spoon run away?' [Well, I don't know. It's just a nonsense song.] 'Perhaps they thought the cow might land on them!' (The illustration, in a colouring book, gives no hint of this possibility; 3–7). To 'Oh where, oh where has my little dog gone' – Ralph: 'How could a tail be "cut *long*"?' (4–10).

It can be seen from these disparate examples that the children attempted to align the stories and pictures with the forms of causation, both physical and social, that they encountered in the external world.

Some developmental psychologists have maintained that even sixth-graders do not have ready access to the category of reality, and Applebee, in his study *The Child's Concept of Story*, remarked 'If Carol White has begun to ask about fact and fiction by the age of five, it will be several more years before most children firmly expect stories to be something "made up" rather than "real" ' (1978: 41). As we have seen, Rebecca and Ralph were able to distinguish between real and pretend characters, and frequently used this as a way of categorising them from 2–10.

It is evident that in the course of their early childhood they grew to an understanding of the reality status of the fictional, secondary world not unlike that of the adult. They understood in which ways the secondary world differed from the external, and when consistency with the external world could be expected. They also recognised the parallels with their own internal worlds, such as dreams.

They had learned to 'suspend disbelief' (Coleridge's term) in the fictional world for the duration of the story, as adults do, while still remaining aware that that was exactly what they were doing. Their readiness to ask logical questions within the context of the imaginative worlds they were engaged with did not affect their enjoyment of books and stories. They knew that the fictional world was apart from the external one, and different in many ways, but found it all the more enjoyable for that.

Several explanations have been given for early understanding of this concept. It has been said that it is anxiety that makes children work out the parameters of the reality-status of frightening books (Morison and Gardner 1978: 648), and they proceed to apply the knowledge to other books as well. This could apply to Ralph. Similarly, it has been suggested that it is in the playing of co-operative imaginary games that an early understanding comes, which applies to any child with an older sibling. On the other hand, it has been suggested that children who play symbolic games frequently, even alone, grasp the difference between real and pretend at a young age (McGhee 1980: 30), which would of course apply to Rebecca.

Other theorists have realised that children are very often underestimated in this area because it is so difficult to test. Children often have difficulty in articulating the difference between real and pretend (or 'they can't *tell* the difference'), although it is the expression of the concept that is the problem, rather than the concept itself. Flavell *et al.* (1986) showed that children of even 6 and 7 had great difficulty in recognising (or, to be more accurate, articulating) the difference between real and pretend when dealing with things which appeared exactly the same as each other but, on handling or otherwise manipulating, proved to be models only. Their most cited example is a sponge that resembles a rock (ibid.: 31). Children of 7, after they know it is a sponge, have difficulty saying it 'looks like a rock', saying only that it 'looks like a sponge'. Flavell *et al.* do not take into account the fact that young children are constantly learning about their world with new names and terms for things. Now that they know it is a sponge, they just say it looks like a sponge – meaning that particular type of rock-resembling sponge. Children are constantly being corrected this way by adults or by experience when learning labels, and this experiment could be more usefully interpreted as an illustration of the way they learn. Flavell *et al.*'s experimental milk which appears red when it has a filter in front of it (ibid.: 8) is even more ambiguous. In everyday life we do not normally say something 'looks red' but that it '*is*' red', if that is how it looks. The inability to articulate these differences does not necessarily imply an inability to distinguish, as Flavell would have it, but rather that this is the way language is commonly used. This is a problem in experimental situations. Most famously, Piaget stated that no pre-operational child (under about 7) could understand the concepts. Many people (e.g. Donaldson 1984) have subsequently demonstrated how far he underestimated young children in this as well as many other areas.

Those who have actually listened to children talking spontaneously with adults have recorded early use of the words and the concepts. Woolley and Wellman (1990) for instance, analysed the speech of six children between the ages of 1 and 6. They discovered eleven ways in which they discussed reality. The ones of most relevance here are those of 'pictorial representation' ('That ain't a *real* skunk, that's only in the book') and 'fiction', as in contrasting a fictional character with reality ('Joey says that King Kong isn't *real*'; ibid.: 950). They concluded that the young child would be likely to refer to things being 'real' or 'not real', or use the adjective 'really' in this sense, every two or three days on average (ibid.: 954). Some of the children in Woolley and Wellman's study were able to do so at 2–6, and all had done so by 3–4 (ibid.: 951).

My two children also demonstrate that the concept is well within the grasp of young children, and if they are given the terminology, or given adults who are listening for evidence of the understanding, they have no trouble articulating it either.

5 'He's looking the wrong way'

Picture conventions

The aspects of the relationship between pictures and reality which I discuss here are conventions of illustration: perspective, missing parts of characters and objects, and the direction of regard and point of view. Some of the behaviour discussed happens before age 2, so could have been included in Chapter 3. However, these behaviours are all part of a continuum of learning, so I have chosen to include them here to illuminate the processes. Actual recognition of objects and characters in illustrations is covered in Chapter 3, because this is usually accomplished well before 2. There are many other conventions of illustration that I could have explored: the lines representing noise or movement, representation of water, colour variations and the three-dimensionality of buildings and containers (e.g. 'It's round, you know', as Rebecca explained of the cut-away Space Ark in *Barbapapa's Ark*, 4–0) or multiple pictures to show time passing – but space is limited.

Perspective

The children's awareness of perspective was the earliest response to an illustrative convention, probably because the adjectives and the concepts ('big' and 'little') appear very early in a child's language acquisition (although note that only two perspective examples were recorded for Anna, *Prelude*: 147). Many books emphasise the size relationship, especially between young and adult forms of animals. As early as 1–9, Rebecca described the cover of *Baby Animal ABC*: 'Big one. Little one. Daddy one. Decca [i.e. Rebecca] one. Tiger.'

One of the first pictures that caused confusion (although the child herself was not aware of being confused) was *The Twelve Days of Christmas*, in which 'Seven swans a-swimming' are illustrated with swans in various positions on a lake. 'Big swan. Little swan,' Rebecca said at 2–0. There is no way she could have known that adult swans are always the same size. No doubt our response would have been something like 'Yes, they look bigger. That's because they're closer to us.' Ralph made this same mistake pointing to the wasps and bees in the foreground as 'daddy' ones at 2–2 (*Picture Stories*) and was still doing so at 2–10.

Animals that have different juvenile forms like swans and bees were a confusing example, because the children wrongly interpreted the smaller ones as younger. The convention was easier to grasp in other situations. When Ralph was 2–9 I commented on the smallness of the car in the first opening of *The Elephant and the Bad Baby*, and he told me it was ' 'acause the elephant [in the foreground] is near'. Rebecca had the convention internalised by 2–11, saying 'Those are the closest' to the large cheeses in the foreground in *The Cow Who Fell in the Canal*, and at 3–0 'The [toy] sailboat is closer' (than the rowing boat, which is shown larger) in *Amanda Has a Surprise*.

The relationships between things of different size could be a stumbling block. Looking at the endpapers showing the kitchen in *Blueberries for Sal*, Rebecca and I discussed whether all the blueberries were finished, because Sal's mother is pouring the last of a saucepan into a jar. I pointed out the other pot still on the stove, suggesting that there might be blueberries there too, but Rebecca countered that there were not enough jars for that many berries. Then she added thoughtfully 'But perhaps they [jars] look bigger when you are close up – when you are in the house' (3–9). She had internalised 'closer looks bigger', but did not understand that things stay in relative proportion to each other.

Ralph expressed the idea clearly at 3–1. He had identified himself as the largest whale in *Whale's Way*, and remarked on several pages 'that's me looking little' when it was further away. His phraseology showed that he was aware that it was appearance that is illustrated, not relative size. His change in understanding can be demonstrated by a series of pictures in *Muffel and Plums* (Fromm) in which Plums, running with his butterfly net, gets closer and closer to the picnic and to the reader, until disaster actually strikes (Figure 5.1). At 2–6 his comment was 'He's getting bigger and bigger' but nine months later he phrased it as 'closer and closer' (3–3). Often, at around 3–11, as he ran as fast as he could down the path to my open arms, he would shout with delight 'You're getting bigger and bigger!', demonstrating that although perspective is a convention of illustration, it does after all have a counterpart in the external physical world.

The convention of being smaller in the distance is usually combined with being further up the page, to fit in with our natural line of sight. Both children expressed this awareness in their own creations, with Rebecca drawing at 4–7: 'If you want to draw things in the distance, you draw them higher up', and Ralph at 4–9, making a picture on a felt board: 'That's in the distance. Things in the distance are sometimes higher up.'

The size of characters in comparison with objects in the 'real' world sometimes reflected on their reality status, as is discussed in the context of the Moomintroll series (pp. 134–137).

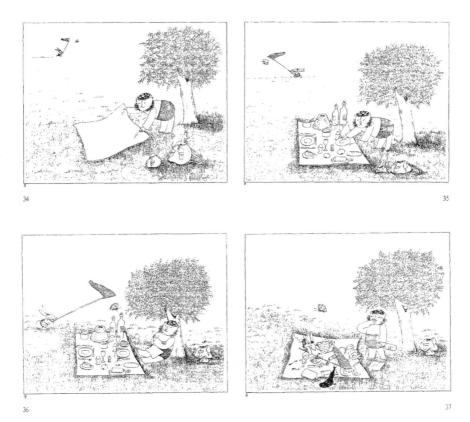

Figure 5.1 Muffel and Plums Lilo Fromm.

Missing parts

Another convention of illustration which could cause confusion is that of objects and characters with parts obscured. Partially seen figures and objects are everyday experiences, part of the external world, and very soon babies understand that the object still exists in its entirety even if it cannot all be seen. This is common in pictures also, where part of the subject or figure is hidden, either by the edge of the page or by something overlapping it, or even by the style of illustration.

This 'missing parts' problem has been recorded as causing distress in some children. Carol White was 'worried', asking 'Where are the little boy's legs?' when they were hidden in water (*BbF*: 22). Anna Crago commented on it from 1–9 on, occasionally with distress (M. Crago 1979). Ralph would often remark on missing parts, but showed no distress. I always assumed his 'no head', for instance, was a shortened way of saying 'there is no head showing in this picture'. Both Rebecca and Ralph articulated their understanding of the convention quite early.

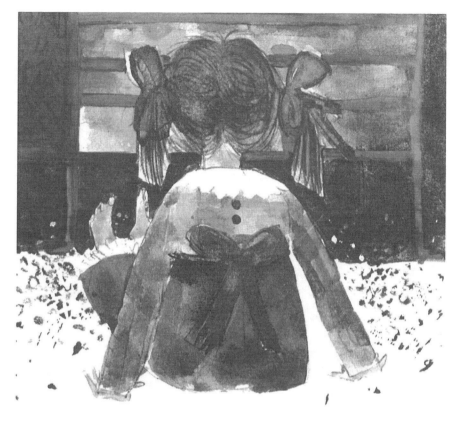

Figure 5.2 Mother Goose Brian Wildsmith.

The earliest recorded example of this having been a problem was with Rebecca. At 1–2 she was enjoying finding 'feet' and 'shoes' when asked, but Polly in Wildsmith's *Mother Goose* confused her. She sits among the cinders with her back to us facing the fire, her feet in front of her at about waist level (Figure 5.2). When asked where her feet were, Rebecca hesitated and then pointed to her bottom (i.e. her feet should have been below her). By 1–4 she could locate them without hesitation. Ralph also pointed first to her bottom at 1–5, but corrected himself at once. At the same age, to the child kneeling in Burningham's *The Cupboard*, Ralph located the feet behind him at once, adding 'boo' [shoe] for good measure.

It is not uncommon to illustrate a person or another animate creature by its head alone, so I was not surprised that Rebecca could locate the dog at 1–1 in *Angus and the Ducks* from his head only.

Recognising a character without the head is a different matter. *Whistle for Willie* offers a good example in Peter hiding under a carton, then standing up, both times with his head hidden (Figures 5.3 and 5.4). Rebecca at 1–4

Figure 5.3 Whistle for Willie Ezra Jack Keats.

Figure 5.4 Whistle for Willie Ezra Jack Keats.

was amused and pointed at the shoes and legs showing beneath each time. Ralph, one month younger (1–3), shouted 'Dere!' just as he did playing hide and seek, and pointed to Peter's legs when standing. Peter, as he appears on most pages, is unambiguously a little boy – or the picture of a little boy. But when it is just his feet and legs showing, the usual cues are missing – face, hands and overall body shape cannot be seen. And with a picture there are not the opportunities of moving to see behind it, or moving it to see the rest of the figure, as in the external world. In fact, at 1–5 Ralph appeared to be trying to push the carton away to see Peter's head, and at 1–6 even demanded 'door' (his word for 'open') as he pushed at the pictured edge.

The concept of something partially hidden being part of a game recurred often to Ralph, who often played peep-oh (peek-a-boo) with Rebecca. This certainly seemed to help his interpretation. At 2–3 he pointed to the man hiding his head in the picture for 'Fee Fi Fo Fum' and told me he was playing peep-oh (*Fee Fi Fo Fum*). In *The Elephant and the Bad Baby* Ralph located the elephant's eyes (without being asked) hidden behind the fruit barrow, pointed at them and shouted 'pop!' as he did when his head emerged from the neck of a jumper (1–7; Figure 5.5). When I laughed, he said 'pop!' to each of the legs too.

Figure 5.5 The Elephant and the Bad Baby Raymond Briggs.

The most widely discussed example of the incompletely seen character is that of Peter Rabbit hiding in the watering can. Carol White had difficulty with this at 2–8, asking 'Where is the rest of him?' (*BbF*: 26), but Cushla, one month older, when asked 'Where's the rest of his body?', pointed to the can at once: 'In there!' (*Cushla*: 50). Anna Crago never asked about it. At 2–3 Ralph volunteered 'Dere y'is!' pointing to the ears showing above the can, on the second reading for one day. At the same age, in a similar Potter scene of a character hiding – Tom Kitten in the bed canopy – Rebecca pointed to the red bulge in the canopy and volunteered 'That's the kitten's bottom' (*Tom Kitten*; Figure 5.6).

Figure 5.6 The Tale of Tom Kitten Beatrix Potter.

Rebecca frequently commented on incompletely seen objects. 'I've never noticed that bicycle before' (3–10) was said to handlebars showing above the water in *Mulga Bill's Bicycle*.

The question of whether there is any more of a picture to be discovered, outside the scene given – perhaps on the back – was explored very early, and is part of the understanding of how a book works. Ralph at 0–11, looking at a photo of Rebecca in a frame, turned it over and appeared to be looking for the back of her head rather than examining the back of the frame itself, just as Vygotsky describes his 5-year-olds doing (1978: 113). Remember that five months previously he had not looked for the back of the Farax baby (p. 38). By 2–2 he had no trouble articulating 'Mi'y in dere' to Mickey's hand showing above the batter in *In the Night Kitchen*.

Wheels shown incompletely are noticeable because the circle is the one shape that demands completion. The Cragos were not surprised that this was the first incomplete figure that Anna commented on: 'Wheel gone. Wheel gone' (1–9, *Prelude*: 155). On the other hand, Rebecca never commented on wheels incompletely drawn, and although Ralph frequently did, it was not until long after his discussions about missing parts of characters had begun. He was fascinated by all forms of vehicles, which had never interested Rebecca. Both knew *Harry the Dirty Dog* well, but it was Ralph who at 2–2 exclaimed of the vehicles in the mud 'Truck wheel fix. Car wheel broke.' By 2–6 he had internalised our explanation for the car wheels, saying 'Stuck in the mud. Can't get out!', but he was still sometimes puzzled by incompletely drawn wheels such as the moon buggy's partly hidden behind a hill in *Meg on the Moon*: 'Why has part of its wheel gone away?' (2–10).

Direction of regard and point of view

In the external physical world it is often vital to know where a person is looking, and who is looking at whom. One of the earliest behaviours of the infant that has made developmental psychologists (and parents) aware of the child's understanding that other people have minds is the ability to follow the direction of regard. Scaife and Bruner (1975) termed this 'shared reference' and found that infants as young as 0–4 occasionally followed line of regard, and that they did so reliably and frequently by 0–9, even turning back to the adult to check they have it right, if they cannot locate what the other person is looking at (Bruner 1990: 75). Children also follow the direction of point by 9 months, and are able to indicate a shared reference as well, to point or 'ask' or 'comment' on something, and expect the adult to follow their line of regard, and also join in a turn-taking 'proto-conversation' (Bretherton 1991: 54; Butterworth 1991: 230).

This skill, which is such an important part of early communication, is also evidenced in book behaviour. I record that at 0–8 Rebecca 'looks at the details I point out with my finger' and by 0–11 she can point herself when asked for 'birds', 'hands', 'the dog', etc. The line of regard is being both followed and used with the pictures.

So, looking at the pictures, pointing to particular aspects of them, and checking that the other is looking at the same place were all well established in the book-reading process. Observing where the actual characters themselves were looking was another step.

Both children seemed well aware that a character's direction of regard could be different from their own as audience. The examples below fail to bear out Piaget's experimental finding that pre-operational children (under 7) cannot take on the point of view of another person (Piaget and Inhelder 1956: 242), though this too has often been challenged since (Grieve and Hughes 1990; Hughes and Donaldson 1979).

Rebecca's first recorded comment on line of regard was at 2–11 to *The Hare and the Tortoise*: 'The woodpecker is looking at that little bird, and the little bird is looking at the woodpecker' (the birds in the upper left corner, Figure 5.7). But then she went on to ask, of the rooster staring out of the frame: 'Who's he looking at?' I answered that I didn't know, what did she think? 'Us!', she replied triumphantly.

It became common with Rebecca, when reading familiar books, to

Figure 5.7 The Hare and the Tortoise Brian Wildsmith.

explore where a character is looking. Two weeks later, regarding *The Cow Who Fell in the Canal*, there were several examples, including 'What is that cat looking at?' (I explained fish bones) and 'That duckling is looking at Hendrika.' Ralph at 3–4 was also recognising that the gaze of the minor characters can be a comment on the main action. In *Harry the Dirty Dog* he remarked that 'Three kittens are watching him run away – two kittens and a mother cat.'

Barbapapa's Ark provided a more complex example. On the opening of the polluted lake (Figure 4.4), various animals are escaping. Two of the extensive barbapapa family have seen what is happening, and look anxious, but the rest are still happily unaware. The problem first occurred to Ralph at 3–6 when he asked of the barbapapas 'Why are they happy and those two sad?' [They can't have seen the sick animals yet.] 'They can't have seen, either' to the canoe-shaped ones further off. 'Stop there,' he said to the distant ones, and put up his hand as a barrier to prevent them coming any closer to the pollution – or perhaps to the disturbing sight. At 4–2 he showed he understood: 'Those ones are happy and those ones – only that and that and that aren't.' [Why are they sad?] 'Because of the pollution.' [Why are they still happy?] 'Because they're not looking. Those ones are happy too. They're very far away.' Two weeks later he was able to articulate the solution without prompting (he identified himself with the furry Barbabeau): 'There's me. Do you know why we are happy? Because we haven't seen what's happening.' He understood that some were not looking, and some were too far away to be able to see.

In *Angus and the Cat*, searching for someone is basic to the plot, so it is not surprising that this was the first book where Ralph remarked 'He's [*sic*] looking at him' of the cat looking at Angus (who cannot see her himself). At 2–5 this is the youngest example in the Reading Journal of commenting on the direction of regard. Angus chases the new cat all over the house, usually able to see but not to reach her. Sometimes she is behind him, following unseen.

Eventually she goes out through the window, and 'no CAT could he see anywhere' as he looks out (Figure 5.8). We can see her hiding, but she is out of sight to Angus, who is also looking in the wrong direction. This proved a difficulty to both children. At first they were not aware that it was a problem. They could see the cat, and assumed that Angus could too, despite the text. When Rebecca first heard the story at 1–8, she would locate the cat on each page. By 1–10 she would laugh when she found where the cat was hiding each time, and said 'funny' at the pages where Angus cannot see her, presumably because the text says Angus could not find her while Rebecca herself could. She did not query it. Even at 3–5 she was still unconvinced that the cat behind the dormer could not be seen. In a half-joking tone, not wanting to accept my explanation, she offered a range of arguments for her opposing conviction, culminating with 'That's a different cat.' [Why do you think so?] 'It's a different colour' (which is patently not so, despite the

into his garden,

Figure 5.8 Angus and the Cat Marjorie Flack.

shadow). The argument ended with her crushing rejoinder: 'You're imagining it!'

Four days later, after yet another reading of *Angus*, she got down on the floor to play with her plastic model animals. She aligned several facing the one way, then explained 'They think there's only one rabbit there. They don't know there are two. They can't see that one behind them', showing she had grasped the concept. At 3–7 she acted out the situation, applying it to herself. She was walking around the house and told me 'I'm pretending we've still got Moushka [our short-lived kitten]. I'm looking for him all over the house. I can't see him because he's following me. Now I turn round and see him. I'm putting him on a furry rug, on your bed.' The book had not been read for two months. When she was 6–4 I tested her [Why can't he see the cat?]. 'Because he's looking that way, and because she's behind there.'

With Ralph the pattern was similar. At 2–4 he was amused and pointed her out; at 2–5, 'Pussy cat sitting dere'; at 3–0: 'There she is!', still not puzzled. By 3–8 he thought 'He could really [see her], couldn't he?' with a laugh. [Could he?] 'Yes, he could turn his head!' He understood that Angus's direction of regard was wrong, but not that the cat would still be hidden. There is no evidence, as with Rebecca, of when he did grow to understand.

The Giant Alexander (Herrmann) has a notice saying 'deep' on the swimming pool, which we discussed. Ralph asked 'What if somebody is on the other side and can't see the notice?' (3–11). At 4–2 in *Moominland Midwinter* where Moomintroll is celebrating the sun's reappearance with a handstand facing away from it, and Little My is watching him crossly (p. 67), Ralph remarked 'They're not looking at the sun. They can't see it' (Figure 5.9). To a character whose leg is showing but unnoticed by the protagonist, he remarked 'He must have seen that!' (4–5). By 5–2 Rebecca was aware not only of what could be seen from the other's perspective, but how it would look from that direction. On *Sesame Street* a baker facing us writes '6' on a birthday cake. Of course it is written to be right way up to the viewer, but Rebecca observed 'He can write upside down!'

Ralph played with the concept of the pictured point of view, just as he was wont to change endings for his satisfaction. At 3–6 he was as eager to see Madeline's scar as her schoolmates were. They have a privileged view, standing on the far side of her bed (Figure 5.10). His suggestion was 'Why weren't they all around here?' – indicating the end of the bed. If they had been there, Madeline would be turned so that the book's audience could see her scar as well (*Madeline*).

A few weeks later he was trying to describe a trilobite, having forgotten its name. 'It might look small, but if you look at its head in a magnifying glass it's big.' This awareness that even our own point of view can be changed almost certainly originated with a book on relative sizes, *How Big is Big?*, which both children spent much time poring over and discussing. This spells out clearly that 'A flea is little. Is there anything smaller than a flea?' and explains how telescopes and microscopes can change the relative sizes for us, or, in other words, our point of view.

In *Angus and the Cat*, Angus was looking in the wrong direction by mistake. However, one can look the wrong way deliberately, as well. The prime example of this in the children's experience was *John Brown, Rose and the Midnight Cat*. When he encountered this at 3–1, Ralph enjoyed locating the

Figure 5.9 Moominland Midwinter Tove Jansson.

Figure 5.10 Madeline Ludwig Bemelmans.

cat on each page, but at 3–2 he first asked 'why?' to 'John Brown would not look'. I explained that he didn't want to see the cat, because he wanted to have Rose to himself, but I was not at all sure he understood. At 3–5 (when he decided briefly that this was his 'favourite book') he remarked 'He's a silly dog, isn't he?' At 3–8, looking at the book alone, he said to the opening where Rose and John Brown look out of the lighted window (Figure 5.11): 'He's looking the wrong way', and was still puzzled at 3–11: 'Why couldn't he see the cat?' Choosing not to observe is a difficult concept for a child. In the end, having tried many ways to explain, I eventually resorted to saying that he pretended he didn't see the cat, which is not quite the same.

These all concern the direction of regard, or viewpoint, of a pictured character. But there is another viewpoint involved in the picture book experience, and that is the one which the illustrator has given to the viewer/reader, the point of view selected for each picture.

At the end of *Barbapapa* (Tison/Taylor) there is an aerial view of the neighbourhood, featuring roads, cars, Francois and Cindy's house, the little house their father built for Barbapapa himself, and a number of people seen from above (Figure 5.12). After the first reading I asked Rebecca about the picture (3–11). She offered first 'That's a sideways picture' [What are those red things?] 'Rooftops' [And what's that?] 'That's Barbapapa's house. It looks sort-of like that', and she turned back to the conventional ground-level picture of it. It is a six-sided construction, and I was interested that she was able to make the connection between the two views. Two days later she also

Figure 5.11 John Brown, Rose and the Midnight Cat Ron Brooks.

located 'a little garage', 'lettuces', 'somebody watering the lettuces', but called the other people 'tortoises'. John suggested that they were 'children looking up' but she insisted that 'that's a kid and those are tortoises'. At 4–1 she no longer insisted on her 'tortoises' theory, and remarked 'We're in an aeroplane.'

Ralph at 1–6 surprised me by identifying ' 'ar' from above. I had expected that wheels would have been essential to his gestalt of 'car', although probably looking down on his toy cars had made the angle familiar. He was confused by the perspective later, though, at 2–5, claiming that Barbapapa had 'turned himself into water' (he could be seen as pond-shaped). The next day Rebecca (5–8) tried to explain it to Ralph as looking down from an aeroplane. At 3–11 he was still unsure, but working towards an understanding. He recognised the man on the 'motorbike', but still had to have the roofs explained. Even after extensive readings I had still to explain it to him, whereas Rebecca, at the same age, had worked it out for herself, first time through.

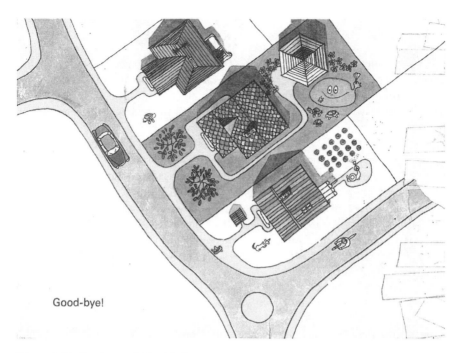

Good-bye!

Figure 5.12 Barbapapa Talus Taylor.

General knowledge and recognition

To some extent, relating pictures to the external world does depend on knowledge of the world, whether it is acquired experientially, through other books or through adult discussion and explanation. One does not have to have seen an actual cow or elephant to believe that such things exist in the external world; the multitude of books that feature them, and the adults' talk about their experiences with them, personally or on television, confirm their 'reality'. However, this reality status can be ambiguous to a child. There are things that appear in books which it would never occur to an adult to stop and confirm. A delightful example is that of Lindsey Wolf when she first encountered a rainbow at 4–5. As Wolf describes it, 'she fell to the ground laughing gaily: "Rainbows aren't real. They *aren't* real! They're only in books!" ' (*Braid*: 17). Different children have different experiences of the world. Lindsey had not seen a rainbow because she had lived in the desert, and Carol White at 4–2 was puzzled by a pictured sunset, never having seen an actual one (*BbF*: 130).

There were similar lacunae in Rebecca and Ralph's knowledge. Ralph said earnestly in *Meg at Sea* that 'There couldn't really be a storm.' [You mean they're only in books?] 'Yes!' This despite the fact that he must have experienced storms by 3–4, though perhaps there had not been lightning within his memory. He exclaimed in surprise at 3–9: 'I only just knowed that there really are dams!' when one was pointed out from the car. He had known of them only through *Barbapapa's Ark*. Rebecca seemed to have had fewer of these problems, or perhaps she was just less likely to express them. She did, however, spell out the parameters of this sort of problem at 4–10, asking 'Are bellows real?' [Yes.] 'But I've never seen them!' Ralph used a similar comeback, demonstrating, though in fun, his criteria for reality with reference to the nonsense song in *Bananas in Pyjamas*: 'Why is there so much cheese on the moon?' [There isn't any.] 'There might be – we haven't been there!' (4–0).

It happened occasionally that the children's general knowledge exceeded that of the illustrator, and they were most surprised to discover that not all illustrators were as well informed as they were. (See pp. 97–100.)

At other times the children insisted that they were correct when they were not. Sometimes this was lack of knowledge on the children's part, sometimes just the drawing style. Examples of this are Rebecca at 4–9 objecting that 'trees aren't white' in *Lord Rex*, or Ralph at 3–6 'Foxes don't really have whiskers' (*One Old Oxford Ox*) and, a few days later, incredulous, 'How can a farm have two tractors?' [Some farms do.] 'No farms do, even giant farms' (which was relevant, as the book was *The Giant Alexander and Hannibal the Elephant*).

In a much more sophisticated area, geographical and ethnic knowledge, and understanding of their reality-status, were also extended by the knowledge acquired from books. For Rebecca, America was the most exotic of locations, because she so loved *Blueberries for Sal* at 2–10. When she begged to pick blueberries herself, I told her that they only grew in America, and it is so far away that you can only get there by plane. From then on, whenever we saw a plane fly over, she would say wistfully 'Perhaps it's going to America, to pick blueberries!' (Lowe 1997b). When she actually did travel on a plane at 4–2, it was to Europe rather than America. She remained unmoved by John's lyrical descriptions of Greece, Italy and France when we flew over them, but as we reached the Netherlands the canals were shining in the sun: 'We're somewhere at last!' (ibid.). 'Holland' had been familiar to her since her first birthday, in *The Cow Who Fell in the Canal*. Later, Finland became her most important foreign country, because of the Moomintrolls (see p. 47).

Ralph's early encounters with other cultures were via myths and indigenous stories: *Arrow to the Sun* and *Anansi the Spider, The Seven Magic Orders, Who's in Rabbit's House?* as well as the Aboriginal Dreaming stories by Roughsey and Trezise. When at 3–7 he heard 'The Teddy Bears' Picnic' sung on the radio, he confided in me 'Mum, you couldn't really go there, 'cause it's in Africa really!' In other words, 'Africa' at that age was the place where fantastic things happened. He was confused about the various peoples acting out the folk stories, because in middle-class Melbourne at that time he saw very few non-Caucasian people. At 4–5 he still used Chinese, Aboriginal, Japanese and African all as interchangeable terms for 'people who look different from us and tell that sort of exciting story'.

Pictures stand in a different relationship to external reality, than language does. The viewer always has to make some adjustment between his or her internal view of the world, and that pictured. The conventions illustrators use to represent these adjustments, for putting three dimensions down into two, and the way the children learned these, are what is demonstrated in this chapter.

6 'The man who drawed it was wrong!'

Authorship, the illustrator's role and artistic style

A work of art is a bridge ... however tenuous, between one mind and another.

Andrew Harrison, quoted in Booth (1988:1)

One aspect of the reality of the text particularly difficult for the child to grasp is the concept of the creator – the roles of the writer and the illustrator. The role of illustrator is the easier to grasp, so precedes that of author (which is covered in Chapter 7). First, however, we must examine the concept of the creator generally, because the author/illustrator's name was the first identification acquired. The roles of writing and drawing in the environment are also relevant.

The understanding that the text – the pictures and the words – have a creator, and that the existence of the fictional world depends initially on another person (or persons) and comes from their thoughts to exist on the page, is an important one in the process of understanding the reality status of stories. As adults we know that the secondary world created when we read is created in our own mind, just as we know that the 'external' world only exists for us as it is transferred by the senses to the mind. Nevertheless, as 'naive realists' (Bruner 1986: 64) we usually talk and behave as if the real world is external to us, and similarly, we talk and behave as if the world of the text is external to us, also. We can speak of it as inhering in the book itself, the artefact or the identity of the book, or we can speak of it as being the author's, as passing from one mind, the author's, to another's, ours.

Authorship, the concept

As they listen to a text, children gain some sense of there being a 'correct' meaning, and eventually come to understand the concept of there being someone who actually wrote the text, who had some meaning in mind.

'We know that to give writing its future, it is necessary to overthrow the myth: the birth of the reader must be at the cost of the death of the Author' (Barthes 1977: 148). 'The birth of the reader' is an apt description of the child's first encounters with books. The importance of their role as reader, which Barthes is emphasising, is something that children take for granted. They know of no interpretation of the text but their own.

Iser (1974, 1978), Fish (1980) and Rabinowitz (1987), like Barthes, take the emphasis from the author's intention and put it instead on the role of the reader in constructing a text's meaning. Both the mediating reader and the child listener construct a meaning. The concept that the text has an author, that an actual physical person wrote it, is an important step in understanding its reality-status. With adults, Barthes could take this understanding as given.

Children do not generally have a concept of the implied author (Booth 1983: 70–71); however, the narrator, the immediate representation in the text itself, is often very visible in children's books, appearing in questions addressed to the audience and other forms of authorial intrusion. There can even be a self-portrait actually appearing in the pictures as well, an aspect of the 'author as guest in his own text' (McHale 1987: 205).

The created mind of the implied author is the one with which we engage in the process of reading. This apparent communication of minds is closer than any other form of communication precisely because while reading we are actually thinking the thoughts of another person, as Booth describes it (1988: 139–141). With adult readers it is often this engagement or 'social relationship' (Meek 1982: 20), this learning how other minds think, that is the attraction of reading. A 'good story' pulls one along through the book, but the ideas shared with the author (or the flesh and blood author's representation in the implied author) are what one gains from the reading process. As Meek says, 'It is consoling to think of reading as friendship, a relationship in which authors and readers expect great things of each other and take mutual responsibilities for the meanings they make' (1990: 111). Young children learn about this relationship through discussion around the text with the reading adult (Dombey 1983: 41, 1992: 35; Wells and Chang-Wells 1992: 149–156).

The relationship between author and reader is vital in the reading process for adults, and also for children. This relationship exists whenever reading takes place, whether aloud by a mediator, or to oneself. The first step in understanding this relationship is knowing that there is an author. Not everyone feels that this is important for the child. For example, Smith argues 'It does not seem necessary for beginning readers to understand that writing is produced by people. How could they easily achieve such an insight?' (1984: 144). On the other hand, Meek points out that it is the book itself, and the process of interacting with it, which teach the author concept (1988: 10). The awareness is not necessarily 'easy', though clearly children in bookish homes do acquire it, mainly through their exposure to many books, many authors and hearing many author statements read.

None of the existing case studies of children and their books follows the child's understanding of this concept in detail. The Cragos devote four pages to their practice of pointing out the author in the author statement or portrait on the cover, and to Anna's growing understanding of the first-person narrator (*Prelude*: 238–241; M. Crago 1978: 77). They did not, however, emphasise the individual writing or illustrative style with Anna, and a footnote comments that my technique of drawing attention to these with Rebecca 'constitutes training in the notion of stylistic signatures' (*Prelude*: 271).

Wolf shows Lindsey's preferences for different styles of illustration, but unfortunately the way these incidents are described gives no indication of whether the child actually knew the illustrator's name, or understood the role (*Braid*: 55, 56), so it cannot be meaningfully compared with the data in this study. In the section 'Echoes of Heard Voices' (*Braid*: 66–77), Wolf discusses the recognition of authorial style through its reproduction in the children's own stories and quotations, but there is little on its relationship to the concept of author as such. Lindsey Wolf did show an awareness of the author concept when at 3–7 she asked 'Who's it wroten by?' (*Braid*: 67). Carol White at 4–3 expressed her developing understanding, asking how '[b]abies and poems and things like that' are made (*BbF*: 125).

The mediator and the author: reading aloud

Understanding the role of the author in the case of the very young child is complicated by the fact that books, or anyway the written part of them, have to be mediated through the reading adult. It is interesting to speculate on where a baby thinks the words come from. The reading voice is the parent's, but is quite different from the normal conversational voice, in inflection, in length of sentence, and in being decontextualised (not referring to the immediate environment, nor being addressed directly to the child). There is a range of discursive features that distinguish spoken from written language, and it is possible that all young children recognise these differences almost from the beginning of hearing stories read.

By the time they have the language to demand a book (in our case, 1–6 and 1–7), they are demonstrating that they expect a pleasant experience and possibly that they know it will not be the parent's own words. Certainly a recitation of the text without the book would not satisfy in this situation. Nor, if they are used to hearing the text, would a simplified retelling: 'Don't tell me all about it. Just read it to me!' (Rebecca, 2–7). It is the whole experience, the pictures and the author's text, that they are requesting. They soon recognise if a word is changed, or if any of the story is skipped, and let the reader know at once.

Apparently, many children think that it is the pictures that an adult reads. This may be an effect of labelling rather than reading the book's actual words. Ralph especially seemed to understand that it was the black marks on the page that carried the words, even at 1–1 (p. 34).

While reading aloud, the adult is communicating to the child their own belief that books can offer pleasure, instruction, comfort; and also the value they put on reading the words of someone else, or thinking the thoughts of someone else.

The discussion with the reading adult which accompanies the text is 'an external model for the internal conversation with the author that is necessary to any but the most superficial reading of a narrative text' (Dombey 1992: 35). This internal dialogue involves the questions that we address to the author (or to the text itself) along the lines of 'Why did she do that?' 'How does he feel now?' and always 'What will happen next?' Although with Rebecca we interrupted the text less than most story readers (our reading was more monologue, less dialogue, than Dombey's example), we did sometimes discuss the story and its meanings before and after the reading. Ralph talked all the way through book readings until he was 2, even though we usually still responded only with the text's words. Rather than just meaning, it was aesthetic pleasure we wanted the children to take from their books.

Authorship at home

Many different aspects of the environment encourage children's understanding of the author-concept, especially in homes where reading and writing are valued, and books are borrowed, bought and discussed. The children whose experiences with books have been studied in detail inevitably come from bookish families. They have seen authorship at first hand in the parents' writing and even being published. They have had books made specifically for them, authored by parents, grandparents or friends. Their own creations have been transcribed and read back – probably even printed. Their paintings and drawings have been on display, so they not only recognise that they them-selves are artists, but have seen the pictures over and over and have the opportunity to remember both the process involved, and the label or story that went with the picture. Parents and even some children meet authors, bringing away books signed by them. They will have listened to, and taken part in, conversations about books and authors. They not only will have had many books read to them, but are likely to have a large collection on hand, for their own use, at any time.

Rebecca and Ralph's knowledge of what authors are, and what they do, was developed thus. By 3–3 Rebecca was aware of my writing 'a book', though not the topic, and when Ralph asked at 4–10, I told him that I was working on a book about what children say about books. There was proofreading of publications – for example, *Adult, Book, Child* (Lowe 1979a) – and Rebecca saw the finished products, with photographs of herself, at 2–5 and 7–5, and Ralph also at 4–2. The actual physical writing of the Reading Journal for this study took a great deal of my time and often occurred in front of the children, especially as they got older.

From time to time the children dictated stories to us, and Rebecca created books herself (see p. 101). I also made books for the children, mainly a series of little 'readers' for Rebecca, beginning when she was 4–8 and continuing for three months. Each contained Rebecca's full reading vocabulary – about 20 words – and had adventures featuring her and Ralph. Her paternal grandmother also made books for her, with pictures cut from magazines, or photographs, and her own verses accompanying them. Ralph, who was denied comics, made his first 'book' in the first few days of kindergarten by cutting out all the serial comics (*Mandrake*) from the back of the *Women's Weeklies* provided, and sticking them into a scrap book as a 'comic book' (3–11). I also produced alphabet books with pictures and drawings of the children's own possessions to label and encourage talk about initial letters.

The book collection itself helped in the development of the author-concept, with a variety of different illustrators and styles to compare. There is also the everyday book-talk between adults, as a model. As soon as they were able, the children began contributing to this ongoing book conversation. The earliest recording of this happening, was Rebecca's contribution '[woo]ff [woo]ff' to the library conversation when she was 1–5 (p. 2). One common form of book conversation was the expression of preferences. For instance, at around 2–3 Ralph insisted that two people could not both 'like' the same book or picture at the same time – if he had opted for one, the conversational partner had to take the other. Later, analytical judgements were offered on style of illustration, writing and even ideology.

Authors as people also existed for the children because they knew that I often met writers and illustrators, and there were books specifically signed for them: 'Signed for Rebecca with love by Edward Ardizzone, May 1973', 'To Ralph with best wishes from Helen Oxenbury 31/8/75', and many others. These were special books, 'the signed books', and kept away from ready access. When they were read, the inscription was read too, and my meetings with these eminent people described. When they were 4–6 (Ralph) and 7–8 (Rebecca) they actually met an author (Ron Brooks) themselves, although Rebecca had also been introduced to Ardizzone as a toddler.

Thus, the living environment was conducive to the growth of the concept of author, which is one reason for Rebecca and Ralph's advanced state of understanding of the author-concept in comparison with what is predicted as the norm by several commentators, including Applebee (1978: 38). See Lowe (1991b, c).

To an adult, the reality-status of a book depends on its creator. With picture books this can be one person (an author/illustrator) or two. Initially, to infants, books must just seem to exist, their production unquestioned. They were part of our children's environment (pp. 13–14). However, young children in a bookish family eventually learn that a picture book has an illustrator, that someone drew or painted the pictures, partly through the author statement having been read aloud each time. Surprisingly soon, they also learn to recognise an illustrator's style, and eventually this recognition is linked with the idea that the same person can draw the pictures for a number of different books. I will discuss the concept of illustrator before that of a writer, because it is easier for a young child to grasp.

Style sensitivity

The illustrator's role is easier to understand than that of the author of the words, because the pictures are there in front of children, in a form they can interpret for themselves. They understand about the process of drawing because they attempt it themselves, and have probably watched an adult do so as well. The pictures clearly belong to the book itself rather than to the outside world, where the adult's voice reading aloud is at first the reality of the text.

Once a person's name is acquired and attached to the book (through the routine reading of the author statement), it is not a big step for the child to understand that a person with that name 'drew the pictures'. The complication of the actual production of the book – that these pictures are printed, not drawn there directly, that it is a manufactured item, like their toys – comes later (and is why some of the children in Kiefer's study, 1993: 278, said the illustrations were made 'by a machine').

The process of understanding the concept of illustrator is aided by the fact that the child may encounter different versions of the same fairy tale or nursery rhyme, which leads to the understanding that the illustrator is interpreting this, creating it from his or her own mind, rather than copying some form of external reality. Mistakes in illustration also foreground their status as creations, as secondary worlds. The child may then go on to compare books by the same illustrator, noting similarities, and gradually learn that artists have their own distinctive style. The concept of the author of the words is more complicated and inevitably comes later.

Cognitive psychologists have done many experiments on children's style sensitivity. Most conclude that young children sort paintings as 'similar' by referring to the subject of a painting when this is available as a cue, and need instruction to recognise the actual style of paintings. Howard Gardner maintained, summarising earlier research, 'It is, in fact, the case that style and metaphor sensitivity is not available in young children' (1977: 270). Subsequent researchers such as Steinberg and DeLoache (1986) and Hardiman and Zernich (1985) have shown that young children are more sensitive than Gardner believed, as long as the subject cues are not there to distract the sorting process. There has also been a lot of work done to establish the painting styles that children prefer. All this is useful information for teaching the visual arts, of course, but it does not relate directly to picture books.

Most of this research has been carried out on children's reactions to single pictures, or groups of three or four, never to the work of art that is the multi-media picturebook. It has been shown that exposure to many pictures by the same artist can be equivalent to training in recognition of style (Johnston *et al.* 1988). This is exactly what exposure to picture books offers. The average picture book has at least fifteen illustrations by the same artist, and this succession must influence children's ability to recognise the style, especially when they are also exposed to other books by the same illustrator. Another aspect is that the cognitive experiments have been done using reproductions of paintings, while it is more often drawing rather than painting that is the distinctive style in picture books.

On the other hand, there have been studies of the picture book as an artistic medium, though not carried out by psychologists – usually by experts in children's literature. A recent and exciting one of these is *Children Reading Pictures*, by Arizpe and Styles (2003), but there are also the ones by Kiefer (1995), Holland *et al.* (1993), Watson and Styles (1996) and Baddeley and Eddershaw (1994). These demonstrate a great acuity in young children, even kindergarten children, in understanding the pictures, and talking about them, even if they are not able to articulate recognition of style as such. Arizpe and Styles hint at earlier recognition by describing a 4-year-old's delight at finding a decontextualised picture by a familiar illustrator (2003: 51).

Most children who have been read to extensively from an early age will be able to perform this 'style sensitivity' task frequently and with ease. My study confirms this.

Style sensitivity in picture books is about recognising illustrative styles rather than formal painting styles or the artistic design of the whole book. Illustrators often use several different styles in different books (changing media, for instance), but it is the way they draw characters, put the features and expressions on people or animals, that children take as the clues ('They've got the same noses'). Sometimes the style of the book's layout is also a hint, if it is part of a distinctive series. Another stylistic aspect is playing with perspective in original ways, such as David McKee's flattened-out versions of the three-dimensional scenes. Not only the protagonists but incidental background details can also be distinctive – 'It's got the same clouds in' (Rebecca, 4–11).

There are a number of different aspects of book exposure that lead to this understanding:

- the name of the creator;
- same character, different book;
- different characters, same artist;
- comparing artistic styles;
- different version, same story;
- fallible illustrators;
- the children as artists and recognising artists.

The name of the author or illustrator

Books were usually referred to by title, and both children could recognise favourites in this way (see Rebecca on *The Sailor* at 2–0, p. 11). Others were referred to by the author/illustrator's name. The easiest way to recognise an illustrator's style is in series. On rushed evenings there might be time to read only 'a quick Dick Bruna' (these are very short). This term was picked up by the children. 'Dick Bruna' was used, not necessarily with reference to the author/illustrator, but rather as a generic term for the square, brightly coloured little books, which were shelved together. They used the term themselves at 2–11 (Rebecca) and 3–3 (Ralph). Often it would go like this:

Parent: There's time for a quick book.
Child: A quick Dick Bruna!

And the child would fetch one (or several) of them.

One night, when she was 3–9, Rebecca and her father went to the bedroom to select books for the evening reading: [Time for a quick Dick Bruna.] '*You're* Dick Bruna!' [What does that make you? Miss Bruna? or Rebecca Bruna?] 'No, I'm a girl. I'm going to put you on the shelf.' It seems clear from this that she had no concept (anyway at that moment) of 'Dick Bruna' as a person, as someone who created the familiar books, but rather saw it as a term for the books themselves. She is a *girl*, not a *book*, as she had suggested her father was. Notice that John speaks of Bruna as a person, even though Rebecca responds as if it is one of the books.

Another generic term was 'Beatrix Potter', again because the books were identifiable by their uniformity and by their being shelved together. Rebecca was 2–6 when, asked what book she wanted for the evening reading, replied 'I want two Be-ix Potters', and Ralph at 3–3 remarked 'More Potter books' to a pile of them on the floor. When Rebecca was 3–10 she was trying to make me remember a library book we had once borrowed 'a long time ago'. She described it as about 'a cat and a mouse. . . . The mouse sat down in front of the fireplace'. The cat 'caught it in a bag'. Eventually I asked her 'What colour cover did it have?' and only then did she say 'It had a white cover. It was a Beatrix Potter', and I at last recognised *The Story of Miss Moppet*, which we had borrowed six months previously. It had not occurred to me to ask her the author, as one would an adult.

The 'Beatrix Potters' and 'Dick Brunas' series each have some characters in common who were talked about – Peter Rabbit, Jemima Puddleduck, Tom Kitten in Potter, and Miffy in Bruna – but the children's early recognition was as much of the physical structure of the books as of the characters or the illustrative style.

However, Ralph's first author's name belonged to a specific book, rather than a series, *Richard Scarry's Best Word Book Ever*. My somewhat dismissive attitude towards this book was shown by my referring to it as 'Scarry'. At 2–5 he would ask for 'dat big Scarry book', as a byname, but by 2–11 had extended this to others: 'We've got a new Scarry, John C!' he enthused to an adult friend. It is notable that, unlike the Brunas and the Potters, the Scarrys Ralph knew were not uniform in size and shape, not recognisable as a set, but recognisable only in their drawing style and in that we adults read the author statement at each reading. When Ralph was 3–4, Rebecca brought home a sheet of busy-work from school, and along the top were the familiar Scarry figures – photocopied line sketches in black and white, and quite out of context. However, Ralph recognised them at once without any prompting: 'That's Scarry! Lucy [his friend] has got that in a book.' By now this term was clearly applied not just to the books, but to the style of drawing, although it was still the generic term for that sort of picture, rather than for the person who created them. At 3–7 I noted that 'whenever I mention "bookshop" he says "I can look at the Scarry books!"' 'At 4–3, though he had many more sophisticated favourites, still there was magic in the Scarrys. As he looked at four of them spread out on the sunroom floor he chanted 'Scarry, Scarry, Richard Scarry' over and over, enjoying the sound of the words, just as Lindsey Wolf had with 'Trina Schart Hyman' (no age given, *Braid*: 68).

Same character, different book

Series in which there were familiar characters, apart from the Potters and the Brunas, were the Angus books (Flack), Gretz's bears, *Madeline* (Bemelmans) and *Orlando the Marmalade Cat* (Hale). We owned four of the Orlando books when Rebecca was born, and bought a fifth when Ralph was 1–4. The books themselves, like the Potters and Brunas, are distinctive: identical in shape and size, and cover layout, although each is a different bright colour. We referred to these as 'Orlandos' rather than 'Hales', so this is what the children also called them. If Potter, Bruna and Scarry had written only about a single set of characters (or we had known books about only one of their characters), they would doubtless have been known by the character's name, as the 'Madeline', 'Angus' and 'Orlando' books were. It was because of their diversity that the author's name was in common use.

Recognising illustrations of specific well-known characters is a skill not unlike recognising photos of actual people. The children demonstrated their ability with photos at 0–8 (Rebecca) and 0–6 (Ralph). Experiments have shown that infants can recognise and respond to pictured faces (pp. 37–38).

When Rebecca was 1–7, *Harry and the Lady Next Door* was read on television. I said 'Look, it's Harry!' and Rebecca jumped up and ran to her room, where she pushed all the books off the pile on her table until she located *Harry the Dirty Dog* and came back carrying it triumphantly. She sat in front of the television apparently comparing the two. Fortunately, the last picture is almost the same in both stories, so there she had the satisfaction of matching them. From 2–3 Ralph instantly and without prompting recognised 'Benn' in McKee's series, and he also managed to produce a title. Picking up *Mr Benn Red Knight* he said '*123456789 Benn*' (a title in the series which he had only heard once, several days previously), then went through picking out the protagonist with delight: 'Dere's Benn!' on page after page. This was an isolated incidence of his quoting the title in comparing one book with another, and was not repeated for several months.

Both Rebecca (2–11) and Ralph (3–3) demonstrated their recognition of Peter from *Whistle for Willie*. Rebecca chose *Peter's Chair* from the library because of the recognition, and at home Ralph, offered *The Snowy Day* (also about Peter), demanded 'No, I want *Whistle for Willie*', it not being in the room. It goes without saying that Madeline (Bemelmans), Veronica (Duvoisin), Orlando and his family (Tinkle was always the favourite) and other characters who are consistent from book to book were recognised at once.

Different characters, same artist

Closely allied to recognising the actual character is recognising another character who looks similar. This is the first step in recognition of style. Although most illustrators would say that they have drawn their different characters distinctively, a child can often recognise the similarity at once. In the youngest recorded incidence, Ralph in the library said 'Boy-Boy' to *The Boy with Many Houses* (2–0). This was his name for the similar (nameless) child in *The Boy with 100 Cars*, which he had borrowed several weeks before. It was not a usual term from him.

Sendak's characters are sufficiently alike to remind the child of the other books and hence the style. Ralph shows an interesting progression here. At 3–0, just before the end of *Where the Wild Things Are*, with *In the Night Kitchen* neither present nor mentioned, he announced 'I want Mickey!' Three weeks later, as John started reading him *Wild Things* again, Ralph stopped him. 'I want the book about another boy.' [Suggestion.] 'It's green.' [Suggestion.] Getting more frustrated: 'It's got poems in it.' When *Hector Protector* (Sendak) was finally hit upon, he exclaimed 'That's my favourite', although he had owned it for only ten days, and heard it once. At 3–5 in the library he was excited to discover 'Here's one about Mickey!', coming upon *Some Swell Pup*. Ralph evidenced no confusion, although Ashley Wolf had difficulty distinguishing between the various Sendak characters (*Braid*: 57). By 3–9 it was no longer the actual characters Ralph was identifying, but finer details. To the bean packet on the front cover of *In the Night Kitchen* he said 'There's the Wild Things!' [Where? Is that the Wild Things?] 'It's a jungle, anyway', he replied. The picture on the front of the packet of bean seeds has large leaves, and the grown green beans are hanging down from the branches in a way that must have made him think of Max and the Wild Things swinging from the branches in their Wild Rumpus.

Rebecca at 2–9 represents the youngest unambiguous case of identifying a character by style. Looking through *Veronica's Smile* for the first time, she remarked at the endpapers 'Janet read me a book about Jim one day.' Janet was a friend-babysitter who had brought *Round the Corner* and read it to her once, three months before. Both books are illustrated by Duvoisin, and the boy in *Veronica* does resemble Jim. From 2–10, Rebecca could always recognise Shirley Hughes's pictures, saying that they looked either like Lucy (*Lucy and Tom's Day*) or Mary Kate (*Meet Mary Kate*). Other books in which similar characters were recognised were illustrated by Wildsmith (Rebecca, 2–11; Ralph, 3–0), Newberry (Rebecca, 3–1 and 3–5), and Graham (Ralph 3–11).

In most of these cases the second book was not present. Commonly, the response was a spontaneous comparison on the child's part, though occasionally we would draw their attention to the similarity. At 2–9 Ralph and I were going through *The Mother Goose Treasury* and came upon a red-headed little boy in the rhyme for 'Giant Bonaparte'. When I asked him 'Does that baby remind you of anyone?' he was highly amused and said 'The baby and the ewfewent – the bad baby!' (*The Elephant and the Bad Baby*). I explained they were drawn by the same person (Raymond Briggs). The children soon mimicked this prompting: 'What does that remind you of?' [I don't know.] 'The Grandfather who pulled up the turnip!' Ralph (4–3) was in this case comparing Oxenbury's illustrations to *The Hunting of the Snark* with *The Great Big Enormous Turnip*. He had not seen the latter for five months.

Comparing artistic styles

The children's ability to identify similarities between characters and objects gradually extended to recognising the artist's individual style. One episode illustrates this increasing discrimination with Ralph at 4–2. It was a mistake of mine that foregrounded the issue of artistic style for him.

Figure 6.1 Crazy Cowboy Guillermo Mordillo.

Figure 6.2 Patatrac Jean Jacques Loup.

He had seen and loved Mordillo's detailed colourful cartoon pictures in *Crazy Cowboy* several times over the previous six months, and this book was again on loan from the library when he found *Patatrac* (Loup) in a bookshop. I assumed they were by the same person, and said so. The books are similar in shape and colour, and have similarly busy complete-opening cartoon paint-ings. I had not compared them more closely. It was only on return home with the newly purchased book that I realised my mistake, and told him. I still thought there were no discernible differences in style, but Ralph saw them. When he had compared the two he explained 'In *Cowboy Crazy* [*sic*] they have long eyes. When he shuts them they're long like that' (demonstrates with his hand out from his own eye, to represent the bulging eyes of the characters). He continued to compare them and noted ' 'Cos *Cowboy Crazy* hasn't got long noses – see, there's a long nose. There aren't any of those in *Cowboy Crazy*' (Loup has some long pointy noses, Mordillo large fat ones. Figures 6.1 and 6.2).

One month later (4–3) Ralph acquired what he described as a 'new *Crazy Cowboy* book'. I agreed that it was, but he went on to correct himself (and me?): 'It's more like *Patatrac*', and indeed *The Architect* is by Loup, not

Mordillo. He pursued his investigations of the styles on this occasion by noticing that 'their feet haven't got those holes!' I glossed this stylistic device as heels on the shoes, and he went on to remark that 'they haven't got heels here, either' (in Loup's *Patatrac*), but Rebecca (7–6) thought that they had the same hair and noses. I pointed out the author statements on *Crazy Cowboy* and *The Architect* as final confirmation. Ralph's summation was:

> 'All of them could have been written by the same man but they just didn't do long eyes. Because – do you know what? – it's got the same pictures as his, and because it must be the same. Another [reason] is because that hasn't got any words and this hasn't.'

Because I had initially thought the illustrators were the same, he was still trying to rationalise this, even though he himself had found the distinguishing characteristics.

From this age (4–2) on, Ralph continued to isolate such fine aspects of style in other books, and often pointed them out. 'These are made by the same person 'cause look, they've got the same noses! And that's the same boy as that!' he showed me at 4–4 to Quentin Blake's *Sixes and Sevens* and his illustrations to Hoban's *How Tom Beat Captain Najork and His Hired Sportsmen*. Similarly with books by Peet: 'He's just like the other one – he's got the same bumpy nose and the same points on his head', comparing *Cyrus the Unsinkable Sea Serpent* with the absent *How Drufus the Dragon Lost his Head* (4–11).

Tove Jansson is responsible for both pictures and words in the *Moomintroll* series. Ralph objected to the picture of the Groke in *Moominpappa at Sea* (p. 18; 4–4). 'Is it the Groke?' [Yes. Perhaps we haven't seen her from the back before?] 'Yes we have. It must have been a different person that did it.' [It's the same person who does all the Moomintrolls.] 'But the eyes are different!' It may be that his close attention to the expressions on faces, and the emotion this indicates, led to his careful analysis of detail in illustration of characters, and interpretation of their emotions (pp. 129–133).

The experience of learning to discriminate between the styles of Mordillo and Loup probably prompted Ralph at a considerably younger age than Rebecca to refer to the actual people who did the pictures. Although there is no doubt that we adults referred to the illustrators as people from the beginning, it was not until 4–11 that Rebecca first used 'by the same person'. She said that Burningham's *ABC* was by the same person as *Trubloff the Mouse Who Wanted to Play the Balalaika*: 'It's got exactly the same mouse in', and a week later, of Gag's *Three Gay Tales from Grimm*: 'I know who this is by – it's the *Millions of Cats* person.' [How do you know?] 'It's got the same clouds' (Figure 3.4). From this age on she always referred to the actual author/illustrator as 'the person who . . .' as well as to the title or the characters that were familiar. These were the first examples of her giving a rationalisation for her recognition of style (the mouse, the clouds), whereas this was frequent with Ralph from 4–4 (seven months younger), as shown above. Some other comparisons of Ralph's were: 'One that's by the same person as *Mushroom in the Rain.* You have to guess' (both illustrated by Aruego, 4–6), 'By the same person as the knight who goes to the castle' (McKee, 4–6) and 'Are they written by the same person?' of two Roughsey and Trezise titles (5–2).

Different version, same story

The different ways of illustrating nursery rhymes and fairy tales, and later, for Ralph particularly, myths and legends, helped the children understand that the illustrations are a representation of another person's mental world, that they have a creator who perceives things differently from other illustrators. There is more than one way of illustrating a character, an incident, or a story.

By 2–6 Rebecca could identify Humpty Dumpty in four nursery rhyme books, even though the impressions of him are quite different (Eve, Wildsmith, Buck, Graham). The cover of Tudor's *Mother Goose: Seventy Seven Verses* has a pattern of mainly realistic children, but also a very unusual Humpty in old-fashioned military garb. Ralph saw this for the first time at 3–10 and came running through the house in great excitement: 'Mummy, come and look. Something's gone wrong!' He took my hand, and John's. 'Daddy, come and look', then, as we passed Rebecca, 'Becca, come and look. Something's gone wrong here!' 'What?' she asked. 'Look! Humpty Dumpty!' He was surprised and also clearly pleased with his own ability to recognise this unusual creature.

The children frequently discussed their preferred versions of the illustrations. It was often the version with the most detail that they favoured, or the one that illustrated particular incidents which appealed to them. In this regard the Ladybird versions of Theseus and Perseus (Preshous, *Famous Legends Book 1*) were more popular with Ralph at 3–11 than the stylised simplicity of White and Provensen's versions in their *Myths and Legends*.

It was not only traditional stories in which the different versions were observed. At 4–0 Ralph had three non-fiction books all open on the floor, positioned one above the other. 'Do you know why I've got them all like that? They've all got the same dinosaur in, see?' This was not one of the common species which he could name, but an early one with large scales. It was drawn in completely different styles, but still recognisable.

Fallible illustrators

The concept of a creator is sometimes foregrounded by mismatches between the illustrations and the words, or between one or the other and known external-world facts. If the text and pictures are inconsistent, children often work hard to find an explanation within the world of the story, but sometimes the only answer the beleaguered reader can give is that the author or illustrator 'made a mistake'.

This sort of mistake is particularly surprising (and irritating to the adult) if the author and the illustrator are the same person. Hughes is guilty of inconsistency in *Lucy and Tom's Day*, in that the doll's house is on the table between their beds on the endpapers and on the first opening when the children wake up, but not when they are put down at rest time. Rebecca asked where the doll's house had gone (3–3) and we discussed where it could have been taken – out to the kitchen, perhaps? In this case we were able to stay within the world of the story because there was no real discrepancy; the doll's house could have been moved without being mentioned in the day's activities. Rebecca's explanation was like Cushla's of a missing pattern on a pictured pillowcase: 'I know – she turned the pillow over' (about 3–6, *Cushla*: 78).

Duvoisin in *Lonely Veronica* writes that 'In the morning, two half loaves of bread and two bananas, which dropped on her nose from a hole in the ceiling, woke her up', while his illustration shows *three* bananas. Rebecca at 4–8 devised an explanation: 'Perhaps those [lowest loaf and banana] and those [middle banana and second loaf] dropped on her first' – in other words, that the third banana didn't actually wake her up. This incident was the first discrepancy Ralph noticed, at 3–2. It was the first time he had looked at this library book, and I knew he had not been alerted by Rebecca, because he did not even recognise the stylised bananas until the text was read. 'What's that?' [We'll find out.] I continued to read. 'They're 'wanas!' he realised, pleased, and he interrupted again shortly after: 'There's three 'wanas!' [So there are.] 'But it said two 'wanas!' I had forgotten this in the two years intervening and had to check back. Nineteen days later (3–3) he heard it again, and counted the bananas. 'The man who drawed it was wrong!', he was delighted to announce, doubtless remembering my explanation of the previous discussion.

Gag covers her bare hills with short, horizontal strokes of shading, as opposed to the upright strokes of grass. *Millions of Cats*: 'Each cat ate a mouthful of grass and not a blade was left!' 'Yes there was – look,' Ralph objected at 2–8. By 3–7 he had learned to accept the word of the text and look for a consistent explanation rather than arguing with it, so he asked 'What's that stuff?' My answer referred to the illustrator herself: 'That's just the way she drew the dirt.'

Sometimes, as mediating adults, we would attribute the problem to the printing rather than to the illustrators themselves (Rebecca's badly printed Bunnykins plate is a case in point – see p. 131). This led to the children using this concept, often inappropriately. Rebecca at 2–11 asked of Spier's illustration of the last duckling on a busy page in *The Cow Who Fell in the Canal*: 'Why has he got his wings up?' [Perhaps he's hurrying to catch up.] 'Or perhaps he's badly printed!'

Ralph quite often used this as justification for his own theories, as with an ongoing discussion about which of her hot-water bottles Phoebe received for her birthday: 'It might be the same but they showed it a different colour' (3–11, *Phoebe and the Hot Water Bottles*). I took his 'they' instead of a singular pronoun to mean that he was referring to the people who physically made the book.

A range of different approaches to an illustrator's 'mistake' is shown to *The Mouse with the Daisy Hat* (Hürlimann), a retelling of Aesop's 'The Town Mouse and the Country Mouse'. In this, although the text states that he 'never spilled a drop', Felix is shown with his glass of red wine, clearly spilling. I found this an irritating case of the words and the pictures being at odds with each other (Hürlimann in a recent personal communication says that it is an addition by the translator). I remarked on it to Rebecca to see what she would say. She tried her best to explain it away: 'Perhaps it [the glass] was coloured red, and that [the splashes] is some colour coming off and that is the colour that's left' (4–6). Ralph's understanding of it was quite different. At 3–11 he pointed it out himself, remarking 'splash', then he thought for a moment: 'He thinks he isn't [spilling] but he is.' Only then did I realise that this is exactly right. Slightly tipsy, Felix is unaware of his spills, and here the narrator or translator has taken Felix's own view-point to express this. Rather than its being a mistake, the gap between the

Figure 6.3 The Mouse with the Daisy Hat Ruth Hürlimann.

illustration and the words was to be filled in, just as Ralph did, as a witty comment on Felix's personality and his state of inebriation (Figure 6.3). Ralph recognised the irony in the gap between the picture and the words, where his very literal mother did not. Nodelman (1988, 1996) discusses the irony in the gaps between the pictures and the words in picture books (also Lowe 2002).

Illustrators of Mother Goose are understandably looking for new ways to represent the familiar rhymes, but often the child prefers consistency rather than originality. Oxenbury's treatment of 'Hey diddle diddle' in *Cakes and Custard* has two illustrations, dog and cow, dish and spoon, but 'Where's the cat and the fiddle?' Ralph demanded at 2–7. I replied that they're just not in the picture. 'But the words say it!', he objected.

Another problem arose when the pictures disagreed with what the children knew to be the case in the real world, most commonly when animals were represented incorrectly. This was not a problem when the creatures were imaginary ones such as Seuss's. But when they purported to be animals from our world, and especially in a realistic text, errors were noticed and commented on. It seemed to be the small creatures that illustrators were unsure of. No one makes a mistake illustrating an elephant, but, as the children noticed, ants, bees, spiders and snails seem particularly difficult for some illustrators.

Snails with four eyes (on the stalks and on the sides of the head) were noticed in *Bananas in Pyjamas* at 5–0 (Rebecca) and 4–0 (Ralph). Rebecca also commented out of the blue, with the book not present, at 5–8, 'You know that book *Dinosaurs and All That Rubbish*?' [Yes.] 'Well, the snail in it – the snail on a leaf – it hasn't got stalks for eyes at all!' Spiders with only six legs were a problem in *The Mother Goose Treasury* and Wildsmith's *Mother Goose*, but insects could be a problem, too. There were bees with stings on their noses instead of on the back, as in *Hop on Pop* (as Ralph remarked at 6–7). In Low's *Summer*, a text showing what children do in hot weather, Rebecca (3–11) remarked on the picnic page 'Are those ants?' [Yes.] 'But they've got so many legs!' [You're right! They've got eight legs!] 'Like spiders!' [Do you know, I think the lady who drew them didn't know how many legs ants have!] 'Perhaps she'd never seen one.' [Perhaps.] I was clearly dubious, so a minute later she had thought of another explanation. 'Mummy, perhaps she didn't know how to count?' (Figure 6.4).

The children as artists, and recognising artists

Children can draw long before they can write recognisable stories, and their own attempts at drawing can be related to the pictures in books. They know about making pictures. Rebecca used a new box of watercolours to make a picture in the style of a known illustrator, at 3–0. 'It's Momoko,' she said, and, when it was finished, 'It's Momoko skiing.' Indeed, the watery figure did have a very close resemblance to the free, undetailed style of Iwasaki's little girl in *Momoko's Birthday*, though whether the watercolours inspired her

Figure 6.4 Summer Alice Low/Roy McKie.

attempt or whether it was just that the result was reminiscent of the familiar style, there is no way to know.

The books that Rebecca made and illustrated herself also demonstrate her awareness of the picture-making process. Her first created book was at 3–9, then others in bursts of activity at 3–11, 4–8, 5–5 and 6–1. Sometimes these were miniatures for her doll's house, at other times colouring and puzzle books for friends, occasionally story books. Her most sophisticated publication was a zoological study of bunyips at 7–4 (Figure 6.5), covering what they ate, where they lived and how many babies they had. The bunyips' appearance was influenced by Ron Brooks's *The Bunyip of Berkeley's Creek*, while the written text was a close reproduction of non-fiction discourse. Her books

Bunyin babys

Bunyin babys are born under the ground they are like mice. But they are as big as a baby nunnies. the mother bunyin has two litters the two littlest stay in the nest to take over the nest Wen the mum and dad hav dide.

Figure 6.5 *Bunyips* by Rebecca.

usually had an author statement, and often publication details as well. She often talked about books she was planning to write, including one to be titled 'Dr Seuss's Awake Book' (in contradistinction to *Dr Seuss's Sleep Book*) at 6–3. At 7–7 she decided she would be 'a well-known author' when she grew up, and write lots of children's books, some of which she had already planned. She defined the creative role: 'You're really God to anything you make' (7–7). Ralph, though just as devoted to books, did less drawing and very little constructing, and rarely produced a book himself.

Children learn that books have illustrators, and what they do, by examining different versions of the same rhyme or story or character, different books by the same illustrator, and even the artist's mistakes. Hence, the children achieve an understanding of artistic style.

'The capacity to relate differences between works to differences between artists, to realize that what is distinctive about a particular work derives from the hand that produced it, is also late to develop' – defined in this context as the middle years of childhood (Gardner 1973: 157). Although Gardner found that there was no possibility of a child recognising an illustrator's style prior to 6 or 7 (1970: 819), it is clear that Rebecca and Ralph, along with some of the other studied children, had succeeded in doing so at 3 and 4.

The understanding of the role of the author, anyway one who is not an author-illustrator, is a more complicated task, and will be examined in the next chapter.

7 'A'course I can, read-maker'

The concept of author and ideology

A firm grip on the concept of the illustrator probably helps in an understanding of the writer, although the latter is definitely a more complex cognitive task. Young children can draw and paint, but they do not know how to write. Their pretend-writing scribbles cannot be read back like the print in books. Children in book-oriented families will have their oral stories written down and read back to them, but this cannot be done alone, and probably at first is not seen as closely related to the creative process of the author.

A number of steps can be recognised in the difficult task of understanding the process of authorship. First there is the understanding that words 'belong' to a book, rather than to the actual speaker, either when read from the page or when taken away from it in quotation. The children's own use of quotations demonstrates that they recognised literary discourse as being different from normal speech. The literary shape, as well as the literary language, is also relevant, and is seen in the children's own invented stories. 'Mistakes' – inconsistencies either within the text or in comparison with other known texts – lead to a concept of an author who is fallible, just as mistakes perceived in pictures do. The words and thoughts of a character are first attributed to the character itself, with the child staying inside the fictional world. Later they are seen as belonging to the page or the words, and finally attributed to the author.

One indication to the children that a text does have a creator is the intrusion of the author into it – those moments when the (implied) author actually intrudes 'in person' into the text. In the illustrations, recognising the author's intrusion as self-portraiture is a specialised skill, implying an audience already in the know. This can only happen through the intervention of the adult. There were only two authors whose self-portraits were recognised in texts (although dust jackets and blurbs had portraits sometimes). Ardizzone pictured himself in *Tim's Last Voyage* and was immediately identifiable once one had met the man himself. When the book was borrowed and the children were 8–1 and 4–10, I pointed him out, and discussed the actual person and my encounter with him. The portrait of Beatrix Potter in the background of *Samuel Whiskers* I identified only when Rebecca was 4–6, though she had owned and passionately loved the book for 15 months. Potter also appears on page 22 of *Pigling Bland* (MacDonald 1989: 55). She was a special case for Rebecca because of our visit to Hilltop Farm.

The intrusion of the author into the written text is a different matter, being aimed directly at the child audience. This can happen with a first-person comment from the author, or with a question directed outwards to an audience. Wall (1991: 18) compares this narratorial voice with that of an oral storyteller and suggests children gain a sense of security from it. Cochran-Smith (1984: 152), in her study of nursery school readings, considers the 'open-ended questions' in many picture books as indicating that an adult reader should address the child listeners directly and invite their response. Equally, it is possible to see the questions as a continuation of the tradition of pretending to build a close relationship with the reader in a purely rhetorical way, as did many eighteenth-century novelists with their 'Gentle Reader' comments (Lowe 1986).

Wall (1991) points out that there are multiple voices in texts purporting to be written for the child, because children's authors keep one eye on the adult readers and purchasers of their texts. Today's illustrators like Anthony Browne, John Burningham, Chris Van Allsburg or Shaun Tan say at least as much to the adult as to the young child, though there were fewer of these sophisticated artists making picture books thirty years ago. The level of text aimed at the adults would have been largely irrelevant to my children in their early years, especially because the family practice was to not offer explanations unless they were asked for.

The direct question seems a rather dated stylistic device today, but it is nevertheless frequent with some authors. At first the child may hear it only as the voice of the mediating reader rather than as the author's, although with our reading style it would have been quite different from the voice and body language the adult would have used if they had been asking the question for themselves.

If the children responded, it was usually to answer as if the questions were directed specifically to them. In the youngest example the question was not strictly an authorial intrusion, but was treated as one. In *Whistle for Willie*, Peter, pretending to be his father, asks 'Is Peter here?' At 1–3 Ralph 'answered' by pointing straight to Peter, as he would have if the question had been directed at him.

The rhetorical question about the polluted lake in *Barbapapa's Ark*: 'Why were so many of them sick?' puzzled Rebecca at first: 'Why do they say that?' she asked at each reading (3–6). Hers was not an easy question to answer, and we would have couched our explanation in terms of 'the authors'. Six months later she had stopped asking about the question and instead just answered it, as did Ralph at 2–11 (Figure 4.4).

Rebecca would sometimes reply to questions couched in the second person. *Two Kittens* asks 'Don't you wish you had kittens like me?', to which her firm reply at 3–5 was 'No, I don't!' (Perhaps she sensed that they were dead kittens frozen and photographed? I didn't find this out until several years later.) The lyrical *Green Is for Growing* asks 'Do you swing up high?' 'Not very,' she replied at 3–8, as one who knew her limitations. By 4–3 she usually ignored questions in the text, and I had to repeat the question in my 'own voice' to get a reply. Edwards's style is full of authorial asides in the stories about *My Naughty Little Sister*. When the text comments 'You know what trowels are of course' I had to ask her directly 'Do you?' to find out, before continuing the story, which hinges on this knowledge (4–8). Godden's style is similar: 'It reminded her of something but she could not think what. Can you?' I had to repeat this in 'my' voice to get her reply: 'Yes, the fairy doll!' (5–0; *The Fairy Doll*).

Answering a question posed by the text could be a difficult cognitive task. At 2–0 Ralph expected everything mentioned in the text to be illustrated, and at the same time expected everything in the pictures to be part of the text. Consequently, he had difficulty with Bruna's question to the picture of the egg: 'What do you think was inside it?' (*The Egg*). The story was completely familiar, and he knew that there was a picture of the duck on the next page, but at 2–0 he could only answer with what he knew was inside an egg, any egg: his word for 'water', 'ba'. This continued over several readings through several days. Then at his next encounter, after a gap of three weeks, he again replied 'ba', but as he turned the page and saw the duckling he told himself 'No "ba" – duck!' Two weeks later, now 2–3, for the first time he accepted the title without contradiction. Previously he had always insisted it was called 'Duck' because of the cover picture. In the same reading he showed his understanding of the egg question as well. With a great laugh he anticipated by giving the answer before it was even asked. To the egg picture: 'A duck, a duck,' he shouted in triumph, and had a similar response at the next reading, the following week. From then on he answered 'duck' to the question with casual assurance. Rebecca had had a similar problem at 2–0, with animals mentioned but not pictured, on the page where the duckling first appears. She was able to recite the whole of the book's text, given the beginning word, except for this page: 'It wasn't a cock or a hen, it wasn't a cat or a dog. It was a little yellow duckling with a piece of shell on its head.' Here she could only give 'duck', not the negatives of the text.

Ralph was much more inclined to answer the text's questions than Rebecca, as he was always more interactive. She never replied to 'What did he see on the path in front of him?' in *Benjamin Bunny*, but Ralph answered 'Pussy cat!' They heard it first at the same age, 2–7. Even book titles could be treated as questions, although they were not read with a questioning inflection. 'Who killed Cock Robin?' asks the title of Roffey's picture book. Ralph answered the cover on his first reading at 2–9: 'A bird – a sparrow with an arrow', as he knew from the nursery rhyme.

First-person narration was much more regularly queried in poetry than in narrative prose, possibly because the 'I' is usually not pictured. Carol White's first problem with first-person narration was to Rose Fyleman's 'Mice': 'But I think mice / Are nice.' 'Who thinks?' (4–0; *BbF*: 100). Similarly, Ralph at

3–0 queried Milne's 'Twinkletoes', 'Here I go' with 'who goes?' and at 4–0 was still querying Milne in 'Puppy and I': 'Who says "No not I"?' and, to the little boy's 'I will, I will!', 'Who will?' In the latter two cases the answer is the character illustrated, rather than the author. Sometimes Ralph answered the question directly. To 'Missing' he answered 'Has anybody seen my mouse?' at 2–8 with: 'Here it is! I'm looking at the mouse. It's a sweet little mouse.'

There are first-person comments in picture books too. The first person is not always, nor even usually, the author. It is more likely to be the protagonist that is the 'I', first-person narrator, in a picture book. It is easier to come to terms with when the protagonist is actually there in the illustrations. After all, the more common third-person texts almost always contain dialogue in which the characters refer to themselves as 'I'. From this, it is a small step to understand who the 'I' is, as long as the character is clearly in the pictures. *A Day at Bullerby*, for instance, clearly states 'I'm Lisa' for the protagonist, and this never caused any difficulty for Rebecca, although she had heard it from 1–11.

The first time Rebecca queried the phenomenon of 'I' as narrator was in *The Cupboard*, heard first at 4–0. On her third hearing she repeated the text with a questioning inflection: 'I think of something else to do?', 'I please come back?' It was obviously the 'I' which she was querying. I pointed out the child and explained that it was he who was 'saying' it, using the familiar 'I'm Lisa' from *Bullerby* to explain the concept. At a reading to both children when she was 5–3, she again queried 'Who is "I"?' I had thought it was the simplicity of the text that was letting her explore other aspects of the story. However, latterly she has explained that it was the way the 'I' was worded – 'Mummy says why don't I think of something else to do' sounds as if it is actually dialogue, and she had expected 'Mummy says "Why don't *you* think of something else to do?" ' This is an example in which it is clear that my interpretation was wrong. My 'Lisa' explanation would not have been of any use, but she was obviously not able to explain the problem to me at the time.

Ralph first queried the first-person narrator at 2–10, to the very familiar *May I Bring a Friend?*: 'Then the king played a while / And so did I.' 'Who did?', Ralph asked, though the 'I' is present in the pictures throughout.

Sometimes the first-person narrator points directly to the author, and here the concept of authorship could be reinforced. Kipling in the *Just So Stories* – or rather the annotation to the pictures that accompany them – has a chatty voice, foregrounding the narrator: 'But I am not allowed to paint these pictures.' This may explain why, at 3–9, the narrator was in the forefront of Rebecca's mind. At the illustration to 'The Elephant's Child' Rebecca said something about 'the sea'. I suggested it was the 'great grey-green greasy Limpopo River', but she insisted 'I think it's a sea.' To my ambiguous 'Why?' (meaning, what made her think it was a sea?) she replied 'Because she [*sic*] made it.' [Who made it?] 'The lady who made the book!' The slightly condescending tone of the Ladybird title *At the Zoo* by Gagg was treated by

Ralph at 4–0 with the disdain he felt it deserved: 'Can you see the brown bear?' Having forgotten the word 'author', he replied: 'A' course I can, read-maker', a neologism that encapsulated his understanding of the authorial role. This statement was made following two weeks of extensive storytelling of his own, a phase ultimately eight weeks long (3–11 to 4–1). His own creativity may have sparked a new awareness of other creators.

Rebecca was amused rather than confused by C.S. Lewis's authorial intrusions into *The Lion, the Witch and the Wardrobe* – for example: 'That is how beavers talk when they are excited; I mean in Narnia – in our world they usually don't talk at all', and 'other creatures whom I won't describe because if I did the grown-ups would probably not let you read this book'. This was at her first hearing of the book at 7–2. To 'None of the children knew who Aslan was, any more than you do', Ralph on his third hearing (7–3) replied '*I* know who Aslan is!'.

Beatrix Potter intrudes into her texts, not only into the illustrations. The ends of several have first-person comments that break the illusion of the fictional world, at least to some extent. These are notorious for causing problems with young children. At the end of *Peter Rabbit*: 'I am sorry to say that Peter was not very well during the evening', Lindsey at 3–7 seemed to think first that it was the reading adult ('Are *you* sorry?') and then that 'Beatrix Potter' might be 'a bunny, too' (*Braid*: 67). *Tom Kitten* ends with 'And I think that some day I shall have to make another, longer, book to tell you more about Tom Kitten.' At 3–1 Anna Crago queried 'Who said that?' (*Prelude*: 238). *Tom Kitten* had been Rebecca's favourite Potter for a year when we gave her the sequel, *Samuel Whiskers*. Only when she heard *Tom Kitten* again after hearing the new one did she object to this last sentence: 'You shouldn't read that page now!' [Why not?] 'Because she's made the book.' The 'longer book' is *Samuel Whiskers*, as she recognised. It is of note that although it caused her problems, they were with chronology, rather than with the identity of the 'I', which she seemed to understand.

On our trip to England when Rebecca was 4–6, we visited Potter's home, Hilltop Farm. Rebecca carried her copies of the books with her and compared the interiors, complaining that 'one of the pot plants has gone' from the windowsill, where the 'authorised version', *Samuel Whiskers*, has two. As well as the scenes represented in *Tom Kitten*, *Samuel Whiskers*, and *Jemima Puddleduck*, Rebecca saw the actual pictures Potter had painted. I bought Lane's biography (1970), and we discovered the original version of *Peter Rabbit* there, which I read to her and explained its genesis. Because of this, the ritual name of 'Beatrix Potter', which she had used for so long, became a real person for her, and this author at least, lived.

The concept of literary style and of author

One aspect of literary style is the shape of the story. The children's awareness of this was reflected in the stories they themselves told. There is an extensive literature on children's ability to tell stories in literary mode, with formal openings and closures, third-person narratorial voice and other indicators (see Applebee 1978: 37, 163; Pitcher and Prelinger 1963; and, much more recently, C. Fox 1983, 1989, 1992, 1993). The Cragos discuss the influence of literary style on Anna's storytelling, analysing three monologues created to the pages of books (*Prelude*: 107–140). Both Rebecca and Ralph devised stories to the pages of familiar books. Rebecca even told me, years later, that she sometimes used to start at the back and tell herself a different story, turning towards the front.

Gardner in 1971 and 1975 (with Lohman) found that 6- and 7-year-olds seemed to have no understanding of literary style, but Green, in an interesting though limited study of ten 5-year-olds, found that several could identify the literary style of authors they had heard before. The experiment carefully removed the elements of book design and illustration style by giving the stories on audio tape. She does not, however, consider that the texts and authors might have been familiar to the children tested, stating that she assumes, on the basis of her own storyreading behaviour, that 'the practice of reading the title page is not widespread', even in the university community where she was working (Green 1982: 149), so she does not take a knowledge of the author's name into account.

Literary language was important in the children's language development. Ralph would query an unknown word often, though rarely on the first rendition of a text – plot came first. Rebecca often used unknown words for days or weeks before requesting a definition. Quotations were such a large part of her conversation from 2–2 to 2–9 that it seemed she used the words of her authors to think with rather than her own, especially in unfamiliar situations. Her daily language was also infused with the tones and style of the literary models she heard (see p. 11). It is not surprising, then, that the children's spontaneous stories and songs, to pictures, told to parents, or as monologues to books or in play, contained many elements of the literary.

Wolf gives a beautiful example of Ashley's songs, inspired in form by the nursery rhymes, but in content by the fairy tales that made up a large part of her literary diet, the refrain being 'Don't kiss me! Don't kiss me! / My master's going to kiss me' (4–2 *Braid*: 71). Rebecca and Ralph also created similar adapted or parodied versions. One of Rebecca's, with a refrain and many variations, resonates with her adult conservation activities, including actually living on a platform in a tree at 18. It was sung while sitting up a tree at 4–9, with some influence in wording from *A Birthday for Frances*.

> Living in a tree
> Is how it should be.
> Living in a tree
> Is how it ought to be.
> Living in a tree
> Is how it has to be.

Living in a tree
That is how it ought to be.
How I ought to be
Is living in a tree.
Living in a tree
Is how I ought to be.
Can't you see
Living in a tree –
How I ought to be.
Is just like I have to be,
Doing what I have to do,
Living in a tree
Is all I can do.
When you're up a tree
Living in a tree
Is all that you can do.

Note that she ends it by both wittily and pragmatically stepping outside the frame of the secondary world, into the external.

When much younger, Rebecca had a saga about her three favourite soft toys, continued on each visit to her grandparents' house from 2–5. These tales were told while turning the pages of large coffee-table books with photographs of Australian landscapes. The title, 'read' running her finger along the title on the cover, was always 'Piggy and Possum and Panda'. These were exciting picaresque adventures with little plot. They began with 'one day', continued in the past tense, and involved incidents with lots of dialogue: ' "There's a waterfall," screamed Piggy. "There's another one," said Panda. "The waterfalls have all gone," screamed Piggy.' On the first of these story-telling marathons she went through three books page by page, then closed the last one just before the end, with a sigh. 'I'd better do some work instead of reading books all the time!' (a turn of phrase she had heard many times from her mother).

Ralph's 'joke' story at 3–3 (p. 150) shows his stories already in the past tense, with formalised beginnings and endings, so it fulfils all three of Applebee's story conventions (1978: 36). It has little plot, but at least has central characters and a unified theme. His definitions of 'joke' and 'story' were confused, but he was clear about the reality status of his creation. Fox (1993) and Engel (1995) discuss the stories children tell, but only Fox considers literary influences, on five children who were extensively read to.

It can be said that, not unexpectedly, Rebecca and Ralph, as well as each of the other children studied in this way, were developmentally advanced in storytelling skill, having absorbed the conventions of the story genre. As Rose notes, 'Applebee's model is clearly the "Once upon a time there was . . ." of story-telling, in which the neutrality of the form guarantees the truth and ordering of events' (Rose 1984: 75). Although Rebecca and Ralph were familiar with fairy tales and able to reproduce their form, these did not make up a large proportion of their literary diet.

Their own created story worlds while playing led to many stories. Their styles of play differed. Where Ralph spoke for the toys, giving them voices and moving them through their actions, Rebecca tended to tell the story, while the toys performed it – such as: 'The sheep said . . . And the giraffe looked down at the goose and said . . . Then the elephant said "Have you got any peanuts?" . . .'

Both children peopled these worlds with imaginary creatures. Both also 'became' other people. Ralph was frequently a squirrel (from 2–3 on) or a 'builder man' at 2–11 when we were having an extension built on to the house. His roles were ephemeral and were associated with some game or with a particular mood. Rebecca's, on the other hand, were an assuming of a personality which sometimes lasted over weeks ('Piglet' at 2–11, 'Snufkin' at 6–4). Not all the roles they took on were literary. Daddy going to work inspired both children at 2–3: 'I being Daddy going to work' with a rag held up as 'Daddy's trousers' and a 'briefcase' with lunch (Rebecca), and 'Me a daddy fox, to work . . . Dis a train. Daddy fox on a train', riding a push-along motorbike (Ralph).

Because they heard so many books, the stories the children created them-selves were recognisably literary. One of Ralph's first extended imaginary games, recorded at 2–4, began as a limited acting out (we were all waiting to be served in a restaurant, and he was given milk in a mug): 'Me a man. Me drinking coffee. Me reading a newspaper . . .', but gradually it appeared that the story he was inventing in his head owed more to picture books, because very soon 'Me got a big Mamma car' [Have you? What colour is it?] 'Blue. A picture of a big blue Mamma car going. Got a driver. Outside, dat big blue Mamma car. Me got a bee-baw car [ambulance] as well. Bee-baw car bump a big Mamma car. Moving. Big Mamma car got wheels, tyres . . .' The slip from his owning the *car* to owning 'a *picture* of' the car perhaps shows that, rather than putting himself mentally into the position, he saw himself as a character in a book. Similarly, there is the move from what he was acting out – drinking coffee and reading a newspaper – to a complex story structure in which he is no longer an actor, just an 'owner' and even then perhaps just the owner of the book, or 'picture' itself. These indicate that the literary setting of the story was taking over his play-acting.

They enjoyed making up stories and telling them, many of which were taken down from dictation, then read back and corrected. One of Rebecca's at 3–8 showed her understanding of what was fantastic, or perhaps nonsense, in the story. It included 'And a dodo came to visit the kangaroo. He came rowing a boat over the lake. . . . Then he rowed up a tree and rowed onto the leaves! Then he rowed right up into the sky, then he rowed down again. And the kangaroo got into his boat and they rowed right up into the sky again, and down again to the dodo's house. . . .' The exaggerated tone of her voice signalled that rowing over grass and up into the sky were fantasy, but dodos and kangaroos living in houses and visiting each other were not. Anthropomorphic animals were not fantastic in the story context. This was shortly after she had begun to comment on animals talking in books.

Sometimes they used a book's illustations to invent a completely different story. One of Rebecca's told to baby Ralph using *Where the Wild Things Are* at 3–7 went in part like this:

> 'The purple slater was a naughty slater. There's the purple slater growed up [front cover – Figure 4.1]. Purple slaters are bad things. At night they just get out of bed and bounce on them at night. Mothers watch and criticize them as they fight and hit, and then they fall asleep on the carpet. . . . His mother was cooking tea while he was sailing down the river to his home. He ate it in his bedroom and it was still hot.'

As with fallible illustrators, the children's perception of 'mistakes' in the written text revealed an understanding of the creative process. At 2–8 Ralph attributed a 'mistake' to the book, rather than the author, when he said 'That page doesn't know it' (in *Cakes and Custard* there is no plate and spoon shown for 'Hey diddle diddle').

Ralph was fascinated with the idea that he could know more than an author. The whale in Brunhoff's *Babar's Travels* chases the fish and leaves them stranded on an atoll. Rebecca (7–5): 'Whales haven't got teeth.' Ralph (4–2): 'What are those insects called?' [What whales eat? Plankton.] 'Why does it say he ate fish?' I knew that some whales in fact do eat fish (only the baleen whales survive on plankton), but I chose to go along with what was obviously an exciting and significant discovery on Ralph's part. [Perhaps the author thought children wouldn't know about plankton, or else he really didn't know about it himself.] Hours later he explained to a friend that the author didn't know about plankton, but *he* did, and so he knew more than an author.

An awareness of the author's style gradually appeared, though far behind that of the illustrator. Rebecca seemed attuned to it for several months from 4–3, adopting different discursive forms in her own stories as appropriate. Following her first contact with most of the traditional fairy tales in *The Fairy Tale Treasury*, she told a story that showed their influence in style and subject: 'I found you, Mummy. I found you in a meadow. You were crying, and I brought you home with me to be my Mummy. My other Mummy was dead, so I kept you to be my Mummy.'

She was similarly inspired by our readings of items from *Black's Children's Encyclopaedia* when it was new. She reproduced the register on and off for the whole evening: 'It was in 1978 that the name "pea" was invented. Before that they just ate peas without a name' (4–4). Telling a story looking through the pages of a book also inspired mimicking style. She had been listening to Rumer Godden's *Candy Floss and Impunity Jane* and later picked it up and told a different story to the pictures, which included many rhetorical intrusions: 'Then she bought a doll. Isn't she pretty?' and 'But do you know what? Some boys tried to take them and they were afraid.' These were not part of her usual style, even when she was in 'literary' mode, but closely resembled Godden's. Her consciousness of style was verbalised six months later when, at 4–11, she dictated a story that included the sentence 'Owls sleep in the day, and hoot up their hooting in the night.' When I read the story straight back to her she laughed and said 'That sounds like something in Dr Seuss.' Her competence with the style of non-fiction can be gauged from the page of her 'Bunyips' book (7–4), a page of which is reproduced as Figure 6.5. Ralph at 4–3 did not articulate the comparison as Rebecca had, but, looking through Seuss's *Sleep Book*, he was chanting similar nonsense rhymes, deliberately incorrect.

The way the fictional world is created by the author is another aspect of style. At 4–1 Rebecca, playing with Lego, had made a house. Inside she put one of her little model dogs, but then she wanted some people to go inside as well. I asked why the dog couldn't live in the house by itself, and after some thought she admitted that 'Beatrix Potter's do'. A similar example is Ralph's idea (4–1) that the Moomin world should contain no humans (p. 136).

An understanding eventually grew that the author might have a reason for an element of the text, apart from the plot. Non-fiction is perhaps easier to grasp in this way than fiction. In Macdonald's *Spiders* (p. 18) the text says 'This spider is called a Black Widow. It is very dangerous. It lives in America.' At 5–5 Rebecca observed that 'they say that so you won't worry about being hurt – they tell you it's in America' (still a remote place for her). Lindsey Wolf made a similar comment to the forced rhyme in a Seuss verse: 'He just does it to make children laugh' (*Braid*: 119).

Comments on structure were not infrequent, often inspired by repetition. In *The Mother Goose Treasury*, 'Cock Robin' was enjoyed by Ralph at 4–0, but after yet another repetition of the refrain he asked 'Why do they keep saying that, the ruddy idiots?' and at 4–11 of *The Pirate Book*: 'Why does it keep saying the same words? "Jolly Roger to the top"?' Irritated by the simplistic style of the Ainsworth reader *At the Zoo*, Rebecca said 'Why do they say the same thing over and over?' (5–6), and recast one of the sentences to demonstrate that variation was possible. Ralph noticed in 'Jabberwocky' (Carroll): 'The last part [stanza] is the same as the first. Why?' (7–1). My answer this time was that Carroll thought it sounded right; it rounded off the poem.

Rebecca often commented on the fact that stories (rather than poems) rhyme. She was surprised and pleased by *The Man Who Took the Indoors Out*: 'Mummy, it seems to be rhymes!' (4–8), and even at 6–0 seemed surprised at the rhyming text in *Indian Two Feet and His Horse*.

The actual choice of words that make up a sentence was sometimes noticed by the children, especially once they were reading independently. At 7–4 Rebecca asked me what my favourite word, then favourite sentence, were. Then: 'I know what my favourite sentence is. "Jack was very filthy so Nora had to wait"' (from *Noisy Nora*). To *Father Bear Comes Home*: 'There's some funny sentences in this story, where he hics in the middle of what he's saying' (7–1).

By 7, both children were also commenting on the structure of the work itself, for example at the end of a chapter of *The Lion, the Witch and the Wardrobe*: 'Why do they always end at exciting places?' (Rebecca, 7–2); Ralph (7–1) to an incident in *Midnite*: 'Do you know what that makes me think of? The beginning of the book, when Midnite bushranged Trooper O'Grady!', and indeed the incidents do parallel one another; Ralph 7–9 rejected *Nate the Great and the Lost List*, which I had bought for him to read alone, on the grounds that 'It's too babyish.' [In what way?] 'Well, he has to find the list before lunchtime, so it can't be very complicated.'

References to other known works always aroused discussion. Intertextuality can be seen as situated either within the book's world, or outside its frame. In *Nurse Matilda* there is a sow called 'Aunt Pettitoes'. Rebecca asked 'Why Aunt Pettitoes?' and I answered from within the book world. [They must have read *Pigling Bland*.] 'Who must have?' [The people who owned the pig, or the children.] However, she stepped outside the frame: 'Or the person who wrote the story!' (7–2), recognising that it was she and the author who shared a knowledge of this character (cf. Meek 1988: 21).

Ralph similarly referred to the author's responsibility, with reference to the little creatures in *Moominland Midwinter*. 'It didn't say who those little people were.' I referred to Too-ticky's conversation. 'But why doesn't it say what their names were?' [Well, Too-ticky didn't tell Moomintroll, so we don't know either.] 'Perhaps Tove Jansson didn't know the names herself' (4–2). This implies that there is some form of 'reality' to which the author has privileged, but not omniscient, access – an alternative reality that the author is drawing on and transforming in her own way. This appears to represent a nascent awareness of the unreliable author, or the author-as-narrator – as if there is a story there, and a world, and the author has put it into words, rather than actually creating it.

A progression can be seen through these examples, from attributing the thoughts to the characters themselves (staying inside the fictional world) through attributing them to the page or the words, and finally to attributing them to an author. Once this understanding is reached, it is then possible to again step back into attributing thoughts to the character, though this time with the understanding that this is how the author wants you to read it (as with *The Mouse with the Daisy Hat*, p. 99).

Although outside the age range of this work, it seems relevant to add Ralph's comments on Enid Blyton's style at 10–1. (Both children went through a phase of reading *The Famous Five* when they were still not quite ready to tackle more advanced novels alone.)

Ralph: What I hate about her, she keeps explaining things – it makes it yucky.

Virginia: Like what?

Ralph: Well, it's Christmas and Tim was bounding round everywhere, and she says 'Tim enjoyed it as much as the children' and she put an exclamation mark as if it was surprising. Of course dogs would enjoy it! Look at Lizzy [our dog]! As if dogs were completely unintelligent or something!

And three days later:

Ralph: I hate Enid Blyton. She says perfectly obvious things again and again. As if the readers were babies!

Ideology and the author

Another aspect of the authorial role is the ideology of the writer. Stephens maintains that 'Writing for children is usually purposeful, its intention being to foster in the child reader a positive apperception of some socio-cultural values which, it is assumed, are shared by author and audience' (1992: 3). '[I]deology is an inevitable, untameable and largely uncontrollable factor in the transaction between books and children' (Hollindale 1988: 10). On the other hand, the narrative itself frequently subverts the values of the text. For instance, Peter Rabbit is punished for his disobedience, by his fear, his tummy ache and his missing out on blackberries for supper. The message is that children should obey their parents. At the same time, all readers recognise that Peter's adventures were much more fun than the sedate fruit-picking of his sisters, and this to a large extent subverts the 'good children' moral (Mackey 2002; Lurie 1991: 114; Lowe 1996: 46).

Stephens (1992) argues cogently for the teaching of analytical skills to children, to encourage them to recognise the manipulative strategies of the text, and the ideology of the author behind the story. This can be problematical with young children. Although blind acceptance of the viewpoint and ideology of the author through the narrator or the protagonist may not be a good thing (one would hope for and encourage Hollindale's 'alert enjoyment of stories'; 1988: 14), it seems an essential facet of the reading process and must be firmly established before the distancing from the text, which Stephens (1992: 68, 81) and Nodelman (1981: 182) encourage, can be taught.

As Chambers puts it, 'a requirement of fulfilled readership is a willingness to give oneself up to the book. [Mature readers] have learned how to do this: how to lay aside their own prejudices and take on the prejudices of the text' (1985: 36–37). Children need to learn to become the reader the text invites them to be – the authorial audience, in Rabinowitz's terms (1987: 21). They need to learn to read *with* the author, for the length of the text taking on the ideologies and ideas, both overt and covert, which the text offers. They must temporarily put aside their own feelings and beliefs and let themselves be seduced by the text, as Booth describes the process (1988: 138–142). As do all readers, children then accept or reject the ideology offered, depending on how it fits with their own values and beliefs. Stephens appears to finally acknowledge this in his penultimate words:

> Readers will (re-)construct their 'own' subject position in dialogue with the text. I think myself it is the best and most humane subject position available to us as human beings; I also recognise that in reaching it readers are thoroughly subjected to the text's processes.
>
> (1992: 287)

Stephens advocates teaching children to recognise the ideology of the author, and also to recognise how the text manipulates the reader, how it is constructed to seduce. Referring to a fictional discussion of a reading of Tolkien, he asks 'What, for example, should a reader make of a book which implies that the best way to think about the world is to do so from the perspective of a conservative upper-middle class English male?' (Stephens 1992: 49). Tolkien certainly is a conservative English male, as are C.S. Lewis, A.A. Milne and Kenneth Grahame. However, these authors were all significant in different periods of Rebecca and Ralph's reading lives. I will discuss Tolkien and Lewis, looking at their ideology (overt and covert) and its effect on the children. The recognition of the author's value systems and beliefs (their ideology) is the most complex aspect of understanding the concept of authorship, and in fact is often not seen, or deliberately ignored, by adults. Nevertheless, there are some indications of the children's awareness of this, although it was never taught, as Stephens advocates. Examples of their awareness will be examined mainly though Lewis's *Narnia Chronicles*. The 'conservative upper-middle class males' were not the only purveyors of foreign ideology that Rebecca and Ralph encountered; I had ideological disagreements with several picture books also, but this did not deter me from offering them to the children.

The Hobbit was first heard by Ralph at 4–11, and delighted him. Some of the espoused values, such as Tolkien's androcentrism, his classist attitudes, his hierarchical view of the world, were clearly alien to the family. However, I was pleased that Ralph came into contact with these, as well as the ones I agreed with – that the smallest, least aggressive, but good-with-words, witty, wily and trustworthy, wins out in the end. And after all, Bilbo manages to subvert many of the more conservative views, over and over. I would not have pointed out these aspects to Ralph.

The *Narnia Chronicles* carry a similar load of ideological problems (from my perspective) to those found in Tolkien. These books were even more significant than *The Hobbit* in Ralph's life, and in Rebecca's too. Some explanation of the intensity of their reception is needed, before discussing their ideological influence.

The Lion, the Witch and the Wardrobe was read to Rebecca when she was 7–2. Ralph, 3–1, was fascinated, and often sat through the readings as well. I finished the whole series of seven books in three months. When Ralph was

5–11 I started the series again, and continued to read them aloud regularly until he was 8–6. *The Lion, the Witch and the Wardrobe* was read aloud five times in total, *The Horse and His Boy* and *The Magician's Nephew* twice, and the others four times, over this period.

Many of Lewis's values contradicted those of our family. His devotion to the Christian myths is foreign, as also is his dislike of, even disgust at, the Eastern religions. He is far from current notions of gender equity (despite the fact that Lucy, and later Jill, are the major protagonists and most sympathetic characters). He disapproves of vegetarians and alternative schools. Perhaps most difficult of all is his belief that physical fighting is the highest way of defending the good.

I continued to read and reread the series when they were requested despite all my ideological disagreements. The children gained from the series enjoyment of the worlds, the concepts of space and time manipulation which enabled the characters to enter these worlds, the language, and the adventures. They also enjoyed the strong good-versus-evil, black-and-white morals. And the fighting, too. It was the stuff of role-playing games and of ideas. Although for the duration of the story Lewis's ideology could be accepted, I was also capable of pointing it out on occasions.

Aslan's view is that 'Battles are ugly when women fight.' At the reading when the children were 5–11 and 9–2, we were using a second-hand edition of *The Lion, the Witch and the Wardrobe*. In the margin, someone had commented on Aslan's statement with 'Philosophy, feminist'. Rebecca queried 'Who wrote it?' [An adult, one who was studying children's lit. I guess.] 'What does it say?' ['Philosophy, feminist.'] 'What does it mean?' [Well, I agree with whoever wrote it. She feels C.S. Lewis is wrong to say 'Battles are ugly when women fight.' Battles are *always* ugly, whoever is fighting.] Here I moved into expressing my own attitudes, superimposing my ideological stance on that of the unknown scholiast. Almost certainly she(?) had meant that it is sexist not to let women carry weapons the way men do, but I had quite consciously given it a different interpretation. The discussion continued. Ralph: 'I think they're *better*, 'cause there's more people to fight, with girls in!'

So it was the covert ideology that temporarily influenced the children rather than the overt one. Overtly, 'girls shouldn't carry weapons', but Lewis's covert ideology was that fighting was good, necessary, exciting, made an adult of you, and that evil must to be physically fought against. This is what came over to both. As well as Ralph's comment above, there were Rebecca's endless battle games with Ralph, wielding her plastic sword (bought with her pocket money for 50 cents) and homemade bow-and-feathers, and her saying that what she wanted most for her birthday was 'a set of armour' (7–5).

Eustace and Edmond's antisocial behaviour is blamed on their attending schools that we might describe as 'alternative' in some ways. Lewis expresses his strong disapproval of any form of schooling that deviates from the traditional conservative boarding school, especially at the beginning of *The Silver*

Chair. Rebecca and Ralph never commented on this aspect, despite the fact that they themselves were attending a Montessori school during many of the readings. They did not associate Eustace and Jill's dreadful, bully-run school with their own pleasant one.

Eventually Ralph did recognise and comment on the covert ideology. In *Prince Caspian* the girls pick apples while the boys go off to build the fire. Ralph at 7–4 was hearing it for the third time, and remarked with deep scorn 'Huh! Sexist!'

The children gained richly from their experience of the *Narnia* series. They took ideas from the series, and the language inspired them. The first thing Rebecca always told others about the books, and the first thing she thought about when a new one was started, was how they would get into Narnia this time. She was fascinated that you could go through the back of an ordinary wardrobe and come out in another world, and that no time had elapsed in our world on your return. As she said wistfully at 7–2, 'Perhaps all wardrobes are like that – we just come at the wrong time.' Ralph especially enjoyed the language, waxing lyrical in his response at 7–3 to the description of spring's return in *The Lion, the Witch and the Wardrobe*:

> 'It's beautiful the way I see it in my mind. There's round patches of white and the green, and the white keeps getting smaller and the green larger. It's beautiful. It's like a chess board only instead of black and white it's green and white, and they're round instead of square.'

'Ideology is not something which is transferred to children as if they were empty receptacles. It is something which they already possess, having drawn it from a mass of experiences far more powerful than literature' (Hollindale 1988: 17). Ultimately it was the family ideology that influenced the children, not that of authors they read, however often and with whatever passion. As demonstrated above, Lewis's distrust of alternative schools made no impact on them, even at the time of reading, let alone as a lifelong influence. Stephens seems to believe that children exposed to these ideologies without learning how to recognise them may take them on board, perhaps becoming conservatives (like Lewis), but it is a matter of interest that Ralph has ultimately become a cultural relativist to the very core (not to mention vegan!), and you certainly couldn't consider Rebecca 'conservative' as an adult, either.

There was a gradual progression in the children's understanding of the author concept, but it seems clear that well before the age of 5, they understood that all books have one or more creators. They learned the differences between literary language and that of everyday conversation. They began to express opinions about the authors and their books: 'C.S. Lewis is one of my favourite authors' (Ralph, 7–9) or 'Are there any more books by Anno?' (Rebecca, 6–10).

This knowledge led to an understanding of the 'made-up' quality of the secondary world, in relationship to that of the external world, and was an essential part of their understanding of the reality-status of the text and pictures. The result of this understanding was an enrichment of their pleasure, and they were then in a position to appreciate 'the quality of the author's gift to us' (Booth 1988: 113).

8 'Did he ever think again?'

Characters, emotions and the theory of mind

> Reading, whatever else it is, however described, is a distinctive, verbal way of encountering feelings, understandings, thinking, knowing and imagining.
>
> (Margaret Meek 1992a: 15)

All stories, no matter how simple, depend on what someone thinks. Bruner defines narrative as dealing with 'the vicissitudes of human intention' (1986: 16). It is the desires and intentions of fictional characters that drive the story. Eco goes further, saying that without misunderstandings on someone's part there can be no story; it is someone's mistaken belief, 'various imaginary courses of events' that the characters set up, which drive the plot (1981: 242).

To understand a plot you have to imagine that it is the characters themselves who have thoughts and emotions. You virtually ignore the author. This chapter looks at the fictional characters, and the children's understanding of their motivations, thoughts and emotions.

Unless you understand the motivation of the protagonist, you cannot follow a story. There is no narrative without this understanding. Toddlers happily turn pages in lumps, but very soon, children do grow to understand their stories. If they are familiar with books (and have heard the actual words read), they will have a concept of story well before 18 months, and insist on hearing the whole.

Every story depends on the mental state of the characters. *The Very Hungry Caterpillar* wanted food, Peter Rabbit wanted adventure, Max in *Where the Wild Things Are* learned to control his emotions, or used his imagination, or had a dream – there are hundreds of interpretations. But they all depend on Max's mental state.

Theory of mind

Cognitive psychologists are vitally interested in children's understanding of reality. 'Theory of mind' is the terminology they use to describe the child's understanding that other people have minds and emotions. This contrasts with the Piagetian view of the child as egocentric until about 7. The theory of mind is obviously directly relevant to children's understanding of narrative. It is possible that an exposure to the states of mind of others in the form of story characters might help in the development of the 'theory of mind' with relation to actual people.

Generally, the psychologists conclude that even at 18 months or 2 years, when imaginative play first comes in, children are capable of thinking of themselves as someone else – no longer Piaget's egocentric children, if they ever were – and that between 4 and 5, most come to a clear understanding about the minds, motivations and emotions of other people. This recent work is summarised by Bourchier and Davis (2002), who speak about the paradox between children's early competence in pretence, and difficulty with successfully performing pretence/reality tests even up to middle childhood years. Though their findings overturn much of Piaget's egocentrism ('in certain respects, so grossly, incongruously wrong, yet so durable' as Bruner says; 1987: 85) the 'theory of mind' psychologists such as Flavell *et al.* (1986) and Wimmer and Perner (1983) still underestimate the child's abilities, probably for many of the reasons outlined in Chapter 1 (p. 5–6). However, others, such as Onishi and Baillargeon (2005) and Clements and Perner (1994), are working on finding non-verbal tests for 'theory of mind' experiments, and have brought back further and further the age at which the tests are passed. In fact, some believe that the ability to read others' minds correctly is innate. Gopnik *et al.* have a general overview of infant minds in *How Babies Think* (1999).

Young children are, by and large, obliging and cooperative. If the strange adult wants them to pretend that the toy is a real lamb, they will do so. If they want them to say the milk is actually red, they will do that too (see p. 6). It is just that their perception of what this odd adult is looking for is quite different from that of the cognitive psychologist running the experiment. Little children do not hesitate to say what they think someone else expects them to say, and cognitive psychologists often do not take this into consideration. They seem also not to take young children's difficulty of articulation into account.

They also ignore the fact that young children are quite capable of deciding that the only mind the puppet or doll has is that of its manipulator. So, if the doll hasn't 'seen' where something is hidden, they know the experimenter has, so this test of others' false belief is also flawed. ('Where will Teddy look for his pencils?' when the child and the experimenter, but not Teddy, 'saw' these put into a Smartie box.)

Beginning with Piaget, psychologists have carried out experiments that seem to show that the young child is bound in the solipsism of infancy, with no understanding of 'real' reality, no way of telling the difference between pretence and reality, no concept that other people have minds that might think differently to their own, until perhaps about the age of 7. However, all this goes against common-sense observation. Children play pretend games without attempting to eat the pretend food; they tease and deceive their siblings, and are very aware of what might be in the mind of the sibling or parent (Dunn 1991).

The words and pictures and stories that psychologists use for their tests are as unambiguous as they can make them, and there is little of artistic or literary richness in them. This is where books and reading are vastly superior to the pictures and stories used in experiments. Surrounded by examples of aesthetic worth and ambiguity, with the possibility of multiple interpretations that works of art have, the child can play among these and work out the concepts of reality, and 'theory of mind' as well.

There seems no doubt that at somewhere between 4 and 5, children undergo a big change in showing that they are capable of performing the theory of mind in experiments, but it may be only then that they are able to understand what the experimenter is asking of them. Before then they understood the concept, but not what the correct answer was from the point of view of the experimenter.

Children who enjoy stories are experienced in recognising the emotions and thought patterns of the fictional characters. This comes about through hearing stories read, rather than playing the 'labelling game' to teach vocabulary. Character, personality, motivation, state of mind, need to be drawn in words rather than pictures. Not giving young children the author's words is depriving them of this rich opportunity. Narratives on television will not do this as well as books, either. In cartoons, for instance, there is little discussion of thought processes. Nodelman (1988: 151) argues that picture books are also more about action than 'subtleties of feeling'. Nevertheless, children do learn to predict the personality and actions of different characters when they are met in a number of books in a series, but even if the one book is heard over and over, there is space to think about the character more and more deeply.

This is another reason why listening to the actual words of the story advantages children: they are soon able to enjoy more wordy texts such as *Winnie-the-Pooh* (the original A.A. Milne version, of course). In repeated adventures of the same characters, children get to understand them well, to predict the responses and actions. In fact, the characters most frequently 'identified' with by my children were the ones in longer stories and in series – Piglet from *Pooh*, and Snufkin from Jansson's Moomintroll stories, for Rebecca, and for Ralph Barbabeau (the Barbapapa books), Tinkle (the Orlando books) and Sparrowhawk (from the *Earthsea* trilogy by Le Guin at 7.6 in role-playing games).

The status of story characters has been much discussed. McHale argues that they have a life of their own, independent of the story itself. He says 'Cordelia is still Cordelia, wherever we meet her' (1987: 35). Similarly the children's book characters remain themselves whether found in another book (intertextuality, which was encountered several times) or taken away from the book itself, discussed like an actual person, or acted out by a child.

Booth (1988: 139) says that we have been exhorted to keep an aesthetic distance from the characters when we read, but adds 'Everyone who reads knows that whether or not we *should* imitate narrative heroes and heroines, we in fact do' (1988: 228–229). Both Nodelman (1981: 182–184) and Stephens (1992: 68, 81) see problems inherent in children identifying with characters and being seduced by the text (see pp. 115–116).

Nell (1988) studied adult compulsive readers of fiction (mainly romances). He found that they immerse themselves in the book, lose themselves in the secondary world it presents to them, even undergo a 'consciousness change' and at the same time identify with the protagonist. So why not young children? In fact, it is vital that they do so to enjoy narrative and become committed readers.

All this is related to the understanding of the real world, because understanding people is what most of our commerce with the world is. Listening to stories and understanding the character's motivations is germane to this.

If young children were completely egocentric (as Piaget maintained) and had no concept that others think differently from themselves, they would not be able to appreciate any stories; the motivation, the emotions, the desires of the characters would be a 'closed book'. But children manifestly do enjoy stories, so they must recognise that fictional characters at least do perform actions that are motivated by thoughts.

'Children are aware of their own mental states, and can project them on to other people using a mechanism that depends crucially on the imagination' (Harris 1989: 53). Relevant here is the evidence of infants being able to follow the direction of gaze of the mother, and of being able, when they can talk (after about 2), to use diectic shifters correctly: you/me, here/there, etc.

Emotions are a case in point. Emotions are recognisable in pictures by the character's facial expressions. Many experiments have been done on a child's recognition of expressions – the basic six of sadness, happiness, surprise, anger, anxiety, disgust. And these are clearly demonstrated in the reading context.

Despite Piaget, it has been shown that children can empathise with the emotions of others. Even a neonate will cry when it hears another baby cry, though this is not yet empathy. But Dunn's study of children of 18 months with older siblings shows that they understand the emotions and know how to play on them. They know how to comfort and how to tease, both of which would be impossible if they imagined that their siblings thought just as they do – but they clearly don't (Dunn 1991). Cognitive psychologists expect that mental verbs (think, know, understand, remember, etc.) will come into children's language at about 2–0, while they begin pretence play at about 1–6.

One of the advantages of studying children in a naturalistic setting using real books, rather than in an experimental situation, is that you will get more information from the children during the reading process. In familiar surroundings with a trusted adult, children express themselves openly, so to some extent you can know how their minds work (in a way not available to the cognitive psychologists, who do not know the individual child). Adults can report their own reactions after reading, as H. Crago (1990) and Spufford (2002) report on rereading their childhood books. Nell (1988) collected responses of ludic readers, and G. Fox (1979) of adolescent ones. However, the young child tends to respond throughout the actual reading session. We never asked questions just to test what the children knew, and only occasionally queried what we really wanted to know ourselves – 'What do you think will happen in the next chapter?', for instance.

One of the platforms of Piaget's perception of young children is their animism – speaking and acting as if objects are animate. I personally can't see why this is a problem, because adults do it all the time. 'The cat wants her tea', 'The bus is coming', 'The moon is rising' – all as if they have minds of their own (as the cat does, I guess, but can't speak it), so it is not surprising that children use the same terminology. But also – and here is the flaw – if children could only think egocentrically, they could not ascribe motivation to things either. The fact that they do is a way of representing the other mind – even if it is one belonging to a bus or the moon. Animism is the child's belief that everything happens for a purpose, a reason, but it is another mind's reason.

Eco agrees that it is the character's mind which is important to the story, and he has a term for the world which is in the character's mind, as opposed to that in the mind of the author (or in the book itself, if you like). He called the world in the character's mind a 'monastic construct'. He points out that disguises and tricks are ways of inducing a false belief in others – in the characters of the story (Eco 1981: 338).

As outlined above, cognitive psychologists are now prepared to accept that children understand their own mental states and those of others. This ability is corroborated throughout this study.

Thinking

I will arbitrarily divide the mental processes into thinking and feeling: recognising characters' thoughts and their emotions, while acknowledging that there is really no clear distinction between the two realms – that they overlap (Bruner 1986: 106). I will include the children's understanding of real people's minds, to contextualise their understanding of characters.

It is interesting that Rebecca and Ralph differed in their understanding of these concepts, as in so much else. Partly it might have been the position of elder and younger, but rather I think it was their personalities. Rebecca was much earlier in using the cognitive verbs, and in recognition of them in the stories she heard. On the other hand, Ralph understood, or anyway commented on, many of the emotions at a very much younger age. He was fascinated by facial expressions and what they meant. Ralph was a much more emotional child, and often in trouble too, so his empathy is understandable, but quite noticeable in comparison to Rebecca's.

The first mental word that goes into a child's vocabulary is 'want'. It doesn't even need spoken language but is expressed in universal signs. The clutching hand, the pointing finger, the 'ah' demand, are quite clear indications of 'want'. Similarly, many stories start with a want, a desire or a need. As it is the earliest acquired of the mental concepts, I will begin with this. Rebecca had 'Decca wants a drink' and 'Decca needs Panda' in her vocabulary at 1–11, and Ralph used 'want' at 2–3, though the obverse, 'had 'nough' (i.e. 'don't want'), was in his vocabulary by 2–0.

Rebecca's earliest expressed interest in a character's desires was, oddly enough, a misconstruction. Several of her books had represented characters' desires in a thought balloon, so when she met the picture of Piglet thinking fearfully about the Heffalump, she interpreted this as desire. 'Why did Piglet want to be chased by a Heffalump?', she asked at 3–2. In *In the Forest* Rabbit is looking timid, though the text says 'And Rabbit came too, when I went for a walk in the forest.' Ralph (3–3) asked 'Did it want to?', to which I replied 'Yes, it was just shy.' Another of Ralph's was at 3–7, when he remarked 'The car needs egg, petrol and oil' to *Meg's Car.* Again this is ambiguous, as we would often speak of our car 'needing petrol'. It may not have been the car's need at all, but just a general comment about the physical state of the car, rather than its mental state.

The concept of characters' 'wants' is such a basic aspect of the narrative that it was usually not commented on specifically, but there were numerous other examples in the daily discussions of books, stories and their characters.

Although the metacognitive skills of thinking about thinking are evidenced comparatively late in the child's speech, the concept of others using their minds in some way underpins all of the theory of other minds. Wants are easy to understand because everyone has them all the time, and because in ordinary conversation actions are explained in this way.

The concept that other minds do more than just wanting, but hold ideas different from one's own, comes in quite early too. Bretherton found that 2–6 was the age when words for thinking came into the language of most children (1991: 64). Initially these may have been only learned phrases, but, used consistently, the concepts themselves became available for use and understanding.

Rebecca used 'I know' at 2–1, and 'I think so' and 'I know it' at 2–3. A clear example was at 2–3. I had not cut the fat off the bacon she was given for breakfast and she commented 'I've never seen white bacon 'afore. I put it in my mouth. I thought it was tasty. White bacon is tasty.' She clearly differentiates here between the sensory experience and the thinking of it. At 2–7 she also had the concept of 'wondering' with reference to another person. She told her father one morning 'I was wondering if you wanted porridge, but there's no milk, so we're having eggs.' The complexity of these and similar statements seems to imply that the complexity of the concept is also present. They don't sound like learned phrases. A later example of mental awareness was her response to the sick possum we rescued when she was 4–1: 'I'll remember even when I'm grown up that I had a possum for a pet when I was quite small.'

Ralph typically was a little later with these terms (his language acquisition, though starting younger, was slower – see p. 15). His first noted use of a mental verb is at 2–5 to the cover of a book, pointing to a character. 'What's that?' [I don't know. What do you think?] 'I think it hen, I think it.' A month later he told us, on a windy day, 'I was thinking that the trees might fly away in the wind, I was thinking.' In both cases the repetition of 'think' seems to mark an awareness of the thinking process, though in the initial instance it was clearly sparked by my use of 'think'. At 3–2 he would say 'I can't imagine which is which' and he had 'I wonder' at 3–10. 'Remember' and 'forget' were common from 3–3 also, but perhaps these are special cases, not quite referring to thoughts. At least in the case of 'forgot' it's an action – something like 'I've left it behind.' At 4–1 he first used 'I saw it in my mind.' This was a very common expression of his for years afterwards, and must have described most satisfactorily for Ralph how his mind worked.

Both children used the terms to refer to other people also, with very little lag between the two usages. Rebecca (2–3) had woken and called out at 2 a.m. I went to her and explained that it wasn't morning until the sun was up. When she awoke at a reasonable hour, she called to her father in excitement 'Daddy, Daddy, the sun came up! Mummy thought it would!' She used 'thought' and 'thinking' frequently thereafter, including to the infant Ralph saying 'bup bup' quietly to himself (he 1–0, she 4–1) 'He's thinking about puppy dogs' (this was his term for animals). She always had a very strong view of herself as a thinker. When a visitor remarked to her that Mummy's hands were stronger than hers to open a jar lid, she agreed: 'Yes, but I'm cleverer, but Mummy thinks she's cleverer' (4–1).

How did they use these well-established concepts to refer to book characters?

Angus and the Cat ends with what in fact is quite a complicated piece of mental juggling. 'And Angus knew and the CAT knew that Angus knew that Angus was GLAD the cat came back!' She could recite this at 1–10 – John having stopped at 'And Angus knew' she continued 'that cat knew'. This was probably before 'knew' entered her normal spoken vocabulary.

In *Barbapapa's Ark* there is an unusual illustrative convention for thinking: the question mark over the heads of three characters who are holding a sick hedgehog and a syringe. Rebecca at 4–0 wanted to know 'why is only one of them thinking?', because there is only one question mark. Then she went on to suggest 'that one thinks and then that one thinks . . .' In other words, she saw the question mark as belonging to only one of them at a time. A month later she encountered what she saw as the same convention in a book at kindergarten. She asked me 'What do penguins think?' then explained 'At kinder there was a book telling what animals think.' This was doubtless a title about animals in general, which had various animals on the cover and question marks scattered among them (I never located the actual book). Of the same picture in *Barbapapa's Ark*, Ralph at 3–7 said 'I'm helping them to think' – he was as usual being the black shaggy Barbabeau.

Ralph evidenced anxiety for characters sometimes. At 4–2 on his first Moomintroll novel (though he had previously encountered them frequently in Rebecca's enthusiasm and heard some individual chapters read) he asked of the Groke, 'Has Moomintroll ever seen the Groke before?' and 'Does Moomintroll remember seeing it?', and eight months later, listening to *The Hobbit*, when Bilbo hit his head and 'remembered nothing more', Ralph looked for reassurance: 'Did he ever think again?'

Ralph was also quite clear on the difficulties that would be encountered by the multi-headed troll in D'Aulaires' *Book of Trolls*, explaining that 'his magic might get spoiled if each of his heads thought differently', and, at the next reading 'There'd be trouble with their powers sometimes. Each head would think of things – different things – and they wouldn't know what they should have' (4–9).

Dunn and Brown (1994: 120–121) point out that families differ in the extent to which emotions are discussed, affecting how often emotion is mentioned by the child. I suspect, though I cannot now prove it, that in our household thinking was probably mentioned more often than emotions were named, leading Rebecca to discuss the former more often, although as Ralph talked about emotions often, there may have been no connection. Still, both children had the thinking concepts to play with, and did so consciously in a metacognitive way. Ralph announced at 3–10 that 'I'm thinking about a person thinking about a person thinking about a person . . .' with real delight in the progression. Rebecca at 5–3 was looking at a diagram of the brain. She told me 'you can think about thinking' and explained then that you can think about your brain while you are using your brain to think with.

What the cognitive psychologists refer to as 'false belief' is an essential part of most stories also. In the external world, children discover that what they thought to be so, in fact wasn't – frequently. They know they can be wrong and often are, so presumably have no trouble understanding that others are, also. And they see the surprise and disappointment or relief of other people when they realise that a thought has been incorrect.

At 2–2 Rebecca was telling her father about the large pair of lips I had cut from an ad for her alphabet scrap book: 'I thought it was a ship or a boat, but Mummy said "Noooo, it's a mouth" ', with a clear message in the 'No' implying 'how can you be so silly?' or 'I thought it was obvious'. It was not only her own false belief she expressed her awareness of, but also her understanding that I thought she would recognise the picture at once, in the emphasised quoted speech. Three months later she acknowledged her false belief at an unexpected sight in the playground: 'I didn't realise you could fit on a swing, Mummy!'

There are, in common parlance, two different uses for the word 'think'. It can just be the general activity of the mind, as above in their 'thinking about thinking', but much more commonly it is used as a term for belief. 'I thought you was making eggs, Daddy' (2–4) when Rebecca discovered that the noise in the kitchen was actually him making his own cup of tea. Asked a question, John would often answer truthfully 'I don't know', to which Rebecca would respond with some asperity 'But what do you *think*, Daddy?' (4–1)

Applying the concept of thinking to others, or just as a general exclamation, the children often used learned phrases such as 'You can't believe'. Ralph recognising Graham's dog in *Benjy's Dog House* as resembling *Harry the Dirty Dog*: 'You can't believe it is a story about Harry!' (3–11). At 2–8 Ralph was well aware that different people had different views of the world. I turned down a request of his with a firm 'no', and his reply was 'But many people [would] say OK.'

Book characters could be recognised as having false beliefs as well. The youngest example recorded was at 3–1. 'That snail thinks it's in its shell' in *Mr Jeremy Fisher*. Ralph's meaning was unclear, though, as the snail seems to be in a normal position with just its head out.

Rebecca at 2–9 recognised many of the animals on the title page on *Veronica's Smile* as ones that she had seen four months earlier in *The Rain Puddle*: 'He thought he had fallen into the pond,' she said. 'So did he, and he did, too.' When we got *The Rain Puddle* itself back from the library almost a year from her last hearing, she told her grandmother it was their 'shadow' in the water (3–4). The foolish animals had been suffering under a 'false belief' from which only the return of the sun and the drying of the puddle rescued them. Another of Duvoisin's titles, *Petunia I Love you*, has the wily raccoon deceiving gullible goose Petunia about his intentions. At 3–10 Ralph was similarly deceived, and it took some time (and explanation) before he understood.

The perennial *Barbapapa's Ark* offered examples here too. Of the suddenly stranded spearfisherman in his scuba diving gear: 'He's thinking that he's underwater' (Rebecca 4–10); and 'They didn't know they weren't underwater' (Ralph 4–11). By 5–11 Rebecca was able to articulate the phenomenon even more clearly in *The Moffats*: 'That's how he thought the driver would look,' she explained to Ralph, of the picture of an adult train driver sitting at a little school desk. Rufus had just comforted his friend Hughie by telling him that even the train driver had once been in Room 1. Ralph's response to the spilt wine in *The Mouse with the Daisy Hat* (p. 99) is a case of his recognising false belief in a character.

Rebecca at 7–4 showed a surprising understanding that other points of view could be different even from the human one. She remarked 'You know how we say "people and animals"? Well, giraffes would say "giraffes and animals" and elephants would say "elephants and animals".'

Other mental states evidenced in stories are imagining, dreaming, wishing and remembering. These of course can only be shown in the illustrations as thought balloons or separate pictures – rather difficult for a child to interpret. As Ralph remarked in a different context, 'You can't draw invisibles, can you?' (4–2 of the invisible girl in *Moominland Midwinter*).

Barbapapa's Ark makes extensive use of the thought balloon convention. Both children liked the reader to spell these out: 'Tell me what they're all thinking about' (Rebecca, 4–0; Ralph, 3–4). In one opening, people are hunting animals and their eager thoughts are represented: fur clothes, trophy heads on the wall. At 4–0, after numerous readings, this still puzzled Rebecca: 'How can they make those without having catched them?', apparently not realising that their thoughts were wishes or hopes, rather than the memories which balloons represented on other pages.

Thought balloons can represent dreams or imaginings as well as memories and wishes, as in *The Bears Who Went to the Seaside* and *The Bears Who Stayed Indoors*. Rebecca almost always remarked on these 'He's dreaming about breakfast' (4–7) and 'He's dreaming about the fish he ate' (4–11).

At 3–6 Rebecca was describing *Bill's Balloon Ride*, which she had looked through but not heard. I queried how Bill managed to fly and her reply was 'You'll see, he imagined it!' However, more often than the illustrations, it is the words that spell out the thinking and imagining aspects of the story. Ralph asked of a book Rebecca was telling him he would enjoy: 'Has it got all the exciting bits about how they think?' (7–9)

Feeling

Here I will look at Rebecca and Ralph's responses to the emotions of the book characters they encountered: how they learned to interpret them, and how this helped them in understanding first the character, then the plot (which usually hangs on actions arising from emotions).

The first technique for understanding other people and their minds is to read their facial expressions. Even babies of a couple of months old can respond to different facial expressions on actual people (Astington 1994: 32). We have seen that they understand a picture as a face (for instance, Ralph's response to the Farax baby at 6 months – p. 38). It has been suggested that all recognisable emotional states, across all cultures, are initially perceived in terms of two dimensions: the pleasure/displeasure and the arousal/sleepiness states (Russell 1989: 305). The examples of the two children demonstrate this clearly. The first facial features they noticed (or anyway commented on) were open mouths and closed eyes. Before long, they spelled these out as 'crying' and 'asleep'. As their vocabularies developed, the expressions were spelled out in more detail, with Ralph evidencing much more interest and awareness of them than Rebecca had at the same age.

It is possible that Rebecca, especially, did not hear the names of many emotions. Because we did not often practise labelling, the discussion of pictured incidents was not of the more common variety, 'Which one is angry?', but came from the child asking 'Why does she look like that?' Our reply might have been 'She's angry because . . .', but we would be more likely to have given the cause from the plot, without naming the emotion at all, so Rebecca did not learn the emotions particularly early. The advent of a second child naturally increased the amount of conversation about emotion in the family.

It is difficult to say whether the open mouths and shut eyes were examples of physical behaviour – speaking or sleeping are possible – or of emotions. It is possible that the children's understanding of these blended into each other.

Rebecca's first recorded remark on emotions was at 1–7, when she described an open-mouthed dog in a photo as 'laughing'. Note that this was not a cartoon dog with deliberate humanised expression, but just an animal. She of course knew that animals don't laugh (because of frequent encounters with them, including our pet cat), but on the other hand we adults frequently spoke of animals as if they had human characteristics, so this was not unusual behaviour on her part. My response was 'Yes! She does look happy, doesn't she?'

Ralph's first 'comment' was to the open mouth of a boy in *The Elephant and the Bad Baby*. The boy is pointing at the elephant's trunk, and an adult sees him as surprised. Ralph pointed to the boy's mouth and made a singing noise – singing on a voiced 'ah' with his mouth similarly open but no words (1–8). This was an unusual response, and we replied with something like 'Yes, the boy looks as if he's singing. Or he might just be talking.'

Mouths drawn open seemed to often lead to wrong interpretations, ranging from 'crying' (Ralph 2–0) to Mickey's yawn in *In the Night Kitchen* and 'he's laughing' (Ralph 2–4) to a bear shouting angrily in *The Bears Who Went to the Seaside*. By 3–7 Ralph had no possibility of mistake, however. In *Barbapapa's Ark* all the animals enjoy the stranding of the whaleboat. 'That one's laughing, and that. That one's laughing in the funniest way. All the ones with their mouths open are laughing.'

For a period around 2–11, Rebecca interpreted all open mouths or beaks as speaking, and would ask 'What's he saying?' to many pictures. We usually turned this back on to her: 'What do you think?' She did not always reply within the narrative. To a bird in *The Hare and the Tortoise* she replied ' "I'm under this flower", that's what he's saying.'

Eyes that were either shut or not clearly visible were the next aspect after open mouths which Ralph commented on, especially between 2–0 and 2–3. His confusion here developed into a game. This was partly to make Rebecca respond (which she did, laughing and teasing him), and probably also to irritate the parents, who would doubtless have corrected him each time. It was certainly continued deliberately.

It began with *Harry the Dirty Dog*, in which Harry is shown howling (though the words say he 'danced and he sang'). Looking at the curved eye, Ralph said 'cry' (2–0), and, as the dog does look unhappy, I was impressed. But it transpired that he was interpreting all closed eyes as 'cry' from here on. On the next page Harry's open eyes were 'wake', and through the rest of the book Harry was either 'cry' or 'wake', including the final picture of Harry curled up in his basket. The words we read clearly describe him as asleep, but Ralph again said 'cry'. [Don't you think he might be asleep?] 'No. Cry!'

(firmly). A week later he did the same with *Miffy at the Seaside* and a few days later to *Harry* again. It was clearly a game by now, with a ritualised 'Cry' in a long-drawn-out, lugubrious tone, and 'awake' loud and joyful. On subsequent days he also did it to the Wild Rumpus page in *Where the Wild Things Are* – 'cry' to Max's shut eyes, and 'awake' to all the wild things. By now Rebecca (5–4) was aware of it as a game, and reacted in a satisfyingly amused way. A few days later she was joining with his shouting 'cry – awake', especially when it was completely inappropriate, such as when the eyes are not seen because the character is looking downwards.

This behaviour continued over several weeks. In *1 2 3 to the Zoo*, which included 'Four lions – cry, awake, awake, awake. Five bears – cry. Mouse cry' [Yes, the mouse is on the bear with its eyes shut] and then 'cry – awake' to the two eyes of the winking owl (2–2). I demonstrated winking for him, but at 2–3 it was still causing him some confusion. 'Asleep that eye' he remarked to Mary Anne's wink in *Mike Mulligan and His Steam Shovel*. In the weeks that followed, with his language skills steadily increasing, he said 'Gone to sleep' to one of the dogs in *Harry*, and when I asked [has he?] he was able to correct himself 'No – awake', then he examined the dog's one visible eye very closely and reaffirmed 'awake'. By 2–5 he correctly used 'gone to sleep' instead of 'cry' to the Wild Thing on the cover of *Where the Wild Things Are* (Figure 4.1). Then 'awake' to the two on the title page, and again 'cry' to Max on the first rumpus page. Rebecca, who was at one of these readings, teased 'Are you sure he's not asleep?' (5–8).

This seems to be the last example of the shut-eyes/crying overgeneralisation. Perhaps Rebecca's teasing and laughing, though he enjoyed it, brought the behaviour to an end, or it may just have been his increasing language skill. Nevertheless, I'm sure he very quickly knew it was not an appropriate response, but continued it for the game, anyway. By 2–7 he was no longer playing when he asked of a character who'd had an accident: 'Where's his eyes?' [They're shut.] 'Why?' [He banged his head.]

Rebecca had had a similar misconception (or perhaps merely a game) at 2–3. One of the rabbits around the edge of the Bunnykins plate which she regularly used was badly printed, with just the faintest line for its eye. She often remarked that this one was 'crying' or 'sleeping', but one day she made it into a story: 'All the 'wake bunnies are running to kiss the crying bunny!'

An older example of the open-mouthed convention is Ralph's question about the irritable woman buying bacon in the grocer's shop in *The Elephant and the Bad Baby*: 'Why is she looking mad?' [You tell me.] 'The grocer sells bacon and it cost infinity dollars so she's mad' (3–7).

The convention of tears for crying was less ambiguous. Ralph could identify this correctly in *Scarry* at 2–0. Rebecca's first correct usage is not recorded, but at 2–3, not having yet heard the story, she called *Snuffy and the Fire* 'Snuffy crying' from the most significant picture inside. For Ralph at 2–4 and 2–6, part of the fun of *123456789 Benn* was in locating the prisoners who are crying.

The youngest query as to why an emotion was happening was Ralph's at 2–6. The text of *3 × 3* says 'three tears ran down their faces', and the picture shows it. He queried 'Why?' This is quite a complex point about the mice's distress at having been chased out of their home. It had been queried by Rebecca when she was 4–7. Ralph had been 1–4 at the time, and might possibly have remembered her query. However, as it had been read numerous times in the intervening fourteen months, that is not likely. (Rebecca was still querying it at 5–3.) The word 'cry' itself is ambiguous. At 3–10, when a character 'gave a great cry' Ralph glossed this as 'Not cry with tears but call out.' Rebecca was 6–3 when she first expressed this distinction.

A sad character does not have to be crying, of course, and if it is a realistic animal character, the expression can be quite subtle. Nevertheless, Rebecca was able to select the more miserable of two bear cubs at 3–10, on my request (*Do Bears Have Mothers Too?*). Also, at 3–10 she said of Oxenbury's cat in *Numbers of Things*, which is holding a fish skeleton, 'He doesn't like those bones.' Not until 5–5 did she add the actual name of the emotion: 'He's sad because he's only got bones to eat.'

At 3–6 Rebecca devised an explanation for the coughing/spluttering bird in *Barbapapa's Ark* (Figure 4.4). She obviously at first interpreted his splutter-drops as tears. 'Why is that bird crying? Perhaps he's crying because the animals are unhappy. That frog's crying too.'

Ralph often confused sad and angry expressions, perhaps because angry pictures made him personally feel uneasy or sad. He expressed this at 2–3 in *Emma Quite Contrary* about the pictures where she is being 'contrary': 'Me no like sad ones.' This may have been a misinterpretation of her angry expression, but is just as likely to have been his way of saying 'I don't like pictures that make me feel sad.'

He mentioned 'cross' or 'angry' much younger than Rebecca. Her first recorded remark of this kind was at 3–8, his at 2–6.

Raised eyebrows for surprise was one of the first expressions Rebecca commented on, but it led to complications when a different gesture was used. Ducks, for instance, have no eyebrows. 'I can't see its eyebrows up', she objected (2–3), when I suggested that a duckling was surprised at seeing a cow in the water, in *The Cow Who Fell in the Canal,* and in *Tom Kitten* the three Puddleducks 'had very small eyes and looked surprised'. 'Who looked surprised?' (Rebecca, 3–9). The reverse was when Ralph at the same age commented 'he's got high eyebrows', but I had to explain that this illustrator just drew people that way.

Ralph was able to articulate that it was facial expressions that showed emotion. At 3–7 he was directing me in a role-playing game: 'You be Miss Muffet. Show you're frightened with your face.' In pictures he often described the expression rather than just labelling it: 'Why has he got his mouth like that?' [You tell me.] 'He's saying "heeeeelp" ' (regarding a frightened Humpty Dumpty in *Eve* at 2–7). To an animal character in the background with a line across its eyes looking like a frown: 'What are his eyes saying?' (2–9). These are two of numerous examples at the time. He even sometimes described his own face. He looked depressed one day at 4–10 and I asked if something was worrying him. 'That's why my mouth is always down, even when my eyes are happy,' he replied.

Between 3–3 and 3–6 there was a rapid growth in Ralph's interest in facial expressions, and he began to compare the levels of emotion as well: 'Do you know which of the girls is sad – sadder than the other ones? The one with the crumpled face' (*Madeline in London*), and the next day, to *Meg and Mog*, 'Why is she looking sad there? Why is her mouth straight there? There she's a bit happy and a bit sad.' One character would be 'fiercer', another 'scarier', and about 3–7 he began grading them as well: 'sadder', 'crossest', 'frowningest', 'laughing in the funniest way'. At 3–9 in *Madeline* when the girls 'frowned at the bad' he noticed that 'Madeline is the frowningest – the crossest'. At 4–4 he pointed to the lines on John's forehead 'Little My has those there. She's cross in these books' (the Moomintroll series).

His sudden growth in comments on emotions and other mental and physiological states is reflected in the numbers of entries in the Reading Journal that mention these, specifically during the year he was 3. They go from twenty-six entries in the three months from his first comment (3–0 to 3–3), then eighty-four in the next three months, ninety-three from 3–6 to 3–9, then dropping back to forty-five in the three months until he turns 4, from which time they decreased.

Rebecca, though commenting less on the fine details of the pictures, collected more varied words for the emotions, and applied them outside the books as well. When the *Five Dolls* series was her passion, she was playing with a set of realistic, non-anthropomorphised stick-on plastic animals. 'Which baby one do you like best? I like this tiger. It looks sort-of Amanda-ish' [Like Amanda the doll?] 'Yes – his eyes look mischievous, see? Like Amanda if she was a tiger' (5–1).

It can be seen that an interest in the expressions of book characters was evident from very early in their book experiences, and ways of talking about the emotions developed soon afterwards. This no doubt led to understanding the plot, and to understanding people in the external world as well – and demonstrated clearly the children's 'theory of mind'.

Empathy is a further version of understanding the emotions of other people. Dunn has observed it in very young children, especially if they have older siblings (1991: 53). It involves not only recognising the emotion of another, but reacting to it with an appropriate emotion of your own. This leads on to identification also, or taking on the character and its feelings and acting this out as well. Both of these will be dealt with in Chapter 9.

9 'I'm Tigger pretending to be Eeyore'

Identification and reality

The children's conception of the reality-status of characters did not seem to affect their identification with them, although it is notable that, out of the multifarious Moomintroll characters, the two most lasting role assimilations were the almost-human Little My (Figures 4.2 and 5.9) and Snufkin. A discussion on the reality status of characters, with reference specifically to Tove Jansson's Moomintroll stories, will be followed by a discussion of the theory of identification with book characters, then a study of the seven types of identification that Rebecca and Ralph demonstrated.

Moomintrolls and reality

Tove Jansson's many and varied creatures, both sketched and described in words in the Moomintroll series, provide a synthesis of the criteria used in discussing the reality of characters (see pp. 20–22 for details of the reading sequence of the series). The children's contact with Moominland began with Rebecca hearing the picture book *Who Will Comfort Toffle?* at 4–2, and Ralph overhearing some of the readings of the actual series from 3–1 on. When he began listening to the whole series at 4–2, it was questions of reality that fascinated Ralph, and led to much speculation.

The Moomintroll characters, those unexpected, clearly delineated creatures, made a deep impression on both children. Rebecca, describing the books to people who did not know them, tended to list and describe the characters first, then retell one or two incidents – always with the comet's passing as the first. The Journal records approximately 120 comments of Rebecca's and 320 of Ralph's referring to Moomin characters. Overall, Rebecca specifically mentioned thirty-four of them and Ralph fifty-four. (One is constantly amazed at the sheer size of Jansson's gallery of creatures!)

The villain (if she is one – victim too) is the Groke, threatening, silent, unexpectedly female: 'It's a her and leaves an icy cold spot wherever she sits' (Rebecca's description, 6–5). She was often looked for and discussed, both in the reading sessions and outside them. Her threat was mitigated by talking about her, and she was used as a stand-in ominous character in games – living in caves we passed on a bushwalk, for instance (Ralph 4–4). Neither child took on the role of the Groke, even though Ralph did sing about it once at 4–3, as I went to find the book:

Who will comfort Toffle?
Who will comfort Toffle?
I will 'cause I'm a Groke.
I am so scared,
I am so scared!

They often discussed the characters. The odd little Hattifatteners are silent and electric. Ralph spoke about them often, affectionately: 'Those funny little Hattifatteners' and even 'Dear little Hattifatteners' (both to *Comet in Moominland*, on different occasions). At 4–3 Ralph had asked Rebecca 'What is your favourite thing in the Moomintroll stories?' Her reply (7–5) was 'Perhaps everything.' Not satisfied, he continued 'But what's your very favourite?' 'Perhaps Snufkin.' Then his surprising choice: 'I think – what was it again? Hattifatteners – I think Hattifatteners.' He made this choice only the once, but it does illustrate his fascination with them.

Rebecca identified first with Sniff (in *Finn Family Moomintroll*), and from then on, very intensely with Snufkin, whereas Ralph's love (without overt identification behaviour) was the intrepid Little My.

Little My's size caused much discussion. There is, as Rebecca noticed quite soon, some inconsistency in the books. Rebecca's first mention of her ('That My gets bigger all the time' (6–5)) referred to the picture in 'The Invisible Child' where My stands eye to (invisible) eye with Ninny (*Tales from Moominvalley*). In this case they both appear to be just smallish members of the family. This is in contrast to the My who in *Moominsummer Madness* (which Rebecca had just heard) has her meal set on top of the table, uses a comb to climb to the edge of a cup, and hides and sleeps in Mamma's sewing basket. Rebecca (7–6) retold with amusement the incident where Little My's sister threatens that she might get stung by an ant and swell to the size of an orange, to which she replies 'I want to grow up. I want to grow up' (*Moominsummer Madness*).

Ants are part of the problem with Little My's size. As Ralph remarked, on hearing the incident in *Moominpappa at Sea* where Moomintroll asks My to help him clear the ants from his glade, 'Look how small she is! She's 'bout as small as a big ant' (4–1). He knew this from the picture in *Moominsummer Madness*.

The size of Jansson's varied characters relative to each other was often of interest. 'Is she smaller than Little My?' Ralph asked of Salome the Little Creep (4–2, *Moominland Midwinter*). 'Mummy, did you know that those little things with the long noses were about as small as Moomintroll?' of Thingummy and Bob sitting beside a dejected Moomintroll on the steps (*Finn Family Moomintroll*, 4–2). This is a surprising picture, as we know that Thingummy and Bob were small enough to sleep in the pockets of Moominmamma's handbag.

The size of the characters relative to our own world led to an enunciation of the reality concept. (See p. 54 on what the comet could do to our own house.) Ralph's very first question, at the beginning of the first title he heard (*Moominland Midwinter*, 4–2), was 'How big are Moomintrolls?' Rebecca, who was also present and the acknowledged expert, held her hand about a metre from the floor, but Ralph chose only about 3 centimetres. I said diplomatically that they could be as big as you wanted to think of them. It seems that Ralph continued to think of them as tiny, the way they are illustrated in *Who Will Comfort Toffle?*

Looking at *Who Will Comfort Toffle?* some weeks later led to a discussion on the size of Toffle. 'Those are meant to be weeds – so I know they're very small. And that's meant to be grass – so he [Toffle] is very small!' (4–3). He recognised that several of the houses Toffle is passing are balancing up on grass stems, so that the tininess of Toffle is emphasised.

Both were interested in the few places where the characters are drawn beside recognisable elements of the actual world, such as Little My with the ants. They commented on the picture in *Comet* where Moomintroll and the others are depicted next to a grasshopper: 'Look how small they are. They must be much much smaller than us, 'cause we're bigger than them [grasshoppers], aren't we?' (Ralph 4–3). 'A person smaller than the flowers!', Ralph exclaimed, before he knew Snufkin, to a picture in *Moominland Midwinter* (4–2). After a long walk, having carried him for some way, I put him down, saying he was too heavy: 'Little My wouldn't be heavy! She could go in your pocket. Little My never grows big, does she? I wish I could ride in your pocket!' (4–4).

The same criterion of 'realness' that Ralph applied to Too-ticky despite her paws – that is just the way the artist draws normal human feet, (Figure 4.2) – he also apparently applied to Little My, who is, after all, human-shaped. There was also a creature he discovered at the 'feast' picture in *Finn Family Moomintroll*. He was looking ahead at the pictures, and he drew my attention excitedly: 'Mummy, I think I know something! I know what Little My is – a person – so come here! I think I know something that Moomintrolls have as well. . . . Quick, come quick! I think I see a reindeer! See? Like I know what Little My is!' (4–3). In other words, the reindeer was a genuine animal, just as he had decided My was a genuine person despite her size. On an earlier occasion, on discovering the picture of the hobgoblin in *Finn Family Moomintroll* (before he had heard it read) he asked 'Is this still a Moomintroll story?' [Yes.] 'Well, why is there a man in it?' A month later (4–3) we were reading *Comet* and came to the picture of the Professor. He exclaimed 'They do know what a man looks like!' His conception of the Moomin world had obviously excluded human beings.

Perhaps symptomatic of Ralph's whole view of the reality-status of the text was his attitude to his beloved My's veracity and reliability as a commentator. In *Moominsummer Madness* Little My tells Snufkin that 'Small villains are much better. They break more easily.' Ralph asked 'What are villains?' I glossed them as baddies, or enemies. 'Do they break?' [Well, that's what Little My said.] 'Are all the words that Little My says true?' [I wouldn't believe everything she said, would you?] 'No' (4–4). He may well have been remembering the text three pages before where she had told Snufkin 'untruthfully' of her mother 'Somebody ate her.'

Three days later, near the beginning of *Moominpappa at Sea*, My was not one of the early pictures. 'Little My has come with them, hasn't she?' [Yes.] 'Little My's the funniest. Little My says rotten things – rotten words she says, doesn't she? All the words she says are rotten.' This implies the same unreliability as his former comment, although the phraseology may well have been inspired by her pronouncement three pages before: ' "Maybe some rotter's put it out," suggested Little My.' 'Rotter' was unfamiliar and not glossed.

The children saw the characters as having differing degrees of 'realness'. Certainly Ralph at least proclaimed them to be 'real' if they were human-like, or at least like some recognisable type of animal, such as the reindeer. These were 'real' because they had recognisable counterparts in the actual world, but, like Too-ticky's problematical feet, Little My's size, etc., they were still strange: 'not a real kind of person' (Figure 4.2).

Remarks such as 'I'm Sniff', 'I wish I was really Snufkin', 'Little My is a nice fellow', express the children's empathy, their willingness to take on disparate roles, try on disparate personalities. A series such as the Moomins offers a unique opportunity for understanding characters in depth, in different situations, under different circumstances, to see the character develop and grow. Only a full-length adult novel can do this as well. Certainly not even the best-delineated children's novel standing alone can, nor, obviously, can a picture book. This is one of the aspects that makes any series so valuable to children.

The variety of the characters also inspired the children to think about what is 'real' in a character and what is not. The traits of almost all the characters are very human ones, recognisable to adults as entirely convincing personality types. Rebecca and Ralph's acceptance of them, and fascination with them, probably represents their understanding of this aspect as well. They could recognise realistic personalities when they encountered them, and easily 'suspend their disbelief' to think of them as people, and make them part of their lives.

Identification

Identification is a much discussed term. Should one identify with book characters or not? Some critics are concerned about readers, especially children, being manipulated by the book and taking on its values (or rather, those of the author). As was noted in Chapter 7, I think giving yourself to the text, being manipulated by it, suspending disbelief, are important skills for children to learn if they are to become committed readers. I feel this attitude should be encouraged in the young child, not discouraged. After all, empathy with a character or person is one of the major steps in understanding that other people have minds – minds which hold something quite different to your own.

Empathy is very close to identification, and this aspect of the identification phenomenon will be discussed first. When it has been clarified, the possible effect of author manipulation will be examined. Then the two children's identification with characters will be looked at in the broad sense, both within the reading session and in imaginative play and serious discussion outside it. These examples will be broken down into different categories.

Empathising with a character can be seen as a form of identification, because one has to, in some sense, get inside the character, to be able to feel as they feel, to respond in an empathetic, an appropriate way. In fact, most writing about identification is referring to exactly this. Readers feel they are close to the character, and that they understand the character's thoughts and feelings. Children have many more overt ways of identification.

I will confine my discussion of identification to just those cases where the children directly commented on their relationship with the character, such as 'I'm being . . .', or 'I'm doing this like . . .', or, referring to the illustration, 'I'm that little one.'

'[W]e cannot draw a clear line between what we are, in some conception of a "natural", unstoried self, and what we have become as we have first enjoyed, then imitated, and then, perhaps, criticised both the stories and our responses to them' (Booth 1988: 229), though he remarks that a 'full identity' with the character is not possible (ibid.: 139, note). Britton also comments on how characters affect us: 'Looked back on, the experiences others [either people we actually know, or authors] have related merge into the experiences we have had ourselves: as a basis for making generalisations, judgements, evaluations, decisions, we call upon both' (1992: 116).

There are several different types of 'identification' evidenced in children's behaviour, displaying different levels of involvement. Here seven processes are identified as having been displayed by Rebecca and Ralph, but it is quite possible that these are not all-encompassing. The varieties listed do not include the basic and most general use of the term, in which the reader mentally sees through the eyes of the focaliser, thinks the thoughts given as going through the mind of the characters. One can only assume that the two children felt this basic identification, as adult readers do. However, this is essentially internal; I can only record the cases that the children actually spoke about.

The first three types discussed occur during the process of sharing the relevant book, so are presumably closer to the identification that critics discuss. The latter four occur outside this frame, away from the book, and although this undoubtedly happens with adult readers as well, with young children we have abundant evidence of it.

Empathetic insight into the character, sharing their experience, happens with a young child either within or outside the book-reading session.

Evaluation of the characters is often demonstrated with young children through laughter at the behaviour or predicaments. It may also be expressed as criticism of a character, or by the child's offering an alternative outcome. The children demonstrated their understanding that the characters were not real people, despite the fact that Applebee (1978: 41) and others maintain that children are not capable of this understanding until they reach about 7. Rebecca and Ralph, and also the other children studied in detail, seemed to understand and express this much earlier.

What one takes away from the reading session, and how it affects one's life, are as important as the actual identification during the story. Both Rebecca and Ralph lived with their book characters in various ways, ranging from simple acting out of incidents or whole plots, to such complete identification that a character became the child's alter ego for weeks at a time.

Harding (1962) considered the way in which we read, and how we relate to fictional characters. His concept of the spectator role which we take towards any narrative was extended by Britton:

> I may also become spectator of events that have never happened and could never happen. I do so, in fact, whenever I read – or hear or tell or write – a fairy story or its adult equivalent. The satisfaction I have in the story is the kind of satisfaction I derive, not from having an experience, but from looking back on one I have had; it is as though I were to go back over an experience I have not had!
>
> (1992a: 103)

Types of identification behaviour displayed by the children

The seven types of identification noted in the behaviour of Rebecca and Ralph will be discussed in order of the intensity of the experience.

- superficial resemblances;
- allocating people to characters;
- self–character comparisons: attributes, behaviour or feelings;
- the character quoted or referred to outside the reading session;
- acting out the story;
- 'becomes' the character in daily life;
- extended identification.

Superficial resemblances

The aligning of oneself with a character is an aspect of experiencing narrative that seems to occur early. First it is likely to be an identification on the grounds of relative size and age. The baby of a family is always aware of themselves as being in the role of smallest, though this may be most obvious to the first-born child, when there is only the classic 'mother, father and baby' in the family, as so often in pictures.

Rebecca even used her own name to stand for 'smallest one' or 'baby', no doubt on the model of the big ones being labelled 'Mummy' and/or 'Daddy'. This may have become the first rapport with a character for her, though arrived at almost fortuitously, and through a purely linguistic relationship. On our first reading of McCloskey's *Make Way for Ducklings* (slightly abridged) I pointed out 'the mummy duck' and 'the baby ducks'. Rebecca (1–8) began thereafter to point to them on each page and label the adult one either 'Mummy' or 'Daddy' and the ducklings 'Decca, Decca, Decca, Decca' to each. Five weeks later she named the tigers as 'Daddy one' and 'Decca one' on the cover of *Baby Animal ABC* (p. 67). Ralph at 2–6 was thinking the same way. At that stage he called himself 'Boy', and his comment on the 'three French hens' in *The Twelve Days of Christmas* was 'That's a daddy one, that's a sister one, that's a boy one', but he nominated as 'boy' the larger of the two small ones – obviously wishful thinking at this age. Although this is purely a way of labelling the 'baby one', and possibly even a form of conscious wordplay, it may have led them into thinking of themselves as a character, 'identifying' with the character, and Ralph's later games of allocating familiar people's names to the book characters. By adding 'one' (as no doubt the sharing adult had done), they showed that they understood that it was not, in any sense, their 'Mummy' herself, but just the mother *animal*. In contrast, Ralph's later games made them the specific people: 'That's you, Daddy.'

The most superficial form of identification is comparing the character's appearance, possessions or actions with one's own. This continues throughout life. As mature readers we still have a thrill of recognition when a fictional experience parallels our own. The earliest record of this response was Rebecca's on her second birthday. To the haiku 'The moon in the water / Turned a somersault / And floated away', she laughed 'Decca somersault' and wanted it repeated over and over. She could not be said to be identifying herself with the moon, but was at least putting herself and her experience into the words the book (*In a Spring Garden*) offered her. Much later, she 'became' a Hattifattener each time her hair was charged with static electricity while brushing.

Books featuring children living in a similar way to their own usually inspired much comparison of lifestyles. *Lucy and Tom's Day* (Hughes) involved endless comment from Rebecca, beginning just after Ralph's birth. 'Our cat doesn't do that when we're eating *porridge*', 'Why don't *we* do our peas into the colander?', 'Why haven't *I* got a table to put my dolls' house on?', 'There isn't time to play after *our* tea', were among many in one day at 3–4. In both our family and Hughes's there is a blond bigger girl and a dark smaller boy. I had been helping her make tiny books for her doll's house at 3–11, and as she stuck in one minuscule picture of two children she said that it was a picture of the doll's house dolls. I remarked that you usually don't have pictures of yourself in a book, and her reply, after a moment's consideration, was 'Sometimes I pretend Lucy and Tom are me and Ralphie' (in other words, she *can* see herself in a book).

Allocating people to characters

White describes how Carol at 3 wanted her to name characters in pictures after the children she played with in the street: 'Any omissions are corrected and reproved. "Where's Alan? You haven't said Alan" ' (*BbF*: 37). Rebecca did not play this sort of game until she joined in with Ralph at about 6–8. In fact, at 2–3 she refused to accept as the name of the mother cat in *Angus and the Cat* any name belonging to human or animal in her actual world.

Ralph began to allocate people's names to characters at 2–2. From his babyhood Rebecca had been giving him roles outside the book session, so he must have become used to thinking that he could 'be' characters. 'Try a little celery, Gloria': Rebecca (3–9, adapting *Bread and Jam for Frances*) was already allocating roles for Ralph as he sat in his high chair at 0–6. This may explain why, at 2–2, he began saying, especially to books with a number of similar characters: 'That's me, that's you, Mummy. Which one is Becca?' If there were more names needed than the family could supply, he, like Carol, moved on to the names of friends: 'That one's Lucy, that one's Sarah.' Even within the actual reading session he would remark 'Look what you're doing, Becca' or 'I'm the best painter'. That he was still maintaining an 'aesthetic distance' (Booth 1988: 139) is shown by the fact that sometimes he would say 'That's a picture of me' (e.g. at 2–3 to a spider in Macdonald Starters, *Spiders*, though a couple of days later, he reverted to 'That's me' to the spider on the title page). By 5–2 he could put it more explicitly: 'I'm a person turned into an arrow' (at a reading of *Arrow to the Sun*).

From when Ralph was 3–5 much of the two children's sharing of books involved this allocation of roles, and subsequent discussion of their activities in the pictures. In the Orlando series, for instance, the kitten Tinkle was always Ralph, Blanche was Rebecca and the third kitten was sometimes their friend Lucy, sometimes our own cat, Socks. Similarly, in the Barbapapa series Ralph was the black furry Barbabeau and Rebecca was usually the yellow animal-loving Barbazoo. 'Look what I'm doing. Where's you, Becca? You're telling them where to put the injection.' This role-allocation was sometimes based on behaviour (Tinkle does the naughtiest and funniest things; Rebecca has always loved animals), partly on gender, partly on appearance (Ralph had abundant black hair and both Tinkle and Barbabeau are black and furry). 'Me, the Nightmare, cries, don't I Becca?' (4–0 to *There's a Nightmare in My Cupboard* – another shaggy creature). These responses and comments would sometimes spill over into a session where an adult was reading the book, especially with Ralph from 3–5 on. Sometimes they squabbled about the allocation of roles, both choosing the same character, but usually they negotiated peacefully. Kenneth Grahame's family 'allotted' and 'dealt out' characters in books and pictures in the same way (1995: 55).

It is interesting that Ralph had no hesitation in allocating to himself the role of 'baddie' on occasion. In *Petunia Beware*: 'I'm the raccoon and you're Petunia. Bec is the farmer', giving her the only significant part left (3–10). The raccoon is a trickster, out to get Petunia the goose in any way he can.

Self–character comparison: attributes, behaviour or feelings

Usually the children overtly compared themselves with the character, but sometimes not so directly. Rebecca said 'I feel like that' concerning a description in *Different Peter and Emma*: 'When Emma plays alone all her games seem the same. She knows exactly what she is going to do next – and nothing is ever different.' I interpreted this, and read it, as being rather melancholy, but to Rebecca, playing alone was clearly a matter of satisfaction. I tried to get her to articulate more clearly. 'It's difficult to explain,' she said, and after I read the section again: 'Yes! That's how it is! Nothing is ever different!' (2–9).

Ralph at 4–3 said he was sometimes cross like Little My; however, usually this type of comparison was an older, more complex response. Ralph was 7–8 when he said of Ramona: 'She got into trouble. I feel like that you know. I get into trouble like her' (*Ramona the Pest*), and Rebecca 7–6 when she said 'I like being by myself, like Snufkin' (*Comet in Moominland*).

The character quoted or referred to outside the reading session

The day before his second birthday Ralph heard *Miffy's Birthday* (Bruna) for the first time. Miffy receives a bear as a gift, and takes it to bed with her. As Ralph went off to bed clutching his own bear: 'Mishy bear, me bear' (1–11). This was exactly one day younger than Rebecca's 'Decca somersault', and for both, the first directly stated identification. He was already attempting to identify himself with the character, as he did so often later. He exclaimed during another reading 'No Mishy bear! Me bear!' (2–1) which might be interpreted as 'that's not Miffy's bear, it's my bear', or perhaps 'It's me that's got a bear, not Miffy.'

Simple physical imitation was one of the first behaviours to appear outside the reading session. At 2–2 Rebecca stood on one leg in the slightly odd position of Goldilocks escaping on the last page of Stobbs's *The Story of the Three Bears*, telling us 'Look! I doing this, like Goldilocks.' The similarity was quite clear. At the same age, having learned to hop, she always said that she was hopping 'like Christopher Robin' (from 'Hoppity' in *When We Were Very Young*) and also 'I sneezed, like Peter' (*Peter Rabbit*).

In the Moomintroll series, Ralph's focus, and his dearest love, was the intrepid Little My. At first he assigned himself Moomintroll, presumably because he had been allocated this role by Rebecca when he was only 3–1, and frequently in games thereafter. However, his interest in Little My was evident as soon as he started to hear the books themselves. She features extensively in

Ralph's first title, *Moominland Midwinter*. To the picture of her on page 32, fighting with her torn sleeping bag, he remarked 'I'm the Moomintroll. I very much like her, don't I?' (4–2). Six weeks later, when he had also heard *Finn Family Moomintroll* and *Comet in Moominland* and was part-way through *Moominsummer Madness*, he spelled out some of his feelings about her. All of her pictures were commented on extensively, and at one illustration his monologue went like this: 'Little My again! What's she doing? She's talking to an ant! Little My is always cross. Little people are usually cross. I'm quite cross sometimes.' He even asked, regarding one picture of her in *Moominpappa at Sea*, 'Why isn't Little My cross there?' (4–4). Ralph did have a quick temper, and recognised a soulmate.

The other trait of Little My which appealed to Ralph was her imperturbability. As we were bushwalking along a narrow cliff track (Ralph, 4–4; Rebecca, 7–7), I was cautioning him to be careful, not to run, it was dangerous. His response was 'Little My wouldn't mind it.' A long discussion on her ensued, in the course of which he asserted 'Little My doesn't mind anything! Little My would like sleeping in mud!' (stepping over a muddy patch in the path). 'Little My says silly things! Little My is a nice fellow!'

Immediately afterwards, he suggested 'Let's play Moomintroll.' We all agreed, and I asked him if he was going to be Little My. 'No, I can't be Little My, because she's a girl' was his reply. In this case Ralph decided to be Snufkin, and Rebecca opted for Little My – a complete reversal of their usual allegiances.

It may not have been only gender that deterred Ralph from the Little My role. Someone as brave, intrepid and energetic as she would be difficult to live up to. Rebecca discovered this towards the end of the same walk, when both were getting tired. I had reminded 'Snufkin' that he liked journeys, and persuaded him to 'play' on his grass-straw flute, and sing 'All small beasts should have bows on their tails', which worked quite well for a while. But later still, when Ralph was finally being shouldered the last stretch, I told Rebecca hopefully that Little My never complains. Crossly she replied 'I'm not Little My, I'm Rebecca!'

Towards the end of his Moomin phase, My was still uppermost in Ralph's mind. At 4–5 I had lifted him up on to a branch of the silver birch tree in the front yard, and as I looked up at him, small pieces of bark fell down. Ralph consoled me: 'Little My would like that, when stuff fell in her eyes!' – she thrives on adversity.

Acting out the story

Acting out seems to have been the type of identification most usual with Lindsey Wolf (*Braid*), or perhaps it was the aspect that most interested her mother. Lindsey frequently dressed up and acted out roles, as also did Anna Crago and even Carol White, much more frequently than Rebecca and Ralph.

Both children did act out parts of *In the Forest* in ways that indicate their typical difference. Rebecca was 3–4 when she managed this complicated allocation of roles:

> 'I'm a bear eating peanuts. You're the mother kangaroo and Ralph's the baby. Brownie [imaginary friend] is being a monkey, and Reddy the Horsie [ride-on toy] is the other monkey, and all my friends and relations [other imaginary people borrowed from Rabbit's in *Winnie-the-Pooh*, often cast as extras] are the other animals.'

Once she had allocated the roles, the actual performance of the story was cursory, and happened mainly in her imagination. On the other hand, Ralph after a reading found a paper bag and peanuts which he actually ate from the bag as the bear had, saying 'I'm the big brown bear' (2–9).

Ralph tried jumping like Jansson's Hattifatteners, of whom he was very fond. One of his earliest comments, on the cover of *Finn Family Moomintroll*, was: 'Why haven't they got feet?' [They just haven't.] 'They must jump. But they couldn't jump very high, because to jump high you have to go like this [demonstrating by squatting down, which they don't appear to be able to do]. They must have just jumped little jumps like this.'

In this area of role-playing, as in others, the second child has the advantage of being coached by the first. As well as 'Gloria' at 0–6, Ralph was also allocated 'Little Plums' (*Muffel and Plums*) at 0–7. Rebecca involved him in her games, so he soon came to understand the concept of 'pretend' and to adapt himself to her different roles. He was able to play pretend games by himself as well. At 2–2 he was sitting in a laundry basin which he called a 'sailboat', and said 'Me say-or', from *The Sailor*. At 2–9 and 2–10 he was frequently 'a pet squirrel', especially when he was feeling cuddly. Sometimes the squirrel was called Squirrel Nutkin (from Potter's tale), sometimes not.

Rebecca acted out actual stories, or incidents from them, perhaps more often than Ralph. With an umbrella held aloft at 2–6 she announced 'I'm going to buy some buns', imitating Mrs Rabbit in *Peter Rabbit*, just as Carol White had (*BbF*: 27). Rebecca's favourite Potter title was *Samuel Whiskers*. In a perfectly cheerful tone, but obviously displacing a little sibling jealousy, she suggested that we make the infant Ralph (6 weeks) into a 'roly-poly pudding' by rolling him up in Play-Doh (3–4; Figure A.1 and her comments on p. 166). I compromised by helping roll him in a clean nappy instead. Others of Rebecca's were 'I Swimmy!' [And who am I?] 'The water. Swimmy going in the water' (and climbs on to my lap, 2–3; *Swimmy*), picking blueberries (3–3 to 4–9 *Blueberries for Sal*), and running away to under the dining-room table (4–2, *A Baby Sister for Frances*).

The incidents of Pooh stuck in Rabbit's front door and Eeyore floating down the river on his back were very popular games with both children. Ralph (2–7) and Rebecca (3–3) acted them out physically with enthusiasm (*Winnie-the-Pooh*).

After a performance of The Three Bears, with me as the Big Bear, her toy panda as the Middle Bear, Ralph (1–7) as Little Bear and herself as Goldilocks, playwright, director and producer (4–9), she scripted a number of new versions, including 'Big Bear is doing the washing. She goes outside to the well to get some more water and Goldilocks jumps in the washing machine, then she comes back and finds her. Little Bear is playing with Middle-sized Bear.' As we act this, I discover her in the imaginary, bucket-filled washing machine: [You again, Goldilocks!] 'Yes! I come in whenever you are out.'

As in this example, the personae and their names could be used in games different from the books' stories. Ralph similarly named himself 'the man that fought the Medusa' in a game at 4–1. When he was 7–6 I overheard a friend of Ralph's, in the middle of a complex game with a group of boys, comment that 'You're always Sparrowhawk', although the game had nothing to do with *A Wizard of Earthsea*.

Lindsey Wolf's frequent 'I'm not Lindsey, I'm . . .' in her third year is relevant in this category because it was almost always associated with dressing up and acting out, rather than 'being' in the everyday world (*Braid*: 40).

'Becomes' the character in daily life

Being a different character while going about one's daily life is different from role-playing a book character in a game. Eating porridge, the children both thought of the natural association: Rebecca 'the three bears had porridge – and Goldilocks' (2–7); Ralph 'me a bear' (2–4). Ralph at 3–10 was perfectly happy to 'become' the disgusting Fungus. Even 'We're a family of Fungus the Bogeymen' (*Fungus the Bogeyman*). Age often mattered to Ralph, in his wanting his chosen character to resemble him (or perhaps vice versa). At 3–3 he remarked of Thomas in *Thomas Builds a House*: 'When I've got his number [i.e. age] I'll build a little house.' He often acted Pepito to Rebecca's Madeline (*Madeline and the Bad Hat*), and perhaps this was why he insisted, at 3–4, that Pepito should have four rather than six candles on his birthday cake, to make him closer to his own age.

Sometimes a game or activity would be enough to spark the comparison. Play-Doh led to book games of this sort. Ralph at 3–3 said 'I'm Mickey.' [Is that the morning cake?] 'No, I'm bumping and thumping to make my helicopter' (*In the Night Kitchen*). Bringing me a plate of Play-Doh in bed one morning, Rebecca said 'I've stolen some dough.' I missed the allusion and asked her what she had made: 'Scratchings' she showed me, like Anna Maria's paw marks (3–4, *Samuel Whiskers*).

Extended identification

Although Ralph's identifications with characters within the story, such as Tinkle the kitten, Barbabeau and Zephir in the Babar series, were consistent, lasting through every reading of each book in the series for several years, he never took on an alter ego outside the reading session, except fleetingly, such as when he cuddled up as 'Squirrel Nutkin' at 2–10.

Episodic works like *Winnie-the-Pooh*, and series of longer picture books, both give opportunities to get to know the various facets of a character well, and their different activities. This may be why such characters were often taken on as roles, and also their actions mimicked. Rebecca, however, became much more thoroughly involved with them. The first of her extended identifications, in which she took on a character as an alter ego, answered only to its name and behaved (occasionally) in its fashion, was Tigger (2–10 to 2–11, *Pooh*). 'Tigger *is* a bouncy animal,' as she remarked, suiting word to deed. It was during this period that she made the complicated double allocation of 'I'm Tigger pretending to be Eeyore' (2–10). After a couple of weeks as Tigger she 'became' Piglet. This was an enduring identification, lasting for a full five weeks. When summoned absent-mindedly, she would reply 'Not Becca! I'm Piglet', and to the sketch of Piglet executed by Daddy on her breakfast boiled egg, she would say 'It's me!' One day she said with conviction 'I'm going to be Piglet all days', by which she probably meant 'for ever' (2–11). It is significant that at this age Rebecca was determinedly independent, claiming that she could dress herself, cross roads without holding hands, and perform other grown-up activities. At the same time, for her alter ego she chose the smallest, weakest, least secure of the characters at her disposal, clearly reflecting a conflict within herself.

In the Moomintroll series, Rebecca's first character assimilation was with Sniff. Leading the way through a bushy park to hunt for tadpoles, I suggested that she was like Moomintroll exploring 'mysterious paths' (*Comet*, p. 7; we were part-way through reading this for the first time, and she was 6–4). She agreed 'Yes, but I'm Sniff. Ralph can be Moomintroll.' She was correct about the character in the lead – at this point in the story it is Sniff. Asked who I was, I declined the obvious role of Moominmamma and chose to be Snufkin, adding that he was my favourite. John was happy to be Moominpappa.

The next day she again announced she was Sniff. When I tried to elicit why she had chosen him, her reply was 'Because he's the littlest, and because he doesn't really belong to the family.' This was a surprise, as he is treated as one of the Moomins, and it is only through the pictures that you can see he is different. I asked if she felt sorry for him not belonging to the family, and her 'No!' was emphatic and surprised. That had obviously never occurred to her. Much of his appeal was this very difference.

Over the next few days she found superficial reasons for 'being' Sniff: the privilege of licking out the custard bowl, for instance (as in *Comet*). As I was picking up the book to reread, and giving her the chapter titles, she asked for 'Sniff finds the cave – that's me. I find the cave', showing that she was also identifying with him within the reading session.

However, the next title we read, *Moominsummer Madness*, does not involve Sniff, and she missed him. Her allegiance changed, and once on the first day of reading this, she had already announced that she was Snufkin instead. A week later I queried this allegiance. [I thought you were Sniff?] 'I'm Snufkin and Sniff,' she replied with dignity. By this time she was well into *Tales from Moominvalley*. Gradually her interest in Snufkin displaced Sniff. For instance, the story 'Cedric' was for her 'about how Snufkin first got his mouth-organ – and Sniff'. Sniff and his toy dog Cedric were definitely secondary for her, although they are the main protagonists in the story. By the time we were halfway through *Moominland Midwinter*, she announced plaintively 'I wish I was really Snufkin, Mum' (6–5). I replied that Snufkin was my favourite too. 'Yes, he's my favourite and Jo's favourite' (Jo Goodman is a children's literature expert and an adult friend.) Much of her time she went around blowing either a mouth-organ or a recorder ('flute'), as Snufkin does.

Her competition entry on 'My favourite author' (6–6 – see p. 47) was on Tove Jansson. Part of it explained:

> I play games. One of the people is one person of the Moomin family, and one is the other. I am usually Snufkin in the game. I play my mouth-organ and I pretend I'm going away with my tent.

It was exactly a year later, at 7–6, as she listened again to *Comet* with Ralph, that she said she, like Snufkin, liked being alone. It was Snufkin's independence, and unruffled self-confidence and self-sufficiency, that attracted her. He was just the sort of person she would like to be (see also H. Crago 1993 on her Snufkin identification).

Gender and identification

Rebecca had no problems with taking on a male alter ego. All the most significant lasting ones she adopted were male, though there were plenty of female ones in the incidental games based on books (a Ramona game was popular at 6–9, for instance). On the other hand, Ralph found it difficult if not impossible to take on a female persona. As early as 2–3, listening to *Where the Wild Things Are* and discussing with Rebecca the gender of the different Wild Things, he remarked of Max 'Dat's me. No, dat's a girl. So-yee [sorry].' At 3–2 he asked rather plaintively 'Why is Meg a she?', as he would clearly have liked to 'be' her (*Meg on the Moon*). His disinclination to identify with a female may have been because he felt it was incumbent upon him, as the younger child, to emphasise his difference from the older/wiser/stronger Rebecca, so he needed to reinforce his gender difference along with other differences. No doubt we reinforced this, not for gender reasons, but to help his sense of self. He identified with dark-haired furry creatures (whereas Rebecca had never specifically chosen blond ones) for the same reason. Further, the males are often the more interesting characters. This is so with his long-standing book-identifications, Barbabeau and Tinkle.

On the other hand, Little My, irascible, independent, strong and small, fascinated him. She was the focus of the Moomintroll series for him, but he would never overtly articulate this identification. He never 'became' her, as

Rebecca did Snufkin, despite his close identification ('I'm quite cross some-times'). Similarly, in the Narnia series, which he heard many times from 4–1 on, it has to be Lucy (or in later books, Jill) that one identifies with. Lucy is the strongest, most interesting and most enduring character. Ralph virtually admitted this one day at 5–11 when he asked 'Can we have a chapter of Lucy?' It must be admitted, however, that Ralph never identified with any character, male or female, in the intense way Rebecca took on the mantle of Piglet and Snufkin, so perhaps gender was irrelevant.

A neat summation of one aspect of the gender question, the fact that action-packed, highly amusing books rarely feature females, came one day when Ralph was in his period of passionate devotion to the Mordillo books, including *Crazy Cowboy*. Rebecca (6–10): 'I'm Crazy Cowgirl!' Ralph: 'No! I'm Crazy Cowboy.' Then: 'I'll find you the book about the cowgirl. . . . Here it is. It's an invisible book, Becca!' (3–8).

Villains and identification

Harding remarks that 'the spectator, whether of actual events or representa-tion, is interested in any of the possibilities of human experience, not merely its pleasures' (1962: 138), and this certainly applies to the children's make-believe games. It was not only the admired and enjoyed characters that they imitated and hence, in part, identified with.

Wolves were familiar fairy-tale villains, with the best known in our family being that in *Peter and the Wolf*, which we had both in print form and as a record with Prokofiev's music. One of the first times Rebecca took on this role, it was quite unexpected. 'Hello juicy person,' she remarked conver-sationally to an adult, and to their query explained 'I'm a wolf' (4–0). The actual phrase is a partial quotation from *Snuffy* (Bruna) 'I've only found some juicy leaves to eat, nothing else.' Later, once Ralph was mobile, she often played it with him, especially after her contact with *Clever Polly and the Stupid Wolf* at 4–4. Running out from between the trees, she announced 'I'm a horrible wolf come out of the forest.' Little Ralph (1–1) followed her and I suggested that he was another wolf, but no: 'He's the one I'm trying to catch. Look, I swallowed him!' And a month later: 'I swallowed him alive – in one gulp' (as the wolf does the duck in *Peter and the Wolf*). Chasing him around (gently and to his delight), she explained several days later 'He's the gingerbread boy' (though in this case the villain is a fox).

A playground with a climbing rocket inspired Rebecca to another wolf game: 'This is a chimney and I'm climbing down. There is a pot of boiling water at the bottom. Now someone's put the lid on it!' (as she was almost at the ground). In the same climbing frame the next day, she decided that she had fallen into the water. 'Now they've boiled me and eaten me all up. Now I've escaped!' (4–5). She could also play it the other way round: 'I'm Little Red Riding Hood. You're the wolf, Mummy' (4–5). Once Ralph was able to take a real part, they enjoyed acting out *Peter and the Wolf* while the record played. On one occasion, with Ralph 2–10 and her 6–1, she explained 'He's being the wolf and I'm Peter.' At 3–7 and 6–11 there was a cooperative game in which Ralph was a troll, Rebecca a monster, and they caught, cooked and ate any billy goats that were stupid enough to cross their bridge.

Ralph at 4 also felt able to take the villain's part on some occasions. A childhood-long interest in the Greek and Norse myths began at 3–9, and he was 3–11 when he first met Beowulf and those most fascinating of villains, Grendel and his mother. He approached Rebecca when she returned from school: 'I've got a good idea! I can be the monster that was in the book we read, and you can be the person that kills him! [*Sotto voce*] What was his name, Mummy? Yeah, Grendel!' As it happened, Rebecca, who had not heard the story, was deep in a project of her own, making a horse's mask out of two paper bags, but Ralph was able to incorporate this, explaining that it said that they rode horses. The next day, a Saturday, he was again Grendel, hiding under the double bed from Beowulf, this time Daddy. John obliged by feinting with his 'sword' and spouting alliterative mock Anglo-Saxon verse, especially when Grendel fired off weapons in the form of shoes. The problem was, of course, that if the story is acted out correctly, Grendel cannot win. Beowulf is invincible. Ralph was making himself quite anxious, and insisted that Beowulf look the other way so he didn't notice him emerging to go to the toilet.

Ralph was a child with many fears. Books often caused him anxiety, and he would frequently refuse to hear to the end stories that seemed to threaten his own or the protagonist's security. With his love of the myths, and perhaps also his willingness to act out the monsters' parts, the fears gradually abated (pp. 52–54). By the time he was 5–2 he was able to say 'I've been thinking about *The Quinkins*. 'Cause they've got the sort of feeling I like – sort of scary feeling.' [Is that the sort you like, scary?] 'Yes. I like scary-feeling ones' (Figure 4.3).

The children's awareness of, and reactions to, the fictional characters they encountered support the arguments of those developmental psychologists engaged in pushing back the age of the child's first understanding that other people have minds, that they think and feel – 'theory of mind' (pp. 120–121).

Harding suggests there are four levels of response to the personae in a novel: imaginative or empathetic insight into other people and sharing their experience; evaluation of the participants and what they do and suffer; understanding that these are not real people but only created personae; and an awareness of communicating with an author (1962: 147). Young children can demonstrate all Harding's levels of the spectator role for readers of fiction, though with perhaps only a limited sense of communicating with the authors themselves, or the implied authors. They also imitate the characters extensively outside the reading session, and in the process work on creating their own individuality, their own sense of self. It seems that the ' "natural", unstoried self' does not exist, however young the recipient of narrative.

10 'It was a joke because it couldn't really happen'

Humour and irony

'I'll tell you a joke. Once upon a time there was a poor cow and he was lonely 'cause he didn't have anyone to live with. There was a dog that had puppies, and she went to live with the cow and the dog was the mummy and the puppies were the kids. And the dog was happy and the cow was happy and the puppies were happy. That was a nice joke, wasn't it?' I respond by agreeing that yes, it was a nice 'story', but was rebuffed by Ralph (3–3) with his own definition: 'It was a joke, 'cause it couldn't really happen, could it?'

'The perception of incongruity in a playful context' is Pien and Rothbart's definition of humour (1980: 2), and one widely accepted by most commentators. To recognise something as incongruous, there must be an initial 'congruous' expectation, from which the incongruity is seen to depart. This expectation shows an understanding of what is normal in the external world, or what is canonical (Bruner's term; 1990: 49) in a fictional one. A humorous response indicates an understanding that 'reality' has been overturned. With his definition of 'joke' ('it couldn't really happen') Ralph demonstrated his understanding of the relationship between humour and reality.

The incongruous violates some (usually unwritten) rule. It surprises, even sometimes alarms – and, as a result, often amuses.

It may be that humour, more than any other genre or trope, forces the child into metafictional thinking, into comparing the world of the text, the ontology of the fiction, with the external world, with the world as the child knows it, with the everyday ontology encountered on all sides (Lowe 1995).

'Humour' is the biggest category in the Reading Journal index, with over 1,900 entries. As soon as there is language – first understood language and then language used – it is possible to chart the infant's and the child's concept of the incongruous. The very young child laughs at mastery, at the surprise of recognition and identification, and at the non-threatening incongruous, in real life. As Wellman (1990) has shown, young pre-schoolers (he puts it at around 3, though I have taken it back to around 2) have a clear concept not only of the physical world, but of their own mental world as well, and are beginning to recognise that other people have minds also.

Even before the concept of author or illustrator develops, there is the understanding that the fictional world is a separate world, a cohesive world with a structure of its own, different from the external world, but nevertheless consistent within itself. In this world it may be that animals can talk, or it may be that characters can change their shape at will. Or perhaps it is a world very like the known physical world. But whatever sort of world the story or the picture presents, it holds an expected consistency within it. A step outside this is seen as funny. A kettle singing in a realistic text is funny (Rebecca 2–11, in *Meet Mary Kate*) if the child's general knowledge does not include whistling kettles.

Apart from the incongruity within the fictional world, the other form of incongruity a reader or viewer can recognise is incongruity with the 'external world'. Rebecca's sudden realisation that 'animals can't talk' at 3–7 was accompanied by wild laughter (p. 46). There can also be the realisation that something is funny because the child knows better, knows that this is not how language works, for instance the incongruity of thinking that a babysitter would sit on a baby (Rebecca to *Teddy Robinson Himself* at 4–0).

Most of the case studies make only passing reference to the humorous responses of the children they are observing. The only extended investigation of a young child's reactions is the Cragos' section entitled 'Funny Ha Ha and Funny Peculiar', in which they divide Anna's humour responses into three categories and discuss several examples at length (*Prelude*: 185–199). There is an article that deals with the humour responses of a specific child from 1–3 to 2–6, though not related to books (Johnson and Mervis 1997).

Categorical statements made by critics and reviewers, apparently based only on their own expectations, or on humour studies by developmental psychologists, consistently underestimate children's abilities. It is very commonly stated, for instance, that children prefer physical humour, visual humour, slapstick, until they are quite mature. 'Visual forms of humour generally dominate until the child reaches high school, when verbal humour and wit begin to command increasing attention and gradually become the major forms of humorous behaviour' (Kappas 1967: 70). As Kappas's is still the only closely analysed study of types of humour in children's books, it continues to be influential. Lypp, writing in German, takes a less conservative view, discussing transformation, fantasy and humour, and the subversive (1986).

There are also humour theorists, some of whom choose a specific area such as puns (Redfern 1984). Bergson (1911), Levin (1972) and Nash (1985) have discussed the (adult) humorous novel. Bakhtin (1984) brought humour theory to the fore in literary criticism with his concept of the carnivalesque. Since his study of Rabelais, the concept of the novel, and especially the humorous novel, as being based on aspects of the Carnival has been widely acknowledged and explored. Things of the body – sex, excrement and death – are celebrated in an atmosphere of licensed mayhem. This concept applies to children's books too, where subversion has always been an important aspect.

Here the scatological is usually changed to physical dirtiness, and the subversion is in the escaping of adult strictures (though more recently excrement has become a popular topic in children's books). *Harry the Dirty Dog* and *Tom Kitten* are good examples. Ultimately it is only a licensed, a permitted, freedom, however. Society usually reclaims the rebel, as it does both Harry and Tom. Stephens discusses the carnivalesque in children's stories (1992: 120–157); and see also Lurie (1991) and Lewis (1989).

There are a number of developmental psychologists who examine the humour responses of children in experimental situations and generalise from these. Most notable among these is McGhee (1972, 1979, 1980, 1989), but there are other writers as well who look at different aspects of humour, such as Schultz and Robillard (1980) on verbal humour, and Gardner *et al.* (1980) on the role of metaphor. Relying as they do on the experimental situation, these investigators inevitably miss much of the humour children both create for themselves and respond to. The creation of jokes by children is a complex intellectual task, and quite rare in the child's life (Chaney 1993), and is not likely to be encountered in the limited environment of the test. Also, the research atmosphere is hardly conducive to relaxed responses to humour. The examples used by Pien and Rothbart to examine children's humour are not relevant to the book world, nor are many of McGhee's, which may be why the humour schemata of the developmental psychologists seem so far out of line with observations of children in natural settings.

Playing with language is in one sense playing with reality. The relationship between word play (using language as a 'basic play material'; Whitehead 1983: 52) and reality is that involved in the sign versus the symbol. The child, especially when exposed to decontextualised language in the form of stories or other conversation about non-present things, gradually recognises the arbitrary nature of the word, and may even create his or her own (see Rebecca's neologisms, p. 55). This relationship throws light on how one thinks, and in what sense what *is* is dependent on what it is *called*. The child works this out largely through wordplay.

Humour at home

Recording humour responses is quite difficult, as one can't see the smiles of a child sitting on your lap or beside you. It was only actual laughter or comment that made it to the Reading Journal. We didn't often quiz the children on their laughter either, as explaining might have spoilt the joke. When we did do so, the reply, as we deserved, was usually along the lines of 'I'm just laughing at the story' (Rebecca 4–1).

The family environment was not one filled with laughter. John and I are fairly serious, and there were few wild games and no practical jokes, especially when Rebecca was little. John and I seldom read or tell jokes, though we enjoy wordplay, accidental or deliberate. On principle we did not laugh at Rebecca except when she was being deliberately comical. All this changed with the advent of Ralph. Rebecca reinforced his mistakes with laughter, as well as praising his successes. Even his serious pretence games could be greeted with laughter, in which I occasionally joined. Both Rebecca (6–2) and I had to laugh at his literary description of himself with a straw in his mouth (2–11): 'I'm a gentleman smoking a pipe. I'm very haunted by ghosts.'

The familiar

The first form of incongruity to be discussed is the familiar. This sounds oxymoronic; how can the familiar be incongruous? This is the humour response that the Cragos term 'Like me', and define as 'the laughing recognition of unexpected *congruity*, not unexpected *in*congruity' (*Prelude*: 197). This variety of humour is never touched on by the humour theorists, although James Thurber acknowledged it: 'There is always a laugh in the utterly familiar' (in Cleary 1982: 11). Even in these humour responses there is the recognition that a rule has been violated: the 'rule' that the book world is apart from the actual world. The children show by their laughter that this framing is what they expect. Out of this book frame (or perhaps into it – the metaphor is slippery) steps unexpectedly something directly from the child's own world: a dummy or pacifier (*Fast–Slow*, *High–Low*; Ralph, 1–1), snails (Rebecca, 2–0), people wearing glasses (Ralph, 2–5), a cat's rough tongue (*Come Here Cat*; Rebecca, 2–8), the name of a friend or relative – and is responded to with a bubbling up of spontaneous delighted laughter. Emma's behaviour, especially putting her jeans on her head and sweater on her legs, amused Ralph enormously – something he had tried himself by 2–3 (*Emma Quite Contrary*). All Emma's behaviour is familiar, and any reading of the book with more than one child would include complicit glances from child to child acknowledging the appositeness of calling for a glass of water or to use the potty after being put to bed (for example, Ralph and Rebecca together at 2–11 and 6–2).

Verbal humour

All wordplay involves incongruity, making a word or a sound different from the language's norm. Schultz and Robillard (1980: 60) describe the different linguistic areas and show how a child can play with the language, how the rules can be violated, in the creation of wordplay, or the delighted recognition of it. They extend McGhee's work with a useful schema in which they divide verbal humour into four broad linguistic categories and look at the rule violation that causes the incongruity, the humour, in each. Their categories are phonology (sounds), morphology (words), syntax (sentences and grammar) and pragmatic (chiefly over-lateralization). I could give examples from Rebecca and Ralph in each of his categories, but have decided to categorise the examples in different ways.

Mislabelling of all types was one of Ralph's major forms of humour designed to amuse others, beginning at 1–1 with *Lucy and Tom's Day* (p. 37). From then on he indulged in mislabelling behaviour frequently, to his own amusement as well as Rebecca's. In *Fish Is Fish*, which is ambiguous anyway (featuring pictures of odd fish-like creatures from the fish-protagonist's imagination), he labelled each fishy creature 'bish' (his word for 'fish' – there is one on each page), but then went on to point and say 'bish' to the blank endpapers as well (1–6).

Rebecca seldom pursued this activity, probably because an adult would be less inclined to find it amusing than an indulgent and subversive sibling. She did enjoy mislabelling actual people or characters, though. At 3–10 she insisted that *Lucy and Tom* were in fact called 'Bam and Wam' and asked that Hughes's familiar title be read this way. She often affectionately applied misnomers to Ralph himself: 'You're a little gimlet', 'You're a little minnow' (4–6) and 'Ralph's indigestible – what does indigestible mean?' (4–10), all taken from Potter's rich vocabulary.

Mislabelling makes a much more amusing joke if it goes against the imperative of rhyme as well. Gay's *Look* is written in basic doggerel, which we were accustomed to read with a pause for Ralph to fill in the relevant rhyme at the end of each line. It begins:

> Here's a shy kitten
> Soft and sweet
> And here's a white lamb with
> Four little black –

'wheels!' Ralph supplied on one occasion (2–3), delighting us all. Similarly, Rebecca at 3–9 sang: 'Heigh dee, heigh dee ho / The great big elephant is so – *fast.*'

Mispronunciations are incongruous in their unexpectedness. They were not common in stories, but 'aminal' in *The Funny Thing* amused Rebecca at 2–3. Piglet's 'Help help! a Horrible Heffalump! . . . Hoff, Hoff a Hellible Horralump. Holl, Holl . . .' is funny for its sound, and for Piglet's anxiety, as much as for its mispronunciation, and amused both consistently once the chapter was familiar. Rebecca would invent mispronunciations herself in very familiar books, for instance asking that her father read *The Hare and the Tortoise* as 'mortoise' throughout, and finding this very funny at 2–11. She explained at the end that 'a mortoise is a kind of tortoise', reassuring herself (or John) that despite its misnaming, the pictured protagonist was still a tortoise.

To a child, the experience of misusing a word, or misunderstanding one, must be common, so to be able to understand something that a character cannot is satisfying, empowering, and amusing. The humour is increased by the fact that literary language is usually so sensible, so complete, so 'correct' grammatically and morphologically, that the incongruity is greater than it would be if the mistake had been spotted in the external world. Teddy

Robinson's grasp of language is often tenuous. It was highly amusing that the bear thinks that the holiday they are going to have might 'come in a box tied with ribbon' (Rebecca: 'You can't put a holiday in a box!'). 'Or on a tray? Or will the postman bring it in a parcel? Or will it just come walking in all by itself?' (Rebecca: 'Holidays haven't got legs!' 4–0, with much laughter, *Teddy Robinson's Omnibus*). *Five Dolls* and later *Alice* also use over-literal 'mistakes' as well as other forms of word play.

Homophones in the form of puns were often part of Rebecca's word play. At 2–10 she tricked her father: 'Dear Daddy.' [Dear Becca.] 'The animal deer – that's the one I was thinking of. Deer daddy.' It was not just the words, but the concepts as well, that she played with as she became ever more adept with language. Our cats always had a supply of the dry food known as 'Go Cat' on hand. One morning at breakfast it suddenly occurred to Rebecca that 'Muesli is "Go Human" ' (6–5). The puns and the catchphrases in the Asterix series were a shared delight to the two children between 5–10 and 11–0 (Ralph), with Rebecca 9–1 and up. It is interesting to note that McGhee's method of testing produces stage 4 ('multiple meanings') only at age 6 or 7 (McGhee 1979: 76; Burt and Sugawara 1988: 18).

Rhymes themselves can play an important part in humour. When *Dr Seuss's Sleep Book* was quite new, Rebecca having heard it about three times only (3–3), I read the page preceding the title page for the first time: 'This book is to be read in bed.' 'It rhymes!', she was amused to discover. Rhyme and rhythm emphasise the constructedness of their language, and as such are incongruous when compared with the language of literary prose, let alone with the casual utterances of everyday life. They can amuse for this reason alone. But when words are deliberately strained to fit the rhyme, or unexpected words appear instead of the expected ones, this adds to the amusement. Ralph loved the rough and tumble and rollicking rhymes of Macleod's 'Babies at the Supermarket' (*The Fed-Up Family Album*), reciting it with enthusiasm at 7–1.

Reversing or negating a text was obviously a way of exploring the story and its reality, as well as being hilariously funny. Rebecca enjoyed saying 'No she didn't' after every sentence of *Miffy at the Seaside* until John read it as 'She *didn't* put on her red trunks all by herself' and 'How *hot* the water was!' (2–9). Ralph was different, in that playing with the text was his prerogative. He did not like the reader to change *The Elephant and the Bad Baby* to 'So the elephant *didn't* stretch out his trunk and take some chips for himself' (2–11) even though he had often substituted 'No' for the Bad Baby's 'Yes'. Taylor describes this 'silly' reading as common among parents (1983: 69–70).

Hidden characters

By far the most frequent cause of humour in illustrations, at all ages, was the character who had to be searched for and found. This could take the form of one partially hidden under or in something, such as Peter under the carton in

Whistle for Willie (Figure 5.3), or one who was almost fully visible, but lost among the teeming plenitude of details, such as Orlando or the kitten Tinkle in *Orlando Buys a Farm*. Another example was the elephant 'hidden' behind the fruit barrow in *The Elephant and the Bad Baby* at 1–7. The other examples mentioned in 'Missing parts' (pp. 69–73) were also amusing.

But Where Is the Green Parrot? has a green bird hidden on each page which is most enjoyable to find – eliciting grins rather than hysterical laughter with Ralph at 2–5. Rebecca at 5–2 remarked that 'He's tricking us there! He could look like a stalk' (when it is hiding in the vase of flowers). Cushla had great satisfaction spotting it too (*Cushla*: 37) and is discussed by Kiefer (1995: 8).

The bizarre

The book that caused the most laughter overall was the puzzle book *Wacky Wednesday*. In this, more and more 'wacky' things must be discovered on each page, and many of them were seen as wildly funny: the man driving his car from the back seat, for instance (Ralph, 2–5), or the steps without a door and vice versa (Rebecca, 4–6). The 'wacky' things are incongruous, hence funny, for a variety of reasons relating to social or physical reality. Some are impossible (isolated walls standing above the ground), whereas some are only impossible because we know how things should be, such as the pram with 20 babies in (see p. 52). Rebecca at 4–6 picked up this difference in type, objecting of one 'wacky' but quite possible thing, the boy wearing one sock in the shower, 'But why did he do it himself?' In other words, the other things are fantastic, not within a person's control.

Slapstick

Slapstick is the first sort of humour that springs to many minds, especially when discussing children. It was not absent from Ralph and Rebecca's literary diet. Ralph particularly enjoyed *Scarry*, for example, with its hundreds of little pictures, mostly of accidents. (Klein 2003 looks at the humour inherent in Scarry, but puts it down to the incongruity of animals doing human things, despite the fact that many picture books, quite serious ones – say Potter – have anthropomorphised animals and do not inspire laughter.) Between 4–2 and 4–5 Ralph was passionate in his devotion to *Crazy Cowboy* and *Patatrac*, also full of slapstick disasters, though of a more sophisticated variety (see Figures 6.1 and 6.2). The Berenstain Bears series hinge on misadventures, almost all happening to Dad. Ralph was 2–7 (with Rebecca 5–10) before one of these was recorded as being amusing, although they had enjoyed other titles earlier without laughter. This is subversive humour, as the incongruity of a pompous adult (in this case Dad) brought low is one of the most constantly amusing varieties of slapstick.

The incongruity of slapstick is that it does not happen in the external world, or rarely. Perhaps for the child, not long past the clumsiness of learning to run, climb, ride a trike, there is also a feeling of superiority: '*He's* falling over, not me!'

Character-based humour

Situational humour does not have to be slapstick or pratfall. It is often based on what we know of the personality of the character. The book with the most humour responses recorded for Rebecca up to age 5 was *Pooh*. Eeyore's 'What is?' to Tigger (2–7), Tigger's fight with the tablecloth (4–2), Wol's version of 'Happy Birthday' (4–9) and others amused Rebecca. She and Ralph together laughed uproariously at Pooh sitting on Small (4–2 and 7–5). This sort of humour is closer to the humour of everyday life than many others – certainly than the slapstick which many people see as the best humorous food for children. Everyday life is full of behaviour that makes for shaping into amusing stories, based on the personalities of the people involved, and what they say. We can laugh, often ruefully, as we do in *Pooh*, knowing just how they would feel. Lurie discusses the subversive aspects of *Pooh* (1991: 166–177). How much of its subversive ideology got through to the children is not known.

While he enjoyed stories of mayhem and the subversive, Ralph was often ambivalent about them, and frequently found them anxiety-producing rather than funny. Perhaps it was the implied punishment that disturbed him, even if only in being temporarily in disfavour with one's family, as in his reactions to *Harry the Dirty Dog* (p. 54) and *Tom Kitten* (p. 52). Humour, and subversion as well, are in the eye of the beholder. The subversive in stories leads one to reassess the social reality that surrounds one. The constraints of everyday life are overturned, and the omnipotent adults routed. Other rules are broken too, in the stepping between the world of the text and the world of the artefact, so that these blur, as is the case with the titles discussed under 'Irony' (below).

The examples of the children's cognitive development in the complex area of humour demonstrate how far Rebecca and Ralph were from the accepted norms of understanding of humour. The sheer number of books they heard, and the relative sophistication and length of these, led to a large number of examples of humour being encountered, and at an earlier age than previously recorded. As Vygotsky (1986) clearly explains, it is not just maturation that leads to development, but training, exposure, experience. With humour, as in many other areas, the child's zone of proximal development is much wider, extends much further down, much younger, than has previously been expected.

Irony

Understanding that the author does not always mean what the text actually says is a first step in understanding irony. Irony is complex for children. For years they have had to learn to suspend disbelief while listening to a story in order to enjoy it to the full, to accept that what the words are telling them is true for the world of the story. In cases of irony, however, they are being encouraged to disbelieve the words. To appreciate irony, there needs to be a willingness to question the text of the story, with the confidence that the story (or verse) will not be spoilt by this. The child has to bring his or her understanding of language to the story, against the text's usage, to 'get' the point. Other types of irony ask the children to move outside the frame of the story and confront the external and the secondary world together. 'An understanding of irony requires that one recognise the evaluative incongruity between what is said and what the speaker believes to be true' (Winner 1988: 25). Nodelman (1988: 227–232) even argues that picture books are by nature ironic, that the relationship between text and pictures is such that there are always gaps to be filled in one or the other, and the process involves seeing irony in this. (See Ralph on *The Mouse with the Daisy Hat*, p. 99.) Kummering-Meibaur (1999) discusses children's understanding of the irony in pictures and text (in *Rosie's Walk*, for instance). See also Lowe (2002).

The Cragos note that 'We can say with conviction that no unambiguous example of a response to irony exists' for Anna up to 5–0 (*Prelude*: 198). The sophistication of listening to (or reading) the words on the page, while knowing that something quite different is meant by them, can only come with age and experience. Although Rebecca and Ralph showed some understanding of irony, the books they heard presented many more examples of irony that were missed by the children, with *Pooh* especially affording many examples at different levels.

Irony grows from the initial ability to recognise that the words do not always convey the truth of the fictional world. At 2–4 Ralph listened to *The Bears on Hemlock Mountain* with Rebecca (6–7). At the end we recited together 'There are no bears on Hemlock Mountain . . . No bears at all!' As we finished, wide-eyed and serious, Ralph assured me '*Were* bears on Hemlock Mountain!' Despite the compulsion of the chant and the belief of the protagonist, Ralph was able to state that the reverse was true – a first step in understanding irony.

This is related to the most basic form of irony, which occurs when the words say one thing (usually in children's books coming from a character, rather than the narrator) while the reader/listener realises that quite the opposite is true. In the example above, *Hemlock Mountain*, only the protagonist was deceived, but in true irony it is the audience that is almost taken in. The first and simplest example of this encountered was the nursery song about 'Mr Frog':

> Mr Frog jumped out of the pond one day
> And found himself in the rain.
> Said he, 'I'll get wet
> And I might catch a cold'
> So he jumped in the pond again!

Both children recognised the irony here and were amused by it, Rebecca at 4–8, Ralph at 4–3.

Arnold Lobel is adept at offering children their first taste of irony. Rebecca was given *Frog and Toad Together* at 3–8, and took it away with her immediately on a visit to her grandparents. On her return she told me 'There is one where they are brave', and later the same day, 'They ran away because they were so brave'. When I offered to read 'Dragons and Giants', she told me 'This is the one where they were not afraid' (demonstrating that it was not the definition of 'brave' that was the problem). In the story, Frog and Toad go for a long walk, on the way meeting a snake who greets them with 'Hello lunch!' They run back home and hide in the bed and in the cupboard 'for a long time, just feeling very brave together'. It is possible that Rebecca suspected this was unusual, not fitting her definition of 'brave', because this is the incident and the wording that seem to have impressed her the most. It may also have been that her grandparents glossed it for her, however. It was not until she was 4–10 that she was able to articulate this, and even then it was my query which gave her the clue. [Were they brave, do you think?] 'Yes', then hesitates: 'What do you think?' I returned it to her, and this time she said doubtfully 'No'. Then with confidence and amusement: 'No, they weren't!' Ralph at 4–3 heard it read on the radio, where the reader actually ended by saying 'But they weren't brave really.' There is no record of his coming to this understanding for himself. Winner writes on children's understanding of irony and metaphor, including the difficulty of intentional falsehood (1988: 135), which the *Frog and Toad* example fits well.

The snake's sinister 'Hello lunch!' amused Rebecca enormously at 4–10. She laughed and exclaimed 'They're not lunch!' Lunch for her – and, it must be admitted, for the anthropomorphised Frog and Toad as well – was something in the order of peanut butter sandwiches. The adult is laughing too, but (ironically!) for quite the opposite reason, which I explained to her: 'They would have been the snake's lunch, if he'd caught them!' In 'The List', Toad writes down everything he is to do in the day, but his list blows away. At 4–7 Rebecca was delighted with his 'running after my list is not one of the things on my list': 'I can't stop laughing!' While overseas between 4–2 and 4–6, she had dictated a notebook full of 'Things to do when I get home'. On our return, these had turned out to be difficult in the execution. This experience probably sharpened her ability to recognise the irony here.

Pooh offered examples of irony, also. At 4–11 Rebecca was highly amused by Pooh and Piglet turning up together at Pooh's door, but 'Luckily Pooh was at home just as they got there, so he asked them in.' The irony of him knocking at and opening his own door for Piglet seems to have been clear to her.

There is irony inherent in *Little Bear* when he wants warm clothes for the snow, and eventually his mother suggests he needs a fur coat, so he takes all the clothes off again. Ralph remarked 'That's a silly one, isn't it?' before it was read on one occasion at 3–7, and at the end, when the narrator intrudes to ask 'What do you think of that?', he chuckled, recognising the irony (Lowe 1996).

Another variety of irony that they encountered and enjoyed was when the world or reality of the story intruded into the external world, or alternatively into the reality of the book-as-artefact. Oakley's Church Mice series do this, particularly at 'THE END', where the mice often assemble the letters. All these are delightful, and had been commented on with laughter since the first one encountered by Rebecca at 5–0. Ralph showed he was aware of the same sort of irony at 3–8, when he remarked with amusement of the cover of *Barbapapa's New House* (Tison/Taylor): 'The telescope is looking at words!' Covers often offer this sort of irony. Rebecca was amused by the author (Lobel again) and his characters confronting each other on the back of *Owl at Home*, although not until 7–2.

Another example was the infinite regression of a character reading its own book, as on the last page of *The Tyger Voyage* (Adams), which was commented on right from its first reading (Rebecca, 5–6; Ralph, 2–4). Intertextuality can also be seen as a form of irony, in the unexpected discovery of a reference or a quotation or a character from another book, indicating that the author has read the same book you have (Meek 1988: 21). This was evidenced in *Orlando the Frisky Housewife* (Hale), where Squirrel Nutkin, Toad of Toad Hall and other familiar friends turn up as garden statues, and surprised and amused the children at 5–1 (Rebecca) and 2–10 (Ralph).

The self-referential text is rare in children's books, but recognised as irony when it does appear. In *Teddy Robinson Himself* a cow Teddy encounters says 'Mer' at him. When he asks why she doesn't say 'Moo', she explains that 'I'm a country cow. Only story-book cows say Moo, not real cows!' Rebecca was amused, and pointed to the picture: 'That *is* a story-book cow!' (4–1).

Rebecca's ability to stand outside the text was demonstrated in her amusement at anthropomorphised animals. Laughing at animals talking, as she must have recognised, was going against the spirit of the story. Her delighted 'I've never seen *mice* do that!' at 2–6 was spelt out more explicitly a year later in her laughter at *Miffy at the Zoo*: 'Animals can't talk!'

These and other examples demonstrate that some awareness and appreciation of irony is possible quite early, even if appreciation of the more subtle varieties comes later.

11 'But the words say it'

Conclusion

This study demonstrates that there was never any confusion apparent in the children's minds about the reality of the pictured and narrated worlds. Even (or especially) at 0–6 the picture of a baby on a packet remained exactly that, a picture printed on cardboard. However, the initial articulation of the question of reality came with anthropomorphism – 'Animals can't talk' – perhaps the easiest of the aspects of reality to put into words, the anomaly that foregrounded the reality status for these children, perhaps because they lived with pets. This first awareness as a generalisation occurred at about the same age for both children (3–6, 3–7), although much earlier when referring to specific characters (2–5, 2–6). Both children had periods of intense interest in the topic of reality, Rebecca at 3–7 to 3–9 and again at 4–5 to 4–7, Ralph younger at 2–10 to 3–1 and 3–10 to 4–0.

Comment on anthropomorphism gradually led to the articulation of the reality status of other aspects of the text, and eventually to the query 'is this a real story?' of the whole book, rather than just of specific characters or incidents or objects, and to the statement that 'it's only a pretend book, anyway'. The younger child, coached by his sibling, came to ask 'is this a real story?', and to the understanding that 'it's in a picture, it's not real', at a much younger age.

The children revealed their capacity for a strong interactional relationship with their stories. Rebecca identified with fictional personalities, even taking them as alter egos away from the text, becoming Piglet, Snufkin or 'Tigger pretending to be Eeyore'. However, for her the text was inviolate. Ralph on the other hand felt free to change the story as he saw need, rescuing the little half-chick, or marrying the little lame boy, or disagreeing with the author or with the parental gloss. He wanted to manipulate the story itself, to go inside and solve the problem or change the ending. As he expressed it at 3.4, 'I'd like to go in and think myself out of it.' This was a constructive and creative way of coping with anxiety. His identification with characters was superficial and he did not take on roles, whether masculine or feminine, except strictly and safely within the text, or in games closely based on them. A good example is that, although he could see himself as 'like' Little My, he could not allow himself to 'be' her. These examples demonstrate the highly individualistic way different children may engage with texts.

Rebecca and Ralph differed markedly in other ways also. Some people might put their differences down to gender, but I attribute them more to personality and their position in the family. For instance, Rebecca was not a 'girly' girl – she never cared for dolls, and was known as a tomboy. She refused to wear dresses for several years, and was even known by a boy's name for a year or more at her Montessori school. She was more interested in science topics than her brother, and had a strong spatial sense and secure sense of direction, often seen as masculine traits. She was most interested in the causation aspect of the reality of books, and in talking about ideas, and what the characters were thinking.

Ralph was mercurial. He was much more demonstrative than his sister, both in cuddles and affection, and in anger. Consequently, he was more interested in the emotions of the book characters, and enjoyed fantasy as well as the traditional myths and legends. His pretend friends were ephemeral, small and in need of protection, whereas Rebecca's Brownie was long-lasting and fiercely independent, as she was herself. Ralph's interest in philosophical ideas, great as it now is, developed rather later than Rebecca's.

That the book was an artefact, with one or more creators, was clearly understood by both at 4, the age at which Ralph addressed the intrusive author as 'read-maker'. Both children found satisfaction in spotting the fallibility of the author or illustrator, which also helped their understanding of the author concept.

The creator of the book was first recognised in the illustrator. Despite the fact that some theorists doubt that this understanding is possible in a young child, Ralph could recognise and name one illustrative style at 3–4 (Scarry), and others regularly by 4–2. Rebecca also categorised pictures as being 'by the same person as . . .' before she was 5. This understanding added to their appreciation of books. The comparing and contrasting, and awareness of style and its continuity, were all part of the pleasure of books and pictures. Written style was also recognised, although to a lesser extent, this being demonstrated more frequently in responses to the stories rather than in actual comparative statements, as the recognition of illustrators was.

Although there were no discernible stages in the development of the understanding of the reality-status, there was a growth in the ability to articulate the difference between the fictional (secondary) world and the external one. Contrary to Piaget's findings, the understanding that the picture is a picture, not the thing itself, and that the word is a word, not the thing itself, seemed to be present from the very beginning. In Coleridge's term, the children begin by 'disbelieving' in the fictional world. They have to learn to suspend this disbelief, to believe in the created world for the length of the story, and only after this to analyse it, and return to disbelief. The children presumably pass through the stage of knowing that this is only a picture of something, before they can articulate that knowledge, but they accept that it is spoken of as if it were the real thing, especially in the context of a story. Eventually they come to articulate that it is only a picture or story, not 'real'. In other words, they return briefly, in some stories, for some period of time, to the 'disbelief'. But once they had articulated it (Ralph earliest at 2–7, Rebecca 3–4), they were able to suspend their disbelief again, or rather not bother to articulate it. In the process, none of the enjoyment of the story was lost.

This study has presented evidence against those who claim that children cannot cope with fantasy, or with anything they have not encountered in the physical world, or with complex ideas, or even with unfamiliar vocabulary.

Rebecca and Ralph have grown into strong, independent, thinking, caring adults, taking responsibility for themselves and for the world. Both value books for what they can learn from them about themselves and others. Both are still working at understanding the reality of the text, the reality of the world, the truth of what they are told by different elements in society ('Is this a real story?'). And books are still a favourite source of pleasure.

Times have changed. Today's children take their storytelling from many different media. The record of Rebecca and Ralph can perhaps stand as a benchmark of children exposed only to books. They did have a little television, but few cartoons, and of course no videos or computer games until they reached early adolescence.

Mackey has investigated 'The case of Peter Rabbit' (1998). She followed the various transformations Potter's classic has undergone: simplified versions with and without the original pictures, computer games, audio, video and DVD versions, the ballet, china wind-up figurines (playing different, equally inappropriate tunes), soft toys, brands of baby clothes. She muses on what effect all these various versions would have on children who have never met the original, and also on ones who have.

Mackey tried not to be too negative about the current narrative environment, but Goldthwaite is much more pessimistic. He feels that 'a literary audience became a mass market, make believe became entertainment and encountering the miracles of story became a passive activity'. The role of fantasy, or 'make-believe', is to 'baptise the imagination' (1996: 12) – children need this, as does the whole race. Hungerford has pointed out that if they don't read or listen to children's literature, children today 'are exposed to a fictional life made up almost exclusively of adults' and that 'fictional children are an endangered species', with children's literature their 'conservation area' (1993: 21).

Hollindale, talking of the 'childness' in children's books, says that we need stories not only as escape and entertainment but to give us patterns to 'reinforce the constant work of storying our own lives: we need stories, as we need food, and we need stories most of all in childhood as we need food then, in order to grow' (1997: 70).

These studies, however, preceded the Harry Potter phenomenon, which has revived interest in the printed word. Rowling's books are well written, and they are long, challenging. One cannot help noticing their commoditisation, however – many children who will never read them have to own them. But maybe this in itself is a good thing. With more books sold there are more profits for publishers, which they plough back into encouraging more new writers. There is also a thick book in many a bedroom which the child knows contains an exciting story, and also knows that many of his or her peers have tackled it – despite its weight, it can't be so very difficult?

Of course there has always been change. One can imagine the regret of people in the eighteenth century, when Newbery began his plan of publishing little books for boys and girls (accompanied by a ball or a pincushion), that storytelling was now no longer an oral skill. How could they get their children to sit and listen to Aunt Maggie's stories, when they could go off and read them for themselves? Today's world of multimedia is just another step – though it seems like a major one – in this direction. Perhaps it is no worse than that instigated by Newbery; time will tell. But we book people still hope that books will remain a source of narrative and pleasure, under the individual's complete control, exercising our own creative thinking, for centuries to come.

And the only way to foster this is by encouraging the love of literature in babies and young children. Ply them with books, read the actual words, and thus keep their creativity and imagination alive. They'll even learn what is 'real' in the process, which can only be a good thing.

Afterword

Rebecca Lowe

Virginia has asked me to write an Afterword for *Stories, Pictures and Reality*, to give my view of the study and some background on how I am as a reader now.

I still have a very great love of books. I really enjoy reading and writing – both favourite activities of mine that I never seem to have enough time for.

While I really enjoy them, I very rarely read novels, as once I am into one I become so involved that I cannot put it down, and become very crotchety and unpleasant to be around if I have to. So for my own sake, and the sake of those around me, I deliberately restrict myself to mostly non-fiction, which does not cause the same addictive behaviour. The novel is almost total escapism for me.

In many ways my reading behaviour is very similar to that described in my childhood. I still enjoy reading favourite books and series over and over, both whole books and individual favourite chapters. I also tend to quote them to myself and run the stories through my head while doing other activities. Interestingly, in books I know well that I reread, I tend to skip the 'bad bits' – something that was very much more Ralph's style than mine when we were younger. I read for pleasure, so I would rather not read parts that make me feel sad, angry or uncomfortable, if I know the book well enough for it not to affect the storyline.

I still identify strongly with characters. Although not expressing this with games any more; I still feel as if I 'am' a character that I have been reading about as I go about daily life.

I read with very little speculation and anticipation. Virginia's comment (p. 53) on 'speculation and anticipation – which we all do when we read' made me stop and think. I had not been aware of it before, and I guess I do speculate and anticipate to some extent, but certainly not much. I like to let the flow of the story engulf me without thought on my part. My interaction with the text tends to happen more outside a reading session, in identification with the characters, than it does while I am actually reading. I read very fast and very visually – while I am reading it is like a movie playing in my head, and the actual words, unless it is dialogue between characters, tend to be bypassed by my conscious brain.

I would still much rather listen than talk or ask questions. I identified my tendency to have difficulty asking questions as a problem about halfway through my twenties, and from that point on I have made a deliberate effort to ask questions. While this sometimes works, I still come away from a situation thinking 'Why didn't I ask that?' The question just didn't occur to me at the time, even though I had been puzzling over it while I was listening. Questions just aren't a natural method of sourcing information for me.

With regard to the content of this book, I have found that Virginia's interpretation does not necessarily match up with my childhood memories (which tend to be good) of my thought processes at the time. A good example is of *The Hobbit*, discussed on p. 20. Virginia states that I said I didn't like *The Hobbit* as there were too many battles. I don't doubt that I said this, although I don't recall it, but I do know that this was not my main reason for not enjoying it. I remember asking repeatedly 'When does it start getting exciting?', finding the listening very boring. Eventually Virginia stated that if I wasn't finding it exciting by now I probably wouldn't at all (or words to that effect), and that was the end of my listening to it. I suspect, although I don't remember, that the 'too many battles' comment was given to Virginia as a reason that I felt she would accept better than just 'it's boring', which, apart from anything else, would have required a lot more explaining on my behalf. Whether the repeated 'this is boring' and 'when does it get exciting?', which are my memories of the situation, made it to the diaries or not I don't know, but it was the 'too many battles' comment that Virginia has quoted in this book. I think this illustrates how well I chose the comment – something to grab my mother's attention that she could relate to.

To me, the best illustration of the different ways Virginia and I perceived a situation is the example of the roly-poly pudding (p. 144). I had a fascination with the picture of Tom Kitten being made into the roly-poly pudding by the rats on page 38 of *Samuel Whiskers*. I could not work out how the cylinder shape, which, according to my understanding of the world, would be best created by rolling Tom and his surrounding dough lengthwise along a flat surface, is in the picture being created by rolling a rolling pin crosswise along the top of the dough (see Figure A.1). This was an unresolved problem that I mulled over a lot in my childhood mind. I also experimented physically with the idea, trying with various materials to replicate what the rats were doing to create the cylinder. Consequently, I thought that the ultimate test might be to try it with Ralph, with the supposition that it might work if one is actually enclosing something living.

None of this was ever articulated to Virginia until well into my adulthood, so is not a part of the diaries. In the absence of this explanation for my behaviour she attributes it to 'sibling jealousy' without question. In fact, she even prefaces it with 'obviously', whereas in my mind it had nothing to do with jealousy at all, even subconsciously I expect,

Figure A.1 The Tale of Samuel Whiskers Beatrix Potter.

as it was purely experimental (although of course I wouldn't have thought of it in those terms at that age). In a recent conversation, which would have no doubt have been of great benefit some thirty years ago, Virginia put the behaviour down to 'artistic licence' while John commented that they might be sealing the edges with the rolling pin. Closure at last!

I think that this example is interesting for a number of reasons. First, I think it is a good illustration of the development of my scientific thinking (I went on to do a Bachelor of Science degree). It is also interesting that had Virginia known my thought processes it would have fitted better into the fallibility of the illustrator discussion in Chapter 6, rather than just being classified as acting out.

If Virginia could have such a different take on what happened in this incident, there must be numerous situations right through where her assumptions did not actually match with what was going on in her children's minds. Pondering on how different my childhood thought processes are to my adult ones, I firmly believe that an adult can never hope to understand a child's mind; the differences are just too fundamental.

That said, I think that Virginia has made an admirable effort to understand a child's thinking. Certainly by studying her children in their natural setting, going about their everyday lives, she has been able to come closer to an understanding than most researchers would be able to. I am pleased and proud to be part of this process.

Children's books cited (alphabetically by title)

N.B. Some books are referred to by a shortened title in the main text. See the index for authors and illustrators.

1 2 3 to the Zoo Carle, E.
123456789 Benn McKee, D.
3 × 3 Kruss, J./Rubin, J.
ABC Burningham, J.
Alexander and the Wind-Up Mouse Lionni, L.
Alice's Adventures in Wonderland and *Through the Looking Glass* Carroll, L.
Amanda Has a Surprise Colbert, A.
Anansi the Spider McDermott, G.
Angus and the Cat Flack, M.
Angus and the Ducks Flack, M.
The Architect Loup, J.J.
Arrow to the Sun McDermott, G.
Asterix (series) Goscinny, R./Uderzo, A.
At the Zoo Ainsworth, R.
At the Zoo Gagg, M.E./Driscoll, B.
B is for Bear Bruna, D.
Babar (series) Brunhoff, J. de
Babar's Travels Brunhoff, J. de
Baby Animal ABC Broomfield, R.
A Baby Sister for Frances Hoban, R./Hoban, L.
Bananas in Pyjamas Blyton, C./Barling, T.
Barbapapa Tison, A./Taylor, T.
Barbapapa's Ark Tison, A./Taylor, T.
Barbapapa's New House Tison, A./Taylor, T.
Barbapapa's Voyage Tison, A./Taylor, T.
The Bears on Hemlock Mountain Dalgleish, A./Sewell, H.
The Bears Who Stayed Indoors Gretz, S.
The Bears Who Went to the Seaside Gretz, S.
Benjy's Dog House Graham, M.B.
Berenstain Bears (series) Berenstain, S. and J.

May I Bring a Friend? De Regniers, B.S.
Meet Mary Kate Morgan, H./Hughes, S.
Meg and Mog Nicoll, H./Pienkowski, J.
Meg at Sea Nicoll, H./Pienkowski, J.
Meg on the Moon Nicoll, H./Pienkowski, J.
Meg's Car Nicoll, H./Pienkowski, J.
Meg's Eggs Nicoll, H./Pienkowski, J.
Midnite Stow, R.
Miffy at the Seaside Bruna, D.
Miffy at the Zoo Bruna, D.
Miffy's Birthday Bruna, D.
Mike Mulligan and His Steam Shovel Burton, V.L.
Millions of Cats Gag, W.
Milly-Molly-Mandy Stories Brisley, J.L.
The Moffats Estes, E.
Momoko's Birthday Iwasaki, C.
Moominland Midwinter Jansson, T.
Moominpappa at Sea Jansson, T.
Moominsummer Madness Jansson, T.
Mother Goose Nursery Rhymes Eve, E.
Mother Goose: Nursery Rhymes Wildsmith, B.
Mother Goose: Seventy Seven Verses Tudor, T.
The Mother Goose Treasury Briggs, R.
The Mouse and His Child Hoban, R.
The Mouse with the Daisy Hat Hurlimann, R.
Mouse Tales Lobel, A.
Mr Benn Red Knight McKee, D.
Muffel and Plums Fromm, L.
Mulga Bill's Bicycle Paterson, A.B./Niland, K. and D.
Mushroom in the Rain Ginsburg, M./Aruego, J./Dewey, A.
My Naughty Little Sister (series) Edwards, D.
Myths and Legends White, A.T./Provensen, A. and M.
Narnia Chronicles Lewis, C.S.
Nate the Great and the Lost List Sharmat, M.W./Simont, M.
Noisy Nora Wells, R.
Numbers of Things Oxenbury, H.
Nurse Matilda Brand, C.
Olga Meets Her Match Bond, M.
One Fish, Two Fish, Red Fish, Blue Fish Seuss, *Dr*
One Old Oxford Ox Bayley, N.
Orlando the Frisky Housewife Hale, K.
Orlando the Marmalade Cat Hale, K.
Orlando the Marmalade Cat Buys a Farm Hale, K.
Owl at Home Lobel, A.
The Oxford Nursery Song Book Buck, P.

Patatrac Loup, J.J.
Peter and the Wolf Prokofiev, S./Howard, A.
Peter's Chair Keats, E.J.
Petunia Beware Duvoisin, R.
Petunia I Love You Duvoisin, R.
Phoebe and the Hot Water Bottles Furchgott, T./Dawson, L.
Picture Stories Peppe, R.
The Pirate Book Hellsing, L./Stroyer, P.
Prince Caspian Lewis, C.S.
The Quinkins Trezise, P./Roughsey, D.
The Rain Puddle Holl, A./Duvoisin, R.
Ramona the Pest Cleary, B.
Richard Scarry's Best Word Book Ever Scarry, R.
The River at Green Knowe Boston, L.
Rosie's Walk Hutchins, P.
Round the Corner Showalter, J.B./Duvoisin, R.
The Sailor Bruna, D.
The Secret Garden Burnett, F.H.
The Seven Magic Orders Mui, Shan/Yue Tin
The Silver Chair Lewis, C.S.
Sixes and Sevens Blake, Q.
The Snowy Day Keats, E.J.
Snuffy Bruna, D.
Snuffy and the Fire Bruna, D.
So Small Rand, A./Rojankovsky, F.
Some Swell Pup Sendak, M.
Songs for Children Graham, M.N.
Spiders (Macdonald Starters)
Stone Soup Brown, M.
The Story about Ping Flack, M./Wiese, K.
The Story of Miss Moppet Potter, B.
The Story of the Three Bears Stobbs, W.
Summer Low, A.
Swimmy Lionni, L.
Tales from Moominvalley Jansson, T.
The Tale of Benjamin Bunny Potter, B.
The Tale of Jemima Puddleduck Potter, B.
The Tale of Mr Jeremy Fisher Potter, B.
The Tale of Peter Rabbit Potter, B.
The Tale of Pigling Bland Potter, B.
The Tale of Samuel Whiskers, or, the Roly Poly Pudding Potter, B.
The Tale of Squirrel Nutkin Potter, B.
The Tale of Tom Kitten Potter, B.
The Tale of Two Bad Mice Potter, B.
Teddy Robinson Himself Robinson, J.G.

Teddy Robinson's Omnibus Robinson, J.G.
There's a Nightmare in My Cupboard Mayer, M.
Things I See [Play Joy Books]
Thomas Builds a House Wolde, G.
Three Gay Tales from Grimm Gag, W.
Tim's Last Voyage Ardizzone, E.
Trubloff the Mouse Who Wanted to Play the Balalaika Burningham, J.
The Twelve Days of Christmas Broomfield, R.
Two Kittens Schwalje, M./Tiffany, V.
The Tyger Voyage Adams, R./Bayley, N.
Velvet Paws and Whiskers Chapman, J./Niland, D.
Veronica's Smile Duvoisin, R.
The Very Hungry Caterpillar Carle, E.
Wacky Wednesday Le Sieg, T.
Whale's Way Johnston, J./Weisgard, L.
When We Were Very Young Milne, A.A.
Where Do Babies Come From? Sheffield, M./Bewley, S.
Where the Wild Things Are Sendak, M.
Whistle for Willie Keats, E.J.
Who Killed Cock Robin? Roffey, M.
Who's in Rabbit's House? Aardeema, V./Dillon, L. and D.
Who Will Comfort Toffle? Jansson, T.
Winnie-the-Pooh Milne, A.A.
A Wizard of Earthsea LeGuin, U.
The Wizard of Oz Baum, L.F.

References

Alderson, B. (1973) *Looking at Picture Books 1973: An exhibition prepared by Brian Alderson and arranged by the National Book League*, Oxford: The League.

Applebee, A.N. (1978) *The Child's Concept of Story: Ages two to seven*, Chicago: University of Chicago Press.

Arizpe, E. and Styles, M. (2003) *Children Reading Pictures: Interpreting visual texts*, London: RoutledgeFalmer.

Astington, J.W. (1994) *The Child's Discovery of the Mind*, London: Fontana.

Baddeley, P. and Eddershaw, C. (1994) *Not So Simple Picture Books: Developing responses to literature with 4–12 year olds*, Stoke-on-Trent, UK: Trentham Books.

Baghban, M. (1984) *Our Daughter Learns to Read and Write: A case study from birth to three*, Newark, DE: International Reading Association.

Bakhtin, M. (1984) *Rabelais and His World*, trans. Iswolsky, H., Bloomington: Indiana University Press.

Barrera, M.E. and Maurer, D. (1981a) 'Discrimination of strangers by the three-month-old', *Child Development*, 52: 558–563.

—— (1981b) 'Recognition of mother's photographed face by the three-month-old infant', *Child Development*, 52: 714–716.

Barthes, R. (1977) 'The death of the author', in his *Image, Music, Text: Essays*, selected and trans. S. Heath, London: Fontana.

Bergson, H. (1911) *Laughter: An essay on the meaning of the comic*, trans. Brereton, C. and Rothwell, F., London: Macmillan.

Bissex, G.L. (1980) *Gnys at Wrk: A child learns to write and read*, Cambridge, MA: Harvard University Press.

Bloom, P. (2004) *Descartes' Baby: How the science of child development explains what makes us human*, New York: Basic Books.

Booth, W.C. (1983) *The Rhetoric of Fiction*, 2nd edn, Chicago: University of Chicago Press.

—— (1988) *The Company We Keep: An ethics of fiction*, Berkeley: University of California Press.

Bourchier, A. and Davis, A. (2002) 'Children's understanding of the pretence–reality distinction: a review of current theory and evidence', *Developmental Science*, 5: 397–423.

Bretherton, I. (1991) 'Intentional communication and the development of an understanding of mind', in Frye, D. and Moore, C. (eds) *Children's Theories of Mind: Mental states and social understanding*, Hillsdale, NJ: Erlbaum.

Britton, J. (1992) *Language and Learning*, new edn, London: Penguin.

Bromley, H. (1996) 'Spying on pictures with young children', in Watson, V. and Styles, M. (eds) *Talking Pictures: Pictorial texts and young readers*, London: Hodder & Stoughton.

Bruner, J. (1983) *In Search of Mind: Essays in autobiography*, New York: Harper & Row.

—— (1986) *Actual Minds, Possible Worlds*, Cambridge, MA: Harvard University Press.

—— (1987) 'The transactional self', in Bruner, J. and Haste, H. (eds) *Making Sense: The child's construction of the world*, London: Methuen.

—— (1990) *Acts of Meaning*, Cambridge, MA: Harvard University Press.

Burt, L.M. and Sugawara, A.I. (1988) 'Children's humor: implications for teaching', *Early Child Development and Care*, 37: 13–25.

Butler, D. (1979) *Cushla and Her Books*, Auckland: Hodder & Stoughton.

Butterworth, G. (1991) 'The ontogeny and phylogeny of joint visual attention', in Whiten, A. (ed.) *Natural Theories of Mind: Evolution, development and simulation of everyday mindreading*, Oxford: Blackwell.

Chambers, A. (1985) 'The reader in the book', in his *Booktalk: Occasional writing on literature and children*, London: Bodley Head.

Chaney, C. (1993) 'Young children's jokes: a cognitive developmental perspective', delivered to Western States Communication Association February 14, 1993. ERIC ED 358 967.

Chukovsky, K. (1963) *From Two to Five*, trans. and ed. Morton, M., Brisbane: Jacaranda Press.

Cleary, B. (1982) 'The laughter of children', *Horn Book*, 58: 555–564.

Clements, W. and Perner, J. (1994) 'Implicit understanding of belief', *Cognitive Development*, 9: 377–395.

Cochran-Smith, M. (1984) *The Making of a Reader*, Norwood, NJ: Ablex.

Cohen, L.B., DeLoache, J.S. and Strauss, M.S. (1979) 'Infant visual perception', in Osofsky, J.D. (ed.) *Handbook of Infant Development*, New York: Wiley.

Crago, H. (1990) 'Childhood reading revisited', *Papers: Explorations into children's literature*, 1: 99–115.

—— (1993) 'Why readers read what writers write', *Children's Literature in Education*, 24: 277–289.

Crago, M. (1978) 'Missing home, missing mother: one child's preoccupation with their location in picture books, a case study', *Orana*, 14: 74–78.

—— (1979) 'Incompletely shown objects in children's books: one child's response', *Children's Literature in Education*, 10: 151–157.

Crago, M. and Crago, H. (1983) *Prelude to Literacy: A preschool child's encounter with picture and story*, Carbondale: Southern Illinois University Press.

DeLoache, J.S. (1984) 'What's this? Maternal questions in joint picture book reading with toddlers', ERIC ED 251 176.

Dombey, H. (1983) 'Learning the language of books', in Meek, M. (ed.) *Opening Moves: Work in progress in the study of children's language development*, London: Institute of Education, University of London.

—— (1992) 'Lessons learnt at bedtime', in Kimberley, K., Meek, M. and Miller, J. (eds) *New Readings: Contributions to an understanding of literacy*, London: Black.

Donaldson, M. (1984) *Children's Minds*, London: Fontana.

Dunn, J. (1991) 'Understanding others: evidence from naturalistic studies of children', in A. Whiten (ed.) *Natural Theories of Mind: Evolution, development and simulation of everyday mindreading*, Oxford: Blackwell.

Dunn, J. and Brown, J. (1994) 'Affect expression in the family, children's understanding of emotions, and their interactions with others', *Merrill-Palmer Quarterly*, 40: 120–137.

Eco, U. (1981) *The Role of the Reader: Explorations in the semiotics of texts*, London: Hutchinson.

Engel, S. (1995) *The Stories Children Tell: Making sense of the narratives of childhood*, New York: Freeman.

Fish, S.F. (1980) 'Literature in the reader: Affective stylistics', in Tompkin, J.P. (ed.) *Reader-Response Criticism*, Baltimore: Johns Hopkins University Press.

Flavell, J.H. (2000) 'Development of children's knowledge about the mental world', *International Journal of Behavioral Development*, 24: 15–23.

Flavell, J.H., Green, F.L. and Flavell, E.R. (1986) 'Development of knowledge about the appearance–reality distinction', *Monographs of the Society for Research in Child Development*, 51 (1), serial no. 212.

Fox, C. (1983) 'Talking like a book', in Meek, M. (ed.) *Opening Moves: Work in progress in the study of children's language development*, London: Institute of Education, University of London.

—— (1989) 'Children thinking through story', *English in Education*, 23 (2): 25–36.

—— (1992) ' "You sing so merry those tunes": oral storytelling as a window on young children's language learning', in Kimberley, K., Meek, M. and Miller, J. (eds) *New Readings: Contributions to an understanding of literacy*, London: Black.

—— (1993) *At the Very Edge of the Forest: The influence of literature on storytelling for children*, London: Cassell.

Fox, G. (1979) 'Dark watchers: young readers and their fiction', *English in Education*, 13 (1): 32–35.

Gardner, H. (1970) 'Children's sensitivity to painting styles', *Child Development*, 41: 813–821.

—— (1971) 'Children's literary skills', *Journal of Experimental Education*, 39: 42–47.

—— (1973) *The Arts and Human Development: A psychological study of the artistic process*, New York: Wiley.

—— (1977) 'Sifting the special from the shared', in Madeja, S.S. (ed.) *Arts and Aesthetics: An agenda for the future: based on a conference held at Aspen, Colorado, June 22–25, 1976*, St Louis, MO: CEMREL.

Gardner, H. and Lohman, W. (1975) 'Children's sensitivity to literary styles', *Merrill-Palmer Quarterly*, 21: 113–126.

Gardner, H. *et al.* (1980) 'Children's literary development: the realms of metaphors and stories', in McGhee, P.E. and Chapman, A.J. (eds) *Children's Humour*, Chichester: Wiley.

Goldthwaite, J. (1996) *The Natural History of Make-Believe: A guide to the principal works of Britain, Europe and America*, New York: Oxford University Press.

Gopnik, A., Meltzoff, A. and Kuhl, P. (1999) *How Babies Think: The science of childhood*, London: Phoenix.

Grahame, K. (1995) *Dream Days*, Ware, UK: Wordsworth Editions.

Green, G.M. (1982) 'Competence for implicit text analysis: Literary style discrimination in five-year-olds', in D. Tannen (ed.) *Analyzing Discourse: Text and talk*, Washington, DC: Georgetown University Press.

Grieve, R. and Hughes, M. (1990) 'Postmodernism in picture books', *Papers: Explorations into children's literature*, 4 (3): 15–25.

Hardiman, G. and Zernich, T. (1985) 'Discrimination of style in painting: A developmental study', *Studies in Art Education*, 26: 157–162.

Harding, D.W. (1962) 'Psychological processes in the reading of fiction', *British Journal of Aesthetics*, 2: 133–147.

Hardy, B. (1977) 'Narrative as a primary act of mind', in Meek, M., Warlow, A. and Barton, G. (eds) *The Cool Web: The pattern of children's reading*, London: Bodley Head.

Harris, P.L. (1989) *Children and Emotion: The development of psychological understanding*, Oxford: Blackwell.

Heath, S.B. (1986) 'What no bedtime story means: narrative skills at home and school', in Schieffelin, B. and Ochs, E. (eds) *Language Socialisation across Cultures*, Cambridge: Cambridge University Press.

Hochberg, J. and Brooks, V. (1962) 'Pictorial recognition as an unlearned ability: A study of one child's performance', *American Journal of Psychology*, 75: 624–628.

Holland, K.E., Hungerford, R.A. and Ernst, S.B. (eds) (1993) *Journeying: Children responding to literature*, Portsmouth, NH: Heinemann.

Hollindale, P. (1988) 'Ideology and the children's book', *Signal*, 55: 3–22.

—— (1997) *Signs of Childness in Children's Books*, Stroud, UK: Thimble Press.

Hughes, M. and Donaldson, M. (1979) 'The use of hiding games for studying the coordination of viewpoints', *Educational Review*, 31: 133–140.

Hungerford, R.A. (1993) 'Star Wars and the world beyond', in Holland, K.E., Hungerford, R.A. and Ernst, S.B. (eds) *Journeying: Children responding to literature*, Portsmouth, NH: Heinemann.

Hunt, P. (1991) *Criticism, Theory, and Children's Literature*, Oxford: Blackwell.

Iser, W. (1974) *The Implied Reader: Patterns of communication in prose fiction from Bunyan to Beckett*, Baltimore: Johns Hopkins University Press.

—— (1978) *The Act of Reading: A theory of aesthetic response*, Baltimore: Johns Hopkins University Press.

Jalongo, M.R. (1988) *Young Children and Picture Books: Literature from infancy to six*, Washington, DC: National Association for the Education of Young Children.

Johnson, K.E. and Mervis, C.B. (1997) 'First steps in the emergence of verbal humor: A case study', *Infant Behavior and Development*, 20(2): 187–196.

Johnston, M.C., Roybal, C. and Parsons, M.J. (1988) 'Teaching the concept of style to elementary school age students: A developmental investigation', *Visual Arts Research*, 14 (2): 57–67.

Kappas, K.H. (1967) 'A developmental analysis of children's responses to humor', in Fenwick, S.I. (ed.) *A Critical Approach to Children's Literature: The Thirty-First Annual Conference of the Graduate Library School . . . 1966*, Chicago: University of Chicago Press.

Kiefer, B. (1988) 'Picture books as contexts for literary, aesthetic, and real world understandings', *Language Arts*, 65: 260–271.

—— (1993) 'Children's responses to picture books: A developmental perspective', in Holland, K.E., Hungerford, R.A. and Ernst, S.B. (eds) *Journeying: Children responding to literature*, Portsmouth, NH: Heinemann Educational.

—— (1995) *The Potential of Picturebooks: From visual literacy to aesthetic understanding*, Englewood Cliffs, NJ: Merrill.

Klein, A.J. (ed.) (2003) *Humor in Children's Lives: A guidebook for practitioners*, Westport, CT: Praeger.

Kummering-Meibaur, B. (1999) 'Metalinguistic awareness and the child's developing concept of irony: The relationship between pictures and text in ironic picture books', *The Lion and the Unicorn*, 23(2): 157–183.

Lane, M. (1970) *The Tale of Beatrix Potter: A biography*, rev. edn, n.p.: Fontana/ Collins.

Levin, H. (ed.) (1972) *Veins of Humor*, Cambridge, MA: Harvard University Press.

Lewis, P. (1989) *Comic Effects: Interdisciplinary approaches to humor in literature*, Albany: State University of New York Press.

Lowe, V. (1977a) 'Cushla, Carol and Rebecca', *Signal*, 24: 140–148.

—— (1977b) 'Peter Rabbit lettuces, or, around Europe with a four-year-old book-worm', *Orana*, 13: 21–24.

—— (1979a) *Adult, Book, Child*, 2nd edn, Melbourne: Australian Library Promotion Council.

—— (1979b) 'Where the wild things aren't: Books, fantasy and the three year old', *Kindergarten Teachers' Association of Victoria News*, 4: 12, 15.

—— (1986) ' "A poetical T. Shandy": Byron's *Don Juan* and Sterne's *Tristram Shandy*', unpublished Honours thesis, Monash University.

—— (1991a) 'Snufkin, Sniff and Little My: the "reality" of fictional characters for the young child', *Papers: Explorations into children's literature*, 2: 87–96.

—— (1991b) ' "Stop! You didn't read who wrote it!": the concept of author', *Children's Literature in Education*, 22: 79–88.

—— (1991c) ' "Where's Pat Hutchins?" The young child's concept of author', in *Sharing Adventures in Literacy: Australian Reading Association, Victorian State Conference*, Frankston, Vic.: Australian Reading Association.

—— (1992) ' "I don't like the bitings": Young children's fear reactions to books', in *Towards Excellence in Children's Literature: Proceedings of a conference sponsored by the Graduate Diploma in Children's Literature*, Toorak, Vic.: Deakin University.

—— (1994a) ' "What are you writing?": The parent-observer at home', *Signal*, 75: 182–193.

—— (1994b) 'Which dreamed it? Two children, philosophy and *Alice*', *Children's Literature in Education*, 25: 55–62.

—— (1995) 'The incongruous, the funny and the real: Young children's humour responses to books', in *Making Sense of Humour: Proceedings of the Third Children's Literature Conference . . . Deakin University*, Burwood, Vic.: Centre for Cultural Communication and School of Literature and Journalism, Deakin University.

—— (1996) 'Little fur coats of their own: Clothed animals as metafictional markers and children as their audience', in Bradford, C. (ed.) *Writing the Australian Child: Texts and contexts in fictions for children*, Perth: University of Western Australia Press in association with Centre for Research in Cultural Communication, Deakin University.

—— (1997a) 'An audience of "non-peers": Childist criticism and the case study', in Nimon, M. (ed.) *Old Neighbours, New Visions: Selected papers from the first conference of Australian Children's Literature Association for Research . . . 1997*, Magill, S.A.: Centre for Children's Literature, University of South Australia.

—— (1997b) 'Flying to pick blueberries: Two preschoolers' literary encounters with other cultures', paper presented at the 11th Congress, International Research Society for Children's Literature.

—— (1997c) ' "Is this a real story?" Very young children and the understanding of reality and pretence, of realism and fantasy', in Pope, R. (ed.) *Making It Real: Proceedings of the Fourth Children's Literature Conference, Deakin University*, Burwood, Vic.: Deakin University and the Centre for Cultural Communication.

—— (2002) *Gaps in 'Read-Makers': Young children finding and filling gaps in stories,*

Double Dialogues, 2. Online. http://www.doubledialogues.com/archive/issue_two/lowe.htm (accessed 25 March 2006).

Lurie, A. (1991) *Not in Front of the Grown-ups: Subversive children's literature*, London: Sphere Books.

Lypp, M. (1986) 'Lachen beim Lesen: zum Komischen in der Kinderliteratur', *Wirkendes Wort*, 36: 439–455.

MacDonald, R. (1989) 'Narrative voice and narrative view in Beatrix Potter's books', in Otten, C.F. and Schmidt, G.D. (eds) *The Voice of the Narrator in Children's Literature: Insights from writers and critics*, New York: Greenwood Press.

McGhee, P.E. (1972) 'On the cognitive origins of incongruity humor: fantasy assimilation versus reality assimilation', in Goldstein, J.H. and McGhee, P.E. (eds) *The Psychology of Humor: Theoretical perspectives and empirical issues*, New York: Academic Press.

—— (1979) *Humor: Its origin and development*, San Francisco: Freeman.

—— (1980) 'Development of the creative aspects of humor', in McGhee, P.E. and Chapman, A.J. (eds) *Children's Humour*, Chichester, UK: Wiley.

—— (1989) *Humor and Children's Development*, New York: Haworth Press.

McHale, B. (1987) *Postmodernist Fiction*, London: Methuen.

Mackey, M. (1998) *The Case of Peter Rabbit: Changing conditions of literature for children*, New York: Garland.

—— (ed.) (2002) *Beatrix Potter's Peter Rabbit: A children's classic at 100*, Lanham, MD: Children's Literature Association and Scarecrow Press.

Meek, M. (1982) *Learning to Read*, London: Bodley Head.

—— (1988) *How Texts Teach What Readers Learn*, Stroud: Thimble Press.

—— (1990) 'Keeping company with Wayne Booth – and others', *Signal*, 62: 104–113.

—— (1992a) 'Transitions: The notion of change in writing for children', *Signal*, 67: 13–33.

—— (1992b) 'Children reading – now', in M. Styles, E. Bearne and V. Watson (eds) *After Alice: Exploring children's literature*, London: Cassell.

—— (1995) 'The constructedness of children', *Signal*, 76: 5–19.

Morison, P. and Gardner, H. (1978) 'Dragons and dinosaurs: The child's capacity to differentiate fantasy from reality', *Child Development*, 49: 642–648.

Nash, W. (1985) *The Language of Humour: Style and technique in comic discourse*, London: Longman.

Navarra, J.G. (1973) *The Development of Scientific Concepts in a Young Child: A case study*, Westport, CT: Greenwood Press. Original Publication 1955.

Nell, V. (1988) *Lost in a Book: The psychology of reading for pleasure*, New Haven: Yale University Press.

Nelson, K. (ed.) (1989) *Narratives from the Crib*, Cambridge, MA: Harvard University Press.

Ninio, A. and Bruner, J. (1976) 'The achievement and antecedents of labelling', *Journal of Child Language*, 5: 1–15.

Nodelman, P. (1981) 'How typical children read typical books', *Children's Literature in Education*, 12: 177–185.

—— (1988) *Words about Pictures: The narrative art of children's books*, Athens: University of Georgia Press.

—— (1996) 'Illustration and picture books', in Hunt, P. (ed.) *International Companion Encyclopaedia of Children's Literature*, London: Routledge.

Onishi, K.H. and Baillargeon, R. (2005) 'Do 15-month-old infants understand false beliefs?', *Science*, 308: 255–258.

Paul, L. (1992) 'Intimations of imitations: Mimesis, fractal geometry and children's literature', in Hunt, P. (ed.) *Literature for Children: Contemporary criticism*, London: Routledge.

Piaget, J. (1954) *The Construction of Reality in the Child*, trans. Cook, M., New York: Basic Books.

Piaget, J. and Inhelder, B. (1956) *The Child's Conception of Space*, trans. Langdon, F.J. and Lunzer, J.L., London: Routledge & Kegan Paul.

Pien, D. and Rothbart, M.K. (1980) 'Incongruity humour, play and self regulation of arousal in young children', in McGhee, P.E. and Chapman, A.J. (eds) *Children's Humour*, Chichester, UK: Wiley.

Pitcher, E.G. and Prelinger, E. (1963) *Children Tell Stories: An analysis of fantasy*, New York: International Universities Press.

Rabinowitz, P.J. (1987) *Before Reading: Narrative conventions and the politics of interpretation*, Ithaca, NY: Cornell University Press.

Redfern, W.D. (1984) *Puns*, Oxford: Blackwell.

Rose, J. (1984) *The Case of Peter Pan: or The impossibility of children's fiction*, London: Macmillan.

Rosen, M (1996) 'Reading *The Beano*: A young boy's experience', in Watson, V. and Styles, M. (eds) *Talking Pictures: Pictorial texts and young readers*, London: Hodder & Stoughton.

Rosenblatt, L.M. (1978) *The Reader, the Text, the Poem: The transactional theory of the literary work*, Carbondale: Southern Illinois University Press.

Russell, J.A. (1989) 'Culture, scripts and children's understanding of emotion', in Saarni, C. and Harris, P.L. (eds) *Children's Understanding of Emotion*, Cambridge: Cambridge University Press.

Scaife, M. and Bruner, J.S. (1975) 'The capacity for joint visual attention in the infant', *Nature*, 253: 265–266.

Schickendanz, J.A. (1990) *Adam's Righting Revolutions: One child's literacy development from infancy through Grade One*, Portsmouth, NH: Heinemann.

Schultz, T.R. and Robillard, J. (1980) 'The development of linguistic humour in children: Incongruity through rule violation', in McGhee, P.E. and Chapman, A.J. (eds) *Children's Humour*, Chichester, UK: Wiley.

Sipe, L.R. (2002) ' "Those two gingerbread boys could be brothers": How children use intertextual connections during storybook readalouds', *Children's Literature in Education*, 31: 73–90.

Smith, F. (1984) 'The creative achievement of literacy', in Goelman, H., Oberg, A.A. and Smith, F. (eds) *Awakening to Literacy: The University of Victoria Symposium on Children's Response to a Literate Environment: literacy before schooling*, Portsmouth, NH: Heinemann Educational.

Spufford, F. (2002) *The Child That Books Built*, London: Faber.

Steinberg, D. and DeLoache, J.S. (1986) 'Preschool children's sensitivity to artistic style in paintings', *Visual Arts Research*, 12: 1–10.

Stephens, J. (1992) *Language and Ideology in Children's Fiction*, London: Longman.

Taylor, D. (1983) *Family Literacy: Young children learning to read and write*, Exeter, NH: Heinemann Educational.

Tolkien, J.R.R. (1964) 'On fairy-stories', in his *Tree and Leaf*, London: Allen & Unwin.

Vygotsky, L. (1978) *Mind in Society: The development of higher psychological processes*, ed. by Cole, M., John-Steiner, V., Scribner, S. and Souberman, E. Cambridge, MA: Harvard University Press.

—— (1986) *Thought and Language*, trans., newly rev. and ed. Kozulin, A., Cambridge, MA: MIT Press.

Wall, B. (1991) *The Narrator's Voice: The dilemma of children's fiction*, New York: St Martin's Press.

Watson, V. and Styles, M. (eds) (1996) *Talking Pictures: Pictorial texts and young readers*, London: Hodder & Stoughton.

Wellman, H.M. (1990) *The Child's Theory of Mind*, Cambridge, MA: MIT Press.

Wells, G. and Chang-Wells, G.L. (1992) *Constructing Knowledge Together: Classrooms as centers of inquiry and literacy*, Portsmouth, NH: Heinemann Educational.

White, D. (1954) *Books before Five*, Wellington: New Zealand Council for Educational Research.

Whitehead, M. (1983) 'Proto-narrative moves in early conversations', in Meek, M. (ed.) *Opening Moves: Work in progress in the study of children's language development*, London: Institute of Education, University of London.

Wier, H.R. (1962) *Language in the Crib*, The Hague: Mouton.

Wimmer, H. and Perner, J. (1983) 'Beliefs about beliefs: Representation and constraining function of wrong beliefs in young children's understanding of deception', *Cognition*, 13: 103–128.

Winner, E. (1988) *The Point of Words: Children's understanding of metaphor and irony*, Cambridge, MA: Harvard University Press.

Wolf, S.A. (1988) 'The reader, the poem, and play: The braid of literature in the life of a young child', unpublished thesis, University of Utah.

Wolf, S.A. and Heath, S.B. (1992) *The Braid of Literature: Children's worlds of reading*, Cambridge, MA: Harvard University Press.

Woolley, J.D. and Wellman, H.M. (1990) 'Young children's understanding of realities, nonrealities, and appearances', *Child Development*, 61: 946–961.

Index

'At a time when multi-modal representations of real and fantasy worlds penetrate far into children's lives, this book presents a powerful argument for sharing conventional texts with children. All teachers of young children should read it to give them a sense of the long-term power of the reverberative text.'
Professor Henrietta Dombey, Professor of Literacy in Primary Education, University of Brighton, UK.

Stories, Pictures and Reality is a naturalistic study by a mother who documented her children's encounters with literature from their earliest months to adolescence and beyond. It is ground-breaking in its triumphant challenge to the commonly held belief among cognitive psychologists, that children have no understanding of reality and pretence before they are at least seven. Through a mother's fascinating observations of the development of the love of books in her children, the book becomes a compelling exploration of children's relationships with literature.

Stories, Pictures and Reality records how the children develop an understanding of the way pictures relate to the 'real' world, the role of the author and illustrator, and how (via literary characters) they develop an awareness and sensitivity to other people's thoughts and emotions. Through a convincing demonstration that young children can enjoy complex words and plots, the book places an emphasis on the benefits of actually reading words to young children, rather than just labelling or talking about pictures.

Students, researchers and academics involved in early literacy will value this book, yet anyone with an interest in children's cognitive abilities and children's literature will read the text with fascination and delight. It will develop in the reader an understanding of how brilliantly such young minds can think and reason about subjects that puzzle even the most sophisticated thinkers.

Virginia Lowe is an independent expert on literature for children, and Honorary Associate at Monash University, Australia.

EDUCATION/LITERACY

Cover image: Jacqui Young

Routledge
Taylor & Francis Group

Printed in Great Britain
www.routledge.com/education

ISBN 978-0-415-39724-7

9 780415 397247

an informa business